THE PRESIDENCY
AND BLACK CIVIL RIGHTS
Eisenhower to Nixon

THE PRESIDENCY
AND BLACK CIVIL RIGHTS

Eisenhower to Nixon

ALLAN WOLK

Rutherford • Madison • Teaneck
FAIRLEIGH DICKINSON UNIVERSITY PRESS

© 1971 by Associated University Presses, Inc.
Library of Congress Catalogue Card Number: 70-135029

Associated University Presses, Inc.
Cranbury, New Jersey 08512

ISBN: 0-8386-7805-X
Printed in the United States of America

To Iris
with love

CONTENTS

Acknowledgments   11

PART I   A FRAMEWORK FOR ANALYSIS   15

1 INTRODUCTION   17
    Scope of Study   18
    Theoretical Approach   20
2 THE FEDERAL GOVERNMENT AND CIVIL
    RIGHTS: AN OVERVIEW   29
        I. Presidential, Congressional, and Supreme
            Court Actions   30
        II. Pressure For and Against Civil Rights   41
            Presidential Exertion of Pressure   41
            Congressional Exertion of Pressure   49
            *Pressure Exerted on the President and
            Congress*   51
        Summary   62

PART II   UNITS OF IMPLEMENTATION   63

3 THE CIVIL RIGHTS DIVISION OF THE JUS-
    TICE DEPARTMENT: VOTING ENFORCEMENT   65
    Philosophy   68
    Voting Enforcement   74
    Methods of Operation   81
    Civil Rights Division Staff   91

7

The Civil Rights Division and Pressure Entities 96
Summary 106

4 THE DEPARTMENT OF HEALTH, EDUCA-
TION AND WELFARE: PUBLIC SCHOOL
DESEGREGATION 107
  I. United States Office of Education: Equal
     Educational Opportunities Program (EEOP) 107
       Philosophy of the Department 108
       Inception of EEOP 113
       Methods of Operation 115
       Pressure Exerted on EEOP 122
  II. The Office for Civil Rights 134
       Philosophy 134
       Relationship With the Justice Department 136
       Congressional Pressure 140
       White House Relations 142
       Methods of Operation 143
     Summary 154

5 THE COMMUNITY RELATIONS SERVICE:
IMPLEMENTATION BY CONCILIATION AND
MEDIATION 155
  Inception, and Location in the Department
  of Commerce 156
  Philosophy 158
  Methods of Operation 160
  Transfer to the Justice Department 164
  Summary 173

6 EXECUTIVE COORDINATION 175
  The Subcabinet Committee on Civil Rights 176
  The President's Council on Equal Opportunity 178
  The Attorney General as Coordinator 190
  Bureau of the Budget 197
  Informal Coordination 200
  Summary 204

CONTENTS

PART III   COMPARATIVE ANALYSES   207

7 UNITS OF IMPLEMENTATION   209
   Inception and Location   210
   Philosophy and Methods of Operation   212
   Relations With the President and Congress   215
   Effectiveness   217
8 THE PRESIDENTIAL ROLE IN CIVIL RIGHTS   218
   Conceptions of Office   220
   Methods of Operation   224
   Summary   234

PART IV   CONCLUSION   237

9 CONCLUSION AND RECOMMENDATIONS   239

Appendixes   253
   A. Interviewees   253
   B. Questionnaire   256
   C. Selected Chronology   257

Selected Bibliography   261
   Public Documents   261
   Books   264
   Articles and Periodicals   266
   Newspapers   267
   Reports and Pamphlets   267
   Unpublished Materials   267
   Other Sources   268

Index   269

ACKNOWLEDGMENTS

I HAVE STOOD ON THE SHOULDERS OF MANY IN THE PREPARA-
tion of this study. Research efforts have been greatly assisted by Professor Norman M. Leverett of the City
College library, Irene Feith and Margaret McGee of the
West Point Military Academy library, and Howard Brown-
stein of Bronx Community College. Many thanks also go
to the numerous people within and out of Government
who willingly and patiently submitted to intensive interviews. Elaine Heffernan of HEW's Office for Civil Rights
was invaluable in this regard. I am, moreover, grateful for
the support and encouragement extended to me by Pro-
fessors Louis W. Koenig, James T. Crown, and Robert F.
Cushman of New York University.

One individual, however, stands out among all who have
contributed to the creation of this work—my wife, Iris.
For her understanding, compassion, and warm support
throughout many arduous years, I gratefully dedicate this
book to her.

THE PRESIDENCY
AND BLACK CIVIL RIGHTS
Eisenhower to Nixon

A FRAMEWORK FOR ANALYSIS

A FRAMEWORK FOR ANALYSIS

1

INTRODUCTION

WHAT HAS THE FEDERAL EXECUTIVE DONE TO IMPLEMENT the civil rights laws? What organizational arrangements and methods of operation have been established to enforce these laws? To what degree have these efforts been effective?

Answers to these questions will aid in understanding why there is a wide gap between the law as written and actual compliance with it—why there has been a slip 'twixt the cup and the lip. There is no doubt that the public policy of the United States as expressed in Congressional statutes, Presidential Orders, and Judicial decrees states that there should be equal rights for all. Yet, theory and practice are far apart, because political, social, and economic equality for the Black man has not been fully made a reality.[1] Negroes, for example, on the Missis-

1. A January 16, 1969, *Release* of HEW, Office of the Secretary, stated that "preliminary analysis of the 1968 data on school desegregation in the 11 states of the deep South shows that 20.3 percent of the 2.5 million Negro students in these districts or a total of 518,607 Negro children are attending schools with white children." This percentage,

17

sippi delta, in the rural regions of Alabama and Georgia, and in many other areas of the South cannot freely seek employment, choose schools for their children, use public facilities, get a fair trial, or move into a white neighborhood.[2]

SCOPE OF STUDY

This study will examine and analyze efforts made by the Executive Branch of the Federal Government to effectuate compliance with the civil rights laws. Governmental

---

according to HEW officials, was increased to between 33 and 40 percent for the 1969–70 school year. *New York Times,* September 14, 1969. In the area of voting, registration figures in the 11 Southern states as reported by the U.S. Commission on Civil Rights and the Voter Education Project of the Southern Regional Council indicate that progress has been made but that much work remains. In November, 1964, the percentage of voting-age Negroes registered in Alabama, Arkansas, Florida, Georgia, Louisiana, Mississippi, North Carolina, South Carolina, Tennessee, Texas, and Virginia totaled 43.3 percent. After the 1965 Voting Rights Act this increased to 57.2 percent by the spring of 1968. The total number of new Negro registrants grew from 2,174,200 to 2,810,763, an increase of 636,563 people who were legally eligible to go to the polls. During spring 1968, 14,750,811 or 76.5 percent of voting age Whites were registered. Figures cited in *Revolution in Civil Rights* by Congressional Quarterly Service, 4th ed. (Washington, D.C., June 1968), p. 115.

Roy Wilkins, Executive Director of the NAACP, believes that the Government's "saddest record" is in the employment field. Personal interview with Roy Wilkins in New York on August 13, 1969, hereafter cited as Roy Wilkins Interview. John Doar, formerly Assistant Attorney General, Civil Rights Division of the Justice Department, rated employment compliance as quite bad and running a poor third behind implementation of voting rights and school desegregation. Personal interview with John Doar in New York on July 24 and August 6, 1969, hereafter cited as John Doar Interview.

2. The provisions against discrimination in housing of the 1968 Civil Rights Act are just beginning to be tested in the courts. A Federal suit filed in Chicago on July 14, 1969, was the first suit filed anywhere under Title VIII of the act. *New York Times,* July 15, 1969.

activities relating to the enforcement of Southern Negro
civil rights in voting and public education will be given
prime emphasis because the Federal enforcement program
was concentrated in these areas.[3] In addition, though
analysis will begin with the Eisenhower Administration
and culminate with the Nixon presidency, close attention
will be given to the Kennedy and Johnson years, when the
greatest bulk of implementation activities took place.

The civil rights laws affected most people employed by
or connected with the Federal Government, and were part
of the responsibilities of numerous agencies.[4] But the

---

3. This study will be primarily concerned with the 11 Southern states
of Alabama, Arkansas, Florida, Georgia, Louisiana, Mississippi, North
Carolina, South Carolina, Tennessee, Texas, and Virginia.

4. This includes a great amount of Federal money that is loaned to
private contractors. The Civil Rights Commission estimated that "nearly
one-third of the Nation's labor force is employed by government contractors . . . [and] a large proportion of the biggest industrial employers
are government contractors." Testimony of Martin E. Sloane, Special
Assistant to the Staff Director of CRC, on December 4, 1968, before an
ad hoc panel of U.S. Congressmen to Investigate the Enforcement of
Executive Order #11246, quoted in Study on Equal Opportunity Programs and Activities of the Federal Government (Washington, D.C.: U.S.
Commission on Civil Rights, April 1969) p. 3, n. 6.

Title VI of the 1964 Civil Rights Act has been the clearest expression
of the National Government to use Federal funds only for projects that
do not discriminate. Section 601 states that "no person in the United
States shall, on the ground of race, color, or national origin, be excluded
from participation in, be denied the benefits of, or be subjected to discrimination under any program or activity receiving Federal financial
assistance." In Section 602 it states that "each Federal department and
agency which is empowered to extend Federal financial assistance to any
program or activity, by way of grant, loan, or contract other than a
contract of insurance guaranty, is authorized and directed to effectuate
the provisions of Section 601 with respect to such program or activity."
78 Stat. 252–53, July 2, 1964. Title VI has been the main force behind
the Government's enforcement activities. Moreover, on December 4,
1964, President Johnson approved departmental civil rights regulations
guiding 21 agencies in their enforcement activities. Federal Register,
Title 45, Subtitle A.

major part of the enforcement operation was within the jurisdictions of a relatively small number of departments and agencies. Thus, certain enforcement units—the Civil Rights Division of the Justice Department, the Community Relations Service, and HEW's two mechanisms, the Equal Educational Opportunities Program, and the Office for Civil Rights—will be the main focus of this study.

These units were integral parts of the total governmental structure and thus had an effect upon and were affected by all activities within this large milieu. The writer, thus, views the units of implementation as "pressure entities" which attempt to satisfy their goals.

THEORETICAL APPROACH

The "process" of implementation is an integral, often indistinguishable part of the "process" of government and is thus similarly part of the ever-present struggle of interest or pressure entities.[5] Replacement of the commonly used term "group" by "entity" helps to create a better understanding of how the enforcement units operated and the environmental conditions they had to cope with. The term "group" connotes pressure activities on the part of more than one person. It does not provide for the individual who may act independently. The term "entity" can be used to describe either the individual or a group. Moreover, the term "group" creates the impression that pressure on the government is an activity principally engaged in by a formal, organized, private interest group. This pic-

---

5. Arthur Bentley saw this action as the "shunting by some men of other men's conduct along changed lines, the gathering of forces to overcome resistance to such alterations, or the dispersal of one grouping of forces by another grouping." *The Process of Government* (Evanston, Ill.: Principia Press of Illinois, Inc., 1908), p. 176.

ture fails to account for pressure exerted by individuals and groups who are within the public sector. It fails to show: the great fluidity of people and groups; the metamorphosis of these entities; the entities of convenience; the temporary nature of ad hoc pressure relationships; the constantly changing alignments which change with the issues; the groups within groups; the innumerable informal entities; and the dynamic qualities of many entities. Thus, the term "entity" allows one to envisage governmental activity as being more encompassing and comprehensive in its scope. It helps create an awareness that pressure activity is a viable, often amorphous type of human relationship.

Moreover, the writer does not view the activities of the Federal Government as a "process," for this implies something planned and methodical. It is rather a continuous series of confrontations of pressure entities seeking to maintain or alter their environments. All involved in the authoritative allocation of values that takes place can be looked upon as pressure entities.[6] One must examine these interests in a relative manner to determine their degree of involvement and influence.[7] However, it

---

6. David Easton believes that "to understand how policy is made and put into effect we must know how people are able to control the way in which others make and execute decisions." He finds that "all those kinds of activities involved in the formulation and execution of social policy . . . the policy-making process, constitute the political system." *The Political System* (New York: Alfred A. Knopf, 1959), pp. 144, 129.

7. Bentley wrote that "no group can be stated, or defined . . . except in terms of other groups. No group has meaning except in its relations to other groups. No group can even be conceived of as a group—when we get right down close to facts—except as set off by itself, and, so to speak, made a group by the other groups." *The Process of Government*, p. 217. Also see David Truman, *The Governmental Process* (New York: Alfred A. Knopf, 1960).

must be borne in mind that these pressure entities, perhaps static on some issues, are more often greatly influenced by changes in their own and related environments.[8]

Consequently, the main parts of Government and their divisions and subdivisions, are considered to be pressure entities. The Supreme Court, for example, is occasionally a monolithic interest entity, but more often it breaks up into several interest entities.[9] Congress has on occasion

---

8. In his classic study, *Southern Politics*, V. O. Key points out that the politics of the South "in its grand outlines revolves around the position of the Negro . . . [and] in the last analysis the major peculiarities of southern politics go back to the Negro. Whatever phase of the southern political process one seeks to understand, sooner or later the trail of inquiry leads to the Negro." However, despite Professor Key's finding that the maintenance of white supremacy is the "single theme" in southern politics, he quickly states that the "politics of the South is incredibly complex. Its variety, its nuances, its subtleties range across the political spectrum . . . further, the South is changing rapidly. He who writes about it runs the risk that change will occur before the presses stop." (New York: Random House, 1949), pp. 5, 6 and ix.

9. The *Brown* decisions serve as solid examples of a united Court while the U.S. *Reports* abound with divided opinions. For insight into the behavior of the Judiciary see: Jack W. Peltason, *Federal Courts in the Political Process* (New York: Random House, 1955); C. Herman Pritchett, *The Roosevelt Court: A Study in Judicial Politics and Values, 1937–1947* (New York: Macmillan Co., 1948); Jack Peltason, *Fifty Eight Lonely Men* (New York: Harcourt Brace, 1961); John R. Schmidhauser, *The Supreme Court: Its Politics, Personalities and Procedures* (New York: Holt, Rinehart and Winston, 1960); Glendon Schubert, ed., *Judicial Decision-Making* (New York: Free Press of Glencoe, 1963); and *Judicial Behavior: A Reader in Theory and Research* (Chicago: Rand McNally and Co., 1964); Theodore L. Becker, *Political Behavioralism and Modern Jurisprudence* (Chicago: Rand McNally and Co., 1964); Walter F. Murphy, "The Lower Court Checks on Supreme Court Power," and Kenneth N. Vines, "Federal District Judges and Race Relations Cases in the South," both in Theodore L. Becker, ed., *The Impact of Supreme Court Decisions* (New York: Oxford University Press, 1969); and David Truman, *The Governmental Process*, chapter 15, "Interest Groups and the Judiciary."

been unified in its action, such as at times of national emergency, but as a rule this pluralistic body is an amalgam of competing interests, with the number of permanent and temporary pressure entities defying calculation. Special coalitions such as the Democratic Study Group in the House of Representatives, the Southern Democrats in both Houses, and the occurrence of party voting on various issues, all attest to the push-pull of competing pressures.[10]

This incomplete description has not accounted for the activities of the staffs of individual Congressmen, of committee staffs, nor of the army of Washington-based, or grass roots, or itinerant professional interest entities.[11] Nor does it take into consideration informal intergroup connections.

The Executive Branch, with its millions of people and its Parkinson-like potpourri of agencies is a scene where one can find pressure entities actively at work throughout its diverse structure.[12] From the White House office to the

---

10. Researchers for the *Guide to Current American Government* found that "party-line voting in 1968 followed Congressional tradition, with party allegiance often outweighed by Members' individual commitments to sectional interests and philosophical positions in such areas as civil rights, housing and gun controls." On roll calls that split the parties, the average Democrat "voted with the majority of his party on 57 percent of the party-unity votes—51 percent in the Senate and 59 percent in the House. The average Republican voted with the party's majority 63 percent of the time . . . 60 and 64 percent" in the Senate and the House respectively. (Washington, D.C.: Congressional Quarterly Service, Spring 1969), p. 64.

11. See L. W. Milbrath's *The Washington Lobbyists* (Chicago: Rand McNally and Co., 1963).

12. Professor Stephen K. Bailey described it well: "The Federal government of 1968 contains: three constitutional branches—legislative, executive, and judicial; an Executive Office of the President with a half dozen major constituent units and scores of minor councils and committees; four operating agencies exclusively responsible to the Congress, which itself is divided into two houses, forty standing committees, and

12 Cabinet departments to the bureaus within each department, and the units within each bureau we find that the activities of pressure entities are a political way of life.

On some issues an entire department may inwardly or outwardly drive as one pressure group, but on other issues divisions with the department struggle to maintain or strengthen their individual positions. Thus, the governmental "process" should be viewed as a whirling kaleidoscopic scene of intertwined pressure-group activities.

One may ask how anything is accomplished.[13] Is power as dispersed and decentralized as Professor Woodrow Wilson initially viewed it?[14] In its desire to create some

---

more than two hundred subcommittees; twelve cabinet departments; fifty independent agencies, nine of which are independent regulatory commissions with both quasi-legislative and quasi-judicial authority; fifty statutory interagency committees; 2.8 million civilian employees, 90 percent of whom are employed in federal field offices outside of the Washington, D.C., area; and 3 million military employees . . . and [this] is only the tip of the iceberg." "Agenda for the Nation" (n.p.: Brookings Institution, 1968) p. 301, as quoted in the *Congressional Record* 115, p. 28, S1789, February 18, 1969.

A clear example of bureau independence is the Federal Bureau of Investigation. J. Edgar Hoover's virtual autonomy was attested to in interviews with former Attorneys General Nicholas Katzenbach and Ramsey Clark. Mr. Katzenbach said that Hoover would do what the Attorney General asked him to do; if Hoover agreed with the order he would put on 100 agents full-time, but if he disagreed he would put one agent on part-time. Moreover, Katzenbach said that he could not tell the agents below Hoover what to do—this had to be done through their chief. Interview with Nicholas Katzenbach in Armonk, New York, on June 24 and July 7, 1969, hereafter cited as Nicholas Katzenbach Interview; and interview with Ramsey Clark in New York on July 10, and August 21, 1969, hereafter cited as Ramsey Clark Interview.

13. See the analysis and suggested reforms of James MacGregor Burns in *Deadlock of Democracy* (Englewood Cliffs, New Jersey: Prentice-Hall, Inc., 1965).

14. In his classic work, *Congressional Government: A Study in American Politics* (New York: Meridian Books, 1956 (republished), Wilson

semblance of responsibility, Congress has given the President powers and obligations to protect the nation physically and financially.[15] These powers have helped make the White House the single existing instrument of governmental coordination. The President is responsible for execution of the laws and the effective operation of Executive units engaged in these efforts. Thus, it should be asked, how did the various enforcement units within the realm of the Chief Executive fulfill their responsibilities?

In this study, these implementation units are viewed as separate yet interrelated entities in a pressure-ridden environment. The method employed to examine their operations observes them in this milieu. Thus, factors relating to conditions that existed at the time of a unit's inception, the locale it was placed in, its philosophy, its methods of operation, and its relations with the White House, Congress, and other pressure entities are diagnosed.

Significant questions that will be asked concerning a unit's inception are: Who sponsored it? What were the reasons for its creation? How did powers in and out of government view the unit? How was this expressed in the law creating it? What were the initial duties and

---

wrote that "the federal government lacks strength because its powers are divided, lacks promptness because its authorities are multiplied, lacks wieldiness because its processes are roundabout, lacks efficiency because its responsibility is indistinct and its action without competent direction." P. 206.

15. The Budgeting and Accounting Act of 1921, for example, was the beginning of White House control over department budgets. See Richard E. Neustadt, "Presidency and Legislation: The Growth of Central Clearance," *American Political Science Review* 48 (September, 1954). The Employment Act of 1946 requires that he submit an annual Economic Report to Congress and it established the Council on Economic Advisers. The National Security Act of 1947 is an overt law giving the President responsibility for the Nation's security.

powers given this unit? What mandates and restrictions were stated in the statute or order establishing it? What type of organizational set-up was allowed? Where was the unit to be established and why? What was its envisaged term of existence? What type of staff and how many staff members was it permitted to have? How large a budget was it given and what were Congressional or Presidential intentions for future appropriations? These questions reflect the writer's belief that the initial structure and sphere of operations of a unit will greatly influence its future operations. That is to say, a unit severely limited at its inception will probably be ineffective in its efforts.

Similarly, the locale an enforcement unit is placed in will greatly affect its work. Is it located in a friendly or hostile environment? What effect does the function and history of the parent department or agency have on the unit's implementation role? What help or hindrance is given the unit by the department's officials and personnel? Thus, if a unit's milieu is inhospitable it will have great difficulty in meeting its responsibilities.

The philosophy of a unit, another diagnostic factor, is critically important for an understanding of its operations. How the unit's policy makers view their roles and determine goals will often be translated into the unit's actions.

A unit's method of operation, the fourth diagnostic factor, will show the actual application of its program. Questions asked will be: What is the organizational structure of the unit? From where and how are its personnel recruited? What are the qualifications of its personnel? What is the relationship between supervisors and subordinates? Does the unit have cohesiveness and *esprit de corps*? Which areas of civil rights does it deal with? How is this determined? What methods are used to bring about compliance with the laws? The writer believes that a unit poorly organized, with unskilled staff and inexperienced leaders, will have little chance to succeed.

Finally, the fifth diagnostic factor, the unit's relations with the White House, Congress, and other entities, will seek answers to the following questions: What is the role of the White House in relation to the unit? Does the President have confidence in the unit? How is this reflected in his actions? How much independence does the unit have from White House control? How does Congress affect the unit's implementation activities through its powers of appropriation and investigation?[16] What type of relationship does the unit have with the Congressional committees that have jurisdiction over it? In another realm, what type of rapport does the unit have with formal interest groups? Can the unit depend, for example, on the support of civil rights groups? Thus, the writer's final hypothesis is: If an enforcement unit does not have at least a working relationship with the White House and Congress, it will have little chance to survive, let alone succeed.

Furthermore, an analysis of the implementing unit's relations with other divisions within the Federal Govern-

---

16. Ramsey Clark told the writer to look at the men who dominate the Congressional committees in order to get an idea of the type of relationship that will ensue. Ramsey Clark Interview. Sherwin T. Montell, Special Assistant to the Staff Director, Civil Rights Commission, believes that "one rough indication of the earnestness of implementation is the extent to which agencies have funds and staff to carry on enforcement activities." His overall impression was that "sums budgeted for Title VI enforcement throughout the Government are very small." Letter to the writer, March 22, 1968. Also see Richard F. Fenno, Jr., *The Power of the Purse: Appropriations Politics in Congress* (Boston: Little, Brown and Co., 1966).

ment and with private interest entities will demonstrate the interrelatedness of governmental activities.

Thus, each unit will be observed as a separate yet interrelated entity that operates in a milieu fraught with pressure activity. This study will attempt to prove that a unit's effectiveness will depend upon, among other factors, restrictions dictated at the time of its establishment (and during its existence), its relationship with official and nonofficial entities, and its methods of operations. Moreover, it will be demonstrated that each unit is part of a large network of competing pressure entities, and, as such, will attempt to gain enough power to survive and meet its responsibilities.

2

THE FEDERAL GOVERNMENT AND
CIVIL RIGHTS: AN OVERVIEW

IN ORDER FOR THE READER TO FULLY UNDERSTAND THE
enforcement aspects of the civil rights picture, it is essential that he have knowledge of the total milieu in which
implementation activities took place. Thus, the first part
of this chapter is a survey of significant Presidential, Congressional, and Supreme Court civil rights actions taken
during the past 30 years. The Executive orders, legislative statutes, and judicial decisions promulgated during
this period were the raw materials used by Federal enforcement units in their compliance efforts.

A detailed description of how civil rights pressure was
exerted on and by the President and Congress, from the
time of the Eisenhower Administration, is presented in
the second part of this chapter. This will help create an
awareness of the total setting in which the enforcement
units conducted their operations. Cognizance of the atmosphere of struggle as portrayed in the strategic maneu-
verings and negotiated compromises that took place in the

political arena, will further aid in understanding complicated factors that were involved in civil rights implementation. The reader, having this total perspective, will be
better able to comprehend the work of the enforcement
units.

I. PRESIDENTIAL, CONGRESSIONAL, AND SUPREME COURT ACTIONS

Since the first slave ships landed on the shores of Virginia the plight of the Black man has become an American
dilemma.[1] Negroes were the subject of a compromise made
during the formulation of the Constitution, and were an
unwitting catalyst in the political battles over states
rights.[2] The South's defeat in the Civil War settled the
question of Federal entry into the realm of Negro civil
rights and soon the 13th, 14th and 15th Amendments were
passed, ratified, and bolstered by implementing legisla-

---

1. See the monumental study on civil rights directed by Gunnar
Myrdal, *An American Dilemma* (New York: Harper, 1944).

2. For the purpose of representation in the House, a slave was to
be counted as three-fifths of a person (though the term "slave" was
never used); and part of Article I, Section 9 states that "the Migration
or Importation of such Persons as any of the States now existing shall
think proper to admit, shall not be prohibited by the Congress prior to
the Year one thousand eight hundred and eight," which Congress
promptly did in that year. It is of interest that Article 6 of the Northwest Ordinance of 1787 states: "There shall be neither slavery nor
involuntary servitude in the said territory, otherwise than in the punishment of crimes whereof the party shall have been duly convicted."
Henry S. Commager, *Documents of American History*, 6th ed. (New
York: Appleton-Century-Crofts, Inc., 1962), pp. 141, 132 respectively.
Moreover, the Missouri Compromise of 1820, the Compromise of 1850,
and the Kansas-Nebraska Act of 1854 all dealt with the question of
slavery.

tion.[3] However, in the years following the end of Federal troop occupancy of the South, action by the National and state governments all but nullified Reconstruction progress.[4] Thereafter, until the end of the second World War, civil rights efforts by the Federal Government were sporadic.

During the Administration of Franklin Roosevelt no civil rights legislation was recommended, nor did Congress enact any on its own initiative. Positive Executive actions were limited to the creation of the Justice Department's Civil Liberties Section in 1939, and the Committee on Fair Employment Practices in 1941.[5]

Presidential involvement increased as exemplified by the program Harry Truman sent to Congress shortly before he ran for a second term. He asked for legislation prohibiting lynching, poll taxes, segregation in transportation, and unfair employment practices.[6] Meeting no success in this sphere, he issued Executive orders relating to desegregation of the armed forces and discrimination in

---

3. Congress enacted five major civil rights and Reconstruction acts between 1866 and 1875. *Revolution in Civil Rights,* 4th ed. (Washington, D.C.: Congressional Quarterly Service, June 1968), p. 2. Sections of this chapter are based on parts of this excellent publication.

4. The Supreme Court did its share in the *Slaughterhouse Cases* in 1872 (83 U.S. 36) and the *Civil Rights Cases* in 1883 (109 U.S. 3); while the 1876 political compromise for the Presidency was a virtual abandonment by the Federal Government of the Southern Negro. See C. Vann Woodward's *The Strange Career of Jim Crow* (New York: Oxford University Press, 1955), for insight into the position of the black man in the South after Reconstruction, and Woodward's *Reunion and Reaction* (New York: Doubleday Anchor Books, 1956), for a concise account of the compromise which settled the Hayes-Tilden election.

5. Executive Order 8802 establishing the Employment Committee said in part that it reaffirmed "policy of full participation in the defense program by all persons, regardless of race, creed, color, or national origin."

6. *Revolution in Civil Rights,* p. 3.

Federal employment and contracts.[7] During the Presidency of his successor, Dwight Eisenhower, the 1957 and 1960 Civil Rights Acts were passed—the first such laws since Reconstruction.

The Civil Rights Act of 1957 established the Commission on Civil Rights, and provided for the Civil Rights Division in the Justice Department by authorizing an additional assistant attorney general. Furthermore, it gave new power to the Attorney General by permitting him to institute voting rights suits to secure injunctive relief. The Federal Government was now empowered to step into certain types of cases to protect the voting rights of individuals.[8]

The main provisions of the 1960 Act gave additional powers to the Attorney General for the protection of voting rights. He could now ask Federal courts to determine whether voting discrimination was in pursuance of a pattern or practice as evidenced by individual court cases. Moreover, the Federal courts were empowered to appoint referees to help them determine qualified voting applicants.[9]

Other actions taken during the Eisenhower Administration included creation of a new Government Contract Committee;[10] an order by the Secretary of Defense calling for an end to segregation in military post schools;[11]

---

7. Executive Orders 9981 and 9980, respectively. Both were issued on July 26, 1948.

8. 71 Stat. 634–38. September 9, 1957.

9. 74 Stat. 86–92, May 6, 1960.

10. Executive Order 10479, August 13, 1953. This abolished the Committee on Government Contract Compliance established by Truman on December 5, 1951 in Executive Order 10308.

11. Ordered on January 12, 1954, to be ended by September 1, 1955. *Revolution in Civil Rights,* p. 36.

and establishment of the President's Committee on Government Employment Policy.[12]

There were few requests made for Congressional laws on civil rights during the Kennedy Administration.[13] However, the comprehensive Civil Rights Act of 1964 was sponsored and pushed to its last stages by Kennedy, and then brought to fruition by his successor. Its eleven titles attempted to correct many civil rights deprivations.[14] Title I prohibited the unequal application of voting registration requirements in Federal elections and stated that an individual's right to vote cannot be denied because of minor registration errors or omissions. It also denied the use of literacy tests as a qualification for voting unless administered in writing, and asserted that a sixth-grade education in English was sufficient proof that an applicant is literate. Furthermore, suits could now be expedited by

---

12. Executive Order 10590, January 19, 1955. This superseded Truman's Executive Order 9980 of July 26, 1948, which had established the Fair Employment Board.

13. John Kennedy was unsuccessful in his bid to require states to accept a sixth-grade education as adequate proof of literacy if such performance tests were given in order to vote in Federal elections. His sponsorship of the Poll tax Amendment covering Federal primaries and elections reached a successful end when it was ratified by the 38th state in 1964. Its main thrust was in the states of Alabama, Arkansas, Mississippi, Texas, and Virginia. Furthermore, the Civil Rights Commission was given a two-year extension until November 30, 1963. *Revolution in Civil Rights*, pp. 47–49.

On the television show "Meet the Press," Theodore Sorensen commented on Kennedy's approach. He said that "in the early years of his Presidency, he pressed hard for action in the civil rights area within the Executive Branch, actions which he could take on his own responsibility. But he did not want to make a lot of bald speeches to the Congress which would result in no action because he knew that would simply increase the frustrations of those who were being denied those rights." *New York Times*, February 24, 1964.

14. 78 Stat. 241–268, July 2, 1964.

the Attorney General, who was empowered to request a three man Federal court.

Title II provided injunctive relief against discrimination in places of public accommodation.

Title III permitted the Attorney General to institute civil actions to help bring about the desegregation of public facilities.

Title IV was an attempt to help segregated school districts desegregate by offering them technical assistance, grants, and aid in special training institutes. The institutes would enable them to "improve the ability of teachers, supervisors, counselors, and other elementary or secondary school personnel to deal effectively with special educational problems occasioned by desegregation, and making available to such agencies personnel of the Office of Education or other persons specially equipped to advise and assist them in coping with such problems."[15] Title IV further placed the Attorney General into what was heretofore primarily a private litigation action by allowing him to file suit for school desegregation.[16]

Title V enlarged the scope and duties of the Commission on Civil Rights, making it a national clearinghouse for civil rights information.

Title VI attempted to prevent racial discrimination in federally assisted programs by directing all Federal departments and agencies to use Federal funds in a nondiscriminatory manner.

---

15. *Ibid.*, Title IV, Section 404.

16. *Ibid.*, Section 407. It said if the Attorney General believes "the complaint is meritorious and certifies that the signer or signers of such complaint are unable, in his judgment, to initiate and maintain appropriate legal proceedings for relief and that the institution of an action will materially further the orderly achievement of desegregation in public education," then suit could be filed by him.

Title VII deals with the area of equal employment opportunity. Its provisions bar employers, employment agencies, and labor organizations from discriminating because of race, color, religion, sex, or national origin. It further established the Equal Employment Opportunity Commission and gave it the power to: work with state, local, and other agencies (private and public), and individuals; furnish technical assistance to help bring about compliance with the act; offer services as conciliators to employers or labor organizations; make technical studies in pursuance of the title's objectives; and refer matters to the Attorney General for possible legal action.

Title X established the Community Relations Service whose function was "to provide assistance to communities and persons therein in resolving disputes, disagreements, or difficulties relating to discriminatory practices based on race, color, or national origin which impair the rights of persons in such communities."[17]

Kennedy officials were far more active in civil rights in the administrative arena than on the legislative front. Executive actions included: establishment of the President's Committee on Equal Employment Opportunity, which replaced the Committee on Government Employment Policy and the Committee on Government Contracts;[18] efforts by Attorney General Robert Kennedy in 1961 to end discrimination in interstate buses, terminals, and airport facilities;[19] greater activity by the Justice De-

---

17. 78 Stat. 267, Title X, Sec. 1002.

18. Executive Order 10925, March 8, 1961.

19. Burke Marshall, head of the Civil Rights Division of the Justice Department and close adviser to Robert Kennedy, said that it was on the Attorney General's "direction that the Department followed up with an imaginative petition asking the ICC to eliminate in one stroke racial discrimination in bus and rail terminals throughout the South." "A

partment in its prosecution of voting vases brought under the 1957 and 1960 Civil Rights Acts;[20] a new HEW policy barring funds to desegregated schools in impacted areas;[21] and issuance on November 24, 1962, of the long-promised Executive order prohibiting racial discrimination in federally assisted housing.[22]

Moreover, many actions taken during the Kennedy years reflected an attempt to create an atmosphere within and outside Government conducive to the furtherance of Negro civil rights. These included overt as well as behind-the-scenes actions.[23]

Recollection of Robert Kennedy as a Lawyer," *The Georgetown Law Journal* (October, 1968), p. 2.

20. Nine voting suits were filed by the Department under President Eisenhower between 1957 and January 19, 1961, while 14 suits were filed in the first ten months of the Kennedy Administration. *Revolution in Civil Rights*, pp. 47–48.

21. HEW Secretary Abraham Ribicoff stated this in a letter to Representative Herbert Zelenko. On May 11, 1962, Ribicoff wrote: "As you know, this Department recently decided to change its interpretation of the 'suitable education' provisions of the impacted-area program and take the position that schools serving the children of parents who live on Federal installations are not suitable within the meaning of the statutes if they are segregated. Beginning in the fall of 1963, these children will no longer be required to attend local schools if they are still segregated but instead will have the alternative, in most instances, of desegregated educational facilities provided through arrangements with the Commissioner of Education." U.S. Congress, House of Representatives, Committee on Education and Labor, *Hearings* before a subcommittee on Integration in Federally Assisted Public Education Programs, part 2, 87th Cong., 2nd sess., 1962, p. 691.

22. Executive Order 11063. Because it did not cover housing financed through savings and loan, and commercial bank loans, this Order applied to approximately 18 percent of new housing, compared to 80 percent anticipated coverage for the 1968 Housing Act. Statistics quoted from *Revolution in Civil Rights*, pp. 52 and 84.

23. A partial list of Negro appointments to high Federal office during the Kennedy Administration includes: Housing and Home Finance Administrator, Justice to the U.S. Court of Appeals, Second Circuit,

During the Johnson Administration, civil rights legislation reached a crescendo with enactment of the omnibus 1964 Act, the Voting Rights Act of 1965, and the Housing Act of 1968.

The Voting Rights Act of 1965 was a major thrust in this area because it had provisions which protected the right to register and vote. Literacy tests or devices deemed prima facie unfair by a "triggering formula," were prohibited, and the Attorney General was empowered to appoint Federal examiners "to prepare and maintain lists of persons eligible to vote in Federal, State, and local elections." They were authorized to "examine applicants concerning their qualifications for voting" whereby "any person whom the examiner finds . . . to have the qualifications prescribed by State law not inconsistent with the Constitution and laws of the United States shall promptly be placed on a list of eligible voters."[24] Other significant provisions extended the 1964 Acts' sixth-grade literacy

Ambassadors to Norway and Niger, district court justices in Illinois and Michigan, Assistant Secretary of Labor, Associate White House Press Secretary, Commissioner for the District of Columbia, Commissioner for the U.S. Commission on Civil Rights, and Deputy Assistant Secretary for HEW. Southern Regional Council, *Executive Support of Civil Rights* (Atlanta, Ga.: Southern Regional Council, 1962), pp. 24–25.

Moreover, Kennedy officials spent a great deal of time talking to various groups of leaders—business, church, labor, attorneys, and so forth, in an attempt to foster grass-roots civil rights activity. The Justice Department was constantly in touch with areas in the South in an effort to expedite enforcement of the laws. She Chapter 3 for details.

24. 79 Stat. 440, Section 6. The "triggering formula," Section 4, came into operation if the Attorney General determined that any state or political subdivision of a state "maintained on November 1, 1964, any test or device, and with respect to which . . . the Director of the Census determines that less than 50 percentum of the persons of voting age residing therein were registered on November 1, 1964, or that less than 50 percentum of such persons voted in the presidential election of November 1964."

presumption to state and local elections, and allowed the Attorney General to assign observers at elections. In addition, Congress required prior approval by the Attorney General or the United States District Court for Washington, D.C., of new voting laws enacted by state or local governments which came under the provisions of the 1965 statute. Moreover, the Attorney General was authorized and directed to institute legal action to end state and local poll taxes.[25]

The first Federal open housing law of this century, Public Law 90-284, signed by President Johnson on April 11, 1968, went far beyond Kennedy's Housing Order by placing within its scope approximately 80 percent of all dwellings.[26] It prohibited, by stages, discrimination because of race, color, religion, or national origin in selling, renting, or advertising the sale or rental of a dwelling. It further prohibited banks or other institutions from discriminating in their loans and forbade "blockbusting." Another part of the law protected civil rights workers, and people who were exercising their civil rights.

Other significant Johnson legislation relating to civil rights included the Economic Opportunity Act of 1964,[27]

---

25. Congress unequivocally stated its intention concerning the poll tax in Section 10 (a) which said: "The Congress finds that the requirement of the payment of a poll tax as a precondition to voting (i) precludes persons of limited means from voting or imposes unreasonable financial hardship upon such persons as a precondition to their exercise of the franchise, (ii) doees not bear a reasonable relationship to any legitimate State interest in the conduct of elections, and (iii) in some areas has the purpose or effect of denying persons the right to vote because of race or color. Upon the basis of these findings, Congress declares that the constitutional right of citizens to vote is denied or abridged" by the payment of a poll tax.

26. 82 Stat. 73. See n. 22 above.

27. This established various anti-poverty organizations which included

and the Elementary and Secondary Education Act of 1965.[28]

The historic role of the Supreme Court in the protection of Negro civil rights has been a varied one ranging from the *Dred Scott* decision (1857) and the *Civil Rights Cases* (1883) to its strong defense of the doctrine of nondiscrimination in the second half of the twentieth century.[29] The Court has been both a hero and a villain, depending upon one's philosophy. Its decisions in the area

---

the Job Corps, Head Start, and VISTA. Such an approach to bringing about equality can be viewed as a "flank" assault while overt Civil Rights Acts can be looked upon as "frontal" assaults. Kennedy aide Arthur M. Schlesinger, Jr. noted that "the President was keenly aware of the larger contexts. When civil rights leaders had reproached him in 1961 for not seeking legislation, he told them that an increased minimum wage, federal aid to education and other social and economic measures were also civil rights bills. He knew that a slow rate of economic growth made every problem of equal rights more intractable, as a faster rate would make every such problem easier of solution. In 1963 he counted on his tax cut to reduce Negro unemployment; he reviewed and enlarged his educational program—vocational education, adult basic education, manpower development, youth employment—to help equip Negroes for jobs; and his concern for the plight of the Negro strengthened his campaigns against juvenile delinquency, urban decay and poverty." *A Thousand Days: John F. Kennedy in the White House* (Boston: Houghton Mifflin Co., 1965), p. 976.

28. Of special importance was Title I, Aid to Educationally Deprived Children. Its first-year billion dollar appropriation was an important weapon in efforts to bring about public school desegregation.

29. After the Court found that it had no jurisdiction because Dred Scott lacked the right of a citizen to sue a citizen of a different state in a Federal court, Chief Justice Roger Taney stated that "the right of property in a slave is distinctly and expressly affirmed in the Constitution." *Dred Scott v. Sandford,* 19 Howard 393, in Commager, *Documents,* p. 345. Moreover, a constitutional scholar holds that "the Civil Rights Cases prevented Congress from exercising disciplinary control over private racial discrimination." Robert E. Cushman and Robert F. Cushman, eds., *Cases in Constitutional Law,* 2nd ed. (New York: Appleton-Century-Crofts, 1965), p. 835.

of public school desegregation offer insight into its erratic journey.

An important step toward the Court's repudiation of the *Plessy* v. *Ferguson* (1896) "separate but equal" doctrine, came in 1938 when the state of Missouri was told to abide by the *Plessy* ruling and admit a black student into its all-white law school because the state did not have a black law school.[30] The Court's change in direction picked up further momentum when it decided, in *Sweatt* v. *Painter* (1950), that an education in a segregated black law school cannot be equal to legal training in a white law school— the University of Texas.[31] The Justices, shortly thereafter, further weakened the *Plessy* doctrine by stating that a Negro, once in a white school, must be afforded equal treatment.[32] It is a noteworthy fact that the above cases dealt with a relatively small area of education—institutions of higher learning, a sphere where few Negroes entered. However, these decisions were incremental steps which led to the precedent-breaking 1954 *Brown* decision.[33] The following year the Court called for desegregation of pub-

---

30. Justice Brown, speaking for the majority in the *Plessy* case (163 U.S. 537), stated the belief that "if the two races are to meet on terms of social equality, it must be the result of natural affinities, a mutual appreciation of each other's merits and a voluntary consent of individuals. . . . Legislation is powerless to eradicate racial instincts or to abolish distinctions based upon physical differences." Cushman, p. 783. The 1938 case was *Missouri ex rel. Gaines* v. *Canada*, 305 U.S. 337.

31. 339 U.S. 629.

32. *McLaurin* v. *Oklahoma State Regents*, 339 U.S. 637 (1950).

33. 347 U.S. 483. Cushman believes that "it is doubtful if the Supreme Court in its entire history has rendered a decision of greater social and ideological significance than this one." He cites three aspects of the case showing the importance given to it by the Justices: (1) unanimity of the Court; (2) one opinion—written; and (3) the fact that the Court waited to state how the decision would be implemented. *Cases*, p. 793.

lic schools with "all deliberate speed."[34] As time passed
with but little Southern school desegregation, the Supreme
Court progressively grew more stringent in its call for an
end to *de jure* segregated schools, until it unequivocally
asserted in October 1969 that public school desegregation
must be brought about immediately.[35]

II. PRESSURE FOR AND AGAINST CIVIL RIGHTS

In many instances, civil rights activity during the Eisenhower, Kennedy, and Johnson years can be characterized
as being either for or against improvement of Negro rights.
The direction and intensity of pressure exerted by the
Chief Executive, for example, often had a telling effect
on the operations of enforcement units.

Presidential Exertion of Pressure

There are often many factors that are involved in Presidential decision-making, one of which is self-pressure.[36] What effect does the knowledge that one is leader
of the strongest nation on earth have on his actions? Does
the office change the man? What effect does his sense of
history have on the choices he makes? President Lyndon
Johnson's behavior in the civil rights sphere was greatly
influenced by his past, so much so that he "bent over back-

---

34. *Brown* v. *Board of Education of Topeka*, 349 U.S. 294 (1955).

35. This case concerned 30 Mississippi school districts. *Beatrice Alexander, et al., petrs.,* v. *Holmes County Board of Education, et al. New
York Times,* October 30, 1969. See also *Cooper* v. *Aaron*, 358 U.S. 1
(1958), *Watson* v. *Memphis*, 373 U.S. 526 (1963), and *Griffin* v. *Prince
Edward County School Board*, 377 U.S. 218 (1964).

36. See eight basic decision-making steps listed by Theodore Sorensen
in *Decision-Making in the White House* (New York: Columbia University Press, 1963), pp. 18–19.

wards" in an attempt to "wipe out the Southern part of his background."[37] He expressed this feeling when he told a group of Congressmen, called in for a special briefing, to push the Voting Rights bill of 1965, because "the ghost of Lincoln is moving up and down the corridors [of the White House] rather regularly these days."[38]

The ability of the President to influence the actions of Congress depends on how he uses the formal tools available, such as the State of the Union address, the annual Budget message and Economic Report, his veto power, and his Constitutional right to call special sessions of the Legislature. Lawrence F. O'Brien, special assistant to Presidents Kennedy and Johnson for Congressional relations, believed that

> the President, after all, gets the attention of the people to a far greater extent than any other leader, and they are interested in his views. They will listen to him. He commands massive audiences on television and radio, and public appearances. And I think that it's an important element in legislative success, the success of the program, to have a President not only advocating initially, but constantly reminding . . . everyone of the program and its meaning, and giving proof positive that he is not only proposing, but he is vitally concerned personally.[39]

In addition, the Chief Executive's arsenal may include having weekly breakfasts with his party's Congressional leaders, and dancing with a Senator's wife in the White

37. Nicholas Katzenbach Interview.

38. *New York Times,* March 13, 1965.

39. Transcript of a television interview over the National Educational Television Network presented on July 11, 1965, as quoted in Congressional Quarterly Service, *Legislators and the Lobbyists* (Washington, D.C.: Congressional Quarterly Service, 1965), pp. 14–17.

House ballroom. Moreover, Congressional willingness to treat the President's program favorably often depends on such factors as legislative makeup and the Chief Executive's current prestige.[40] John F. Kennedy, for example, did not propose major civil rights legislation in the first two years of his Presidency for fear that such an attempt would endanger his entire legislative program. Theodore Sorensen, his Legal Counsel, has written that

> the reason was arithmetic. The August, 1960 defeat of civil rights measures in the more liberal Eighty-sixth Congress— as well as the voting patterns in January of 1961 in the Rules Committee fight in the House and the cloture rule fight in the Senate—all made it obvious that no amount of Presidential pressure could put through the Eighty-seventh Congress a meaningful legislative package on civil rights. The votes were lacking in the House to get it through or around the Rules Committee. They were lacking in the Senate to outlast or shut off a filibuster.[41]

Another White House aide, Arthur M. Schlesinger, Jr., confirmed this and added:

> Moreover, he had a wide range of Presidential responsibilities; and a fight for civil rights would alienate southern support he needed for other purposes. . . . And he feared that the inevitable defeat of a civil rights bill after debate and filibuster would heighten Negro resentment. . . . He

40. Eisenhower, for example, had to deal with a Democratic-controlled Congress six of his eight years in office. Moreover, the Congresses during Johnson's term were more liberal than those that his predecessor had to work with.

See the importance placed on Presidential prestige by Richard E. Neustadt in *Presidential Power* (New York: John Wiley and Sons, Inc., 1960)—a book given careful attention by President Kennedy.

41. *Kennedy* (New York: Harper and Row, 1965), p. 475.

therefore settled on the strategy of executive action. No doubt wishing to avoid argument and disappointment, he did not even establish an interregnum task force on civil rights.[42]

Lyndon Johnson, on the other hand, prodded Senate leaders to use their influence to pass the Elementary and Secondary Education Act, pressed hard for the 1964 Civil Rights Act, and used the power of his office to help bring about passage of the 1965 Voting Rights Act.[43] On May 6, 1964, Johnson said at a News Conference that if the pending civil rights bill was not passed he "would seriously consider coming back here . . . after the Republican convention and, if necessary, coming back after the Democratic convention."[44] The following year he personally delivered a special voting rights message to a joint session of Congress, saying that he would not tolerate their cutting his bill as they had his predecessor's in 1964. He warned them that "this time, on this issue, there must

---

42. *A Thousand Days*, pp. 930–31.

43. Stephen K. Bailey and Edith K. Mosher described factors relating to passage and implementation of the Elementary and Secondary Education Act in their excellent book, *ESEA: The Office of Education Administers a Law* (Syracuse, N.Y.: Syracuse University Press, 1968), p. 64.

44. U.S. President, *Public Papers of the Presidents of the United States* (Washington, D.C.: Office of the *Federal Register*, National Archives and Records Service, 1966), Lyndon B. Johnson, p. 618. Moreover, Clarence Mitchell, NAACP Washington Director, wrote that shortly before passage of the 1964 Act, he had "shared a Capitol subway ride with a distinguished Southern Senator who had long been an opponent of civil rights, but who has usually fought fair. 'We put up a tough fight,' he said, 'but we are going to lose because President Johnson is just putting too much pressure on us.'" "The Warren Court and Congress: A Civil Rights Partnership," *Nebraska Law Review* 48 (1968): p. 99, n. 21.

be no delay, no hesitation and no compromise with our purpose."[45]

Presidential pressure on the Federal judiciary can run the gamut from the Chief Executive's appointment power to his support of court decisions. Use of the Executive sword at Little Rock and the University of Mississippi are illustrations of the dependence of Federal courts on Presidential power. In addition, the philosophical and judicial temperament of a Presidential appointee can have great bearing on future enforcement operations. According to Attorney General Nicholas Katzenbach, the Justice Department, under Kennedy and Johnson, looked throughout the South in order to locate a qualified Negro for a lower court berth, but could not find one. Katzenbach believed it would have been "ridiculous" to look in Mississippi where the Administration "would have tested senatorial courtesy pretty hard," but that they "looked hardest in Florida and Texas," because they could work with Senators Smathers and Yarborough. As for getting enough votes in the Senate Judiciary Committee, Katzenbach found that "Eastland was never any trouble so long as you did not bother Mississippi."[46]

Professor E. E. Schattschneider reportedly believed that the political process is basically a battle between the President and Congress to decide who will control the bureaucracy. His statement is borne out by practical evidence. Presidents come and go periodically, but the staying power of the people that handle the all-important daily operations in and out of Washington is considerably longer. If the man in the White House desires to see his policies carried out he must acquire and maintain control

45. *Public Papers*, Lyndon Johnson, March 15, 1965, p. 283.
46. Nicholas Katzenbach Interview.

over this vast sea of humanity. Kennedy attemped to maintain close relations with the inner layers of the bureaucracy, but appears to have had great difficulty governing the State Department, among others.[47] He tried, for example, to make his Cabinet officers aware of their responsibilities in the area of equal employment by constantly questioning them about the number of new Negro appointees in their departments.[48] Similarly, after President Johnson's 1965 civil rights speech at Howard University, White House sources said that "each Government agency will be asked to review its civil rights, social and economic programs in the light of Mr. Johnson's speech and to see what more can be done by the Government to carry the Negro beyond 'legal equity.' "[49]

Clarence Mitchell, Washington representative of the NAACP and an experienced veteran in the art of the possible related this story of Johnson prodding:

> After passage of the 1965 Voting Rights Act the President invited civil rights leaders to a meeting at the White House. He was in good humor. Noting that some advocates of civil rights seemed to be straying to other fields, he said: 'In my part of the country it gets very cold on the range. The cattle get weary and lie down. If we do not make them stand on their feet they will freeze to death. So we go around and twist their tails until they stand up. That is known as tailing up,' he said. Then pointing to an aide who was present, he said to the group: 'I want him to be in charge of tailing up on civil rights.'[50]

Moreover, when a President feels it is worth his time

---

47. See *A Thousand Days*, p. 681.
48. Roy Wilkins Interview.
49. *New York Times*, June 6, 1965.
50. "The Warren Court and Congress," p. 99.

to follow up a policy decision, it is very difficult for those in the lower echelons to resist his queries. This was experienced by Douglas E. Chaffin when he served as Director of Personnel for the Housing and Home Finance Administration. In an illuminating letter Chaffin recalled that

> starting in the mid fifties, there was a concerted program coordinated by the White House to increase equal opportunity for the employment of negroes [sic] in the Executive Branch of the Government. Responsibility for enforcement was placed on the heads of individual agencies. Yet in 1959, a major center for Federal agencies and employment—the Peachtree Seventh Building in Atlanta—which housed approximately 2,000 employees representing twenty or more agencies, had literally no negro employees, not even custodial on the staffs of these agencies.

Chaffin found, however, that when Norman Mason, Administrator of the HHFA decided that the White House was

> serious about the equal opportunity program, he decreed that it should apply in all of HHFA's regional offices, and he made it clear that he was serious and determined to enforce the program. It was surprising how quickly the administrative obstacles, which had previously barred the employment of negroes, melted away when the top man decided to exert his leadership. . . . I believe that my conclusion that successful enforcement is made up very largely of administrative leadership holds true.[51]

Whitney Young, Executive Director of the National Urban League, commenting on this aspect of enforcement,

---

51. Letter to the writer, March 13, 1968.

stated his belief that there has been a "conscious attempt to bring in people who aren't committed to implement—who don't believe in implementation." He thought the reason for this was that "the Administrations are so sensitive to being accused of having people who are too pro—too much idealistic." He found that "there has developed an obsession with balance," because "on no other commission of Government, except in civil rights, do they get leaders of a program who have reservations of the programs' purpose."[52]

However, a determined President can subtly discourage discriminatory activities by his aides, as illustrated by the following answer given by President Kennedy at a News Conference:

> Question: . . . do you have any feeling about whether members of your administration should belong to the Metropolitan Club here in Washington?
>
> President: It seems to me that where everyone eats and the clubs that they belong to—private clubs—is a matter that each person must decide himself, though I personally approved of my brother's action—the Attorney General.[53]

Or the Chief Executive can directly state the course of action that he wants followed, as exemplified by Postmaster General John A. Gronouski's reaction to an order from President Johnson. Gronouski thereafter issued a directive stating:

> The President has requested that department heads and

---

52. Interview with Whitney Young in New York on August 6, 1969, hereafter cited as Whitney Young Interview.

53. October 11, 1961. John F. Kennedy, *Public Papers* (1964), p. 661. Robert Kennedy had resigned from a private Washington club that prohibited Negroes from joining.

agencies take whatever action is necessary to make certain that Government officials refrain from accepting speaking engagements and from participating in meetings and conferences where segregation is practiced.

Therefore, I am again emphasizing this policy. . . . Officials should not participate in conferences or speak before audiences where any racial group has been segregated or excluded from the meeting, from any of the facilities or the conferences or from membership in the group.[54]

Thus, a President can use many devices to influence others. His relations with organized interest groups, for example, will depend on his ability to control their behavior. The means to accomplish this may entail: awarding Federal grants; giving private audiences; using the prestige and aura of the Presidency to convince; or dialogue intended to spur them on so that they can be of value in helping bring his program to fruition.[55]

Congressional Exertion of Pressure

Congress, in whole and in part, can bring pressure to bear on the President in numerous ways through its powers

---

54. U.S. *Congressional Record*, 88th Cong., 2nd Sess., July 27, 1964, 17063.

55. The NAACP, for example, received a Federal contract for the first time in its sixty-year history when the Department of Housing and Urban Development awarded it $173,760 to survey and analyze minority group building contractors throughout the United States. *New York Times*, July 2, 1969. Moreover, Roy Wilkins lauded the fact that President Kennedy met with the newly created American Negro Leadership Conference on Africa for an "unprecedented thirty-two or thirty-four minutes" interview. More recently Vice President Spiro Agnew spoke before a Southern Governors Conference in an apparent effort to quiet feelings concerning school desegregation. *New York Times*, September 17, 1969.

of appropriation, legislation, and investigation.[56] Woodrow Wilson recognized the power of Congressional chairmen long before he became President. Then, as now, key centers of Congressional power, for and against Negro civil rights, must be dealt with by the President. The Chairman of the House Judiciary Committee, Emanuel Celler, for example, is a liberal Democrat from New York, while the Chairman of the Senate Judiciary Committee, James O. Eastland, is a conservative Democrat from Mississippi.

Pressure exerted on some Congressional entities by other Congressional entities is a legislative way of life. This adversary type of behavior in the area of civil rights is exemplified by the existence of two opposing forces in the House of Representatives—the Southern bloc and the Democratic Study Group. A similar array of interest entities can be found in the Senate.[57] This internal struggle can be readily seen in activities relating to Congress's consideration of the 1964, 1965, and 1968 Civil Rights Acts, as illustrated in *New York Times* headlines:

HOUSE UNIT BALKS MOVES TO SOFTEN CIVIL RIGHTS BILL

2 PARTIES SOFTEN CIVIL RIGHTS BILL: KEY TEST TODAY

SENATE LIBERALS STUDY VOTE PLAN

---

56. In a letter to the writer dated April 11, 1968, Senator Jacob Javits said that Congress "exercises supervision of the enforcement procedures primarily through the appropriations process."

57. *Congressional Quarterly* reported that in the 1964 Congressional session, House and Senate Southern Democrats split 100 percent of the time with Northern Democrats on civil rights votes. On other issues they split 24 percent of the time, for the same year. *Weekly Report*, December 25, 1964, p. 2835.

SENATE REJECTS BAN ON POLL TAX BY VOTE OF 49–45
Southerners and G.O.P. Aid Leadership in Defeating Liberals' Amendment

BAN ON POLL TAX BACKED IN HOUSE
Judiciary Committee Retains Plan Senate Defeated

McCORMACK BACKS BAN ON POLL TAX[58]

MANSFIELD AND DIRKSEN STILL GROPING FOR A RIGHTS COMPROMISE AS SENATE DEBATE ENTERS THIRD WEEK[59]

However, a civil rights leader who has viewed the scene for many years believes that liberals "in Congress don't have the same kind of durability and consistency that the Southerners have." He has observed that "liberals vote for legislation and then take a trip," while "Southerners then sabotage it at appropriations."[60]

Pressure Exerted on the President and Congress
Formal pressure groups played a very important part in the formulation, enactment, and implementation of the civil rights laws. Interest groups, for and against the furtherance of Negro rights, exerted varying degrees of pressure on the President, members of Congress, and the

58. October 23, 1963, October 29, 1963, May 1, 1965, May 12, 1965, May 13, 1965, May 14, 1965, respectively.

59. The maneuvers of Mike Mansfield, Senate Majority leader, and Everett McKinley Dirksen, Senate Minority leader, in the early stages of the 1968 Civil Rights bill illustrate the many roles played in the legislative struggle. The *New York Times* reported that "the stated objective of the two leaders was to 'build a bridge' between the Administration supported bill being backed by the Senate liberals and a substitute measure advanced by Southern conservatives." February 5, 1968.

60. Whitney Young Interview.

Judiciary, in attempts to effectuate their goals.[61] An overall view of their activities is essential for a full understanding of the Federal role in civil rights enforcement.

The anti-civil rights forces, spearheaded by the Southern bloc in Congress, have methodically attempted to weaken Federal programs that are aimed at advancing Negro rights. Their actions to influence the man in the White House have taken such forms as: collective endorsement of petitions opposing Administration enforcement actions, and private meetings with the President protesting school desegregation programs.[62] All Presidents have been aware of the disproportionate legislative strength of the South.[63] In addition, Southern electoral

61. See V. O. Key, Jr., *Politics, Parties, and Pressure Groups*, 5th ed. (New York: Thomas Y. Crowell Co., 1964), especially chapter 6, "Role and Techniques of Pressure Groups," and David Truman, *The Governmental Process*, especially chapters 11 and 12.

62. The *New York Times* reported that on May 2, 1966, 18 Senators from nine Southern states sent a "Most Solemn Petition" to President Johnson, protesting the school desegregation guidelines. It said, in part:

We come to you as Chief Executive of the nation to protest vigorously the abuse of power involved in the bureaucratic imposition of the guidelines and we earnestly beseech your personal intervention to right this wrong and have this order revoked.

A signer, Lister Hill, Democrat of Alabama, commented that "We must fight the President on down." May 15, 1966.

Moreover, Clarence Mitchell, NAACP Washington representative, recalled President Johnson's telling him that Southern officials and others were always "bending his ear" about the guidelines. "Guidelines, guidelines, guidelines, that's all I hear," was Johnson's remark to Mitchell. Interview.

63. In 1966, for example, 10 of the 16 standing committees of the Senate were chaired by Southerners, while 3 of the remaining 6 had Southern Democrats next in seniority. The House standing committees for the same year had Southerners chairing 14 of the 20; and they were second in seniority on 2 of the remaining 6, and third in seniority on the other 4. Statistics based on information in the January 1966 *Congressional*

votes are no longer considered unachievable by leaders of
the Republican Party.[64]

Moreover, Southern opposition has come from coalitions
of Governors, Southern leaders such as George Wallace,
and resolutions by private associations.[65] Pressure from the
area south of the Mason-Dixon line has been constant,
consistent, and intense, coming from both private and
public sectors. The Presidents have been subjected to this
seemingly monolithic barrage.

On the other hand, the loosely knit army pressing for
greater civil rights has had a more difficult time because
they were seeking to change the status quo. It is far easier

Directory (Washington, D.C.: U.S. Government Printing Office, 1966),
89th Cong., 2nd Sess.

64. The South's bloc of delegates at the 1968 Republican Convention
(356) was larger than the East's (355), the Midwest's (352), and the
West's (262). The South tied for third largest in 1952, and was third
again in 1960 and 1964. Statistics based on Congressional Quarterly
computations in New York Times, December 5, 1966.

Furthermore, Clarence Mitchell said that in conversations he had at
the White House with Nixon officials, they admitted that they were
keeping a campaign pledge to Southerners to "keep Thurmond happy,"
and they thought this would be the way "to make Republican inroads into
the South." Interview.

65. At a Southern Governors' conference, Governor Albert P. Brewer
of Alabama presented a resolution protesting to President Nixon the use
of busing to achieve racial balance in the South's public schools. New
York Times, September 16, 1969.

The New York Times' report on television interviews of George C.
Wallace stated that he said he is prepared to run for President again in
1972 "if the Nixon Administration has not handled a half-dozen critical
issues to his satisfaction." July 14, 1969. In a later statement Mr. Wallace
said: "Today, I'm asking the President to tell Mr. Mitchell [U.S. Attorney General] to go back to the Federal courts and ask for the restoration of the freedom-of-choice system." New York Times, September 8,
1969.

A Georgia press association, composed of 227 newspapers, issued a
resolution castigating an action by the Department of HEW. Quoted in
the Congressional Record 112: 20401-2, August 24, 1966.

to block or weaken a new legislative proposal than it is
to get that innovating piece of legislation through Congress. Thus, liberal interest groups struggled to retain
what they had won in the past. Their achievements in the
administrative area of civil rights enforcement have been
quite limited in comparison to their success in the legislative realm. Step by step, from the innovative but weak
1957 and 1960 civil rights laws, to the meaningful statutes
of 1964, 1965, and 1968, they have practiced the art of
the possible with a steady hand. The eventual outcome of
these five momentous bills was contingent upon the support given by the President. Thus, civil rights groups exerted pressure on the White House in the attempt to influence the Chief Executive.[66]

One of these groups, the Leadership Conference on
Civil Rights—a coalition of more than 120 national civil
rights, religious, labor, civil, professional, and fraternal
organizations, was organized to bring about Federal legislative and executive action to assure equal civil rights.
Marvin Caplin, its Washington office director, wrote that

> the Conference, about three years ago, established a Com-
> mittee on Compliance and Enforcement, under the chair-
> manship of James Hamilton, Director of the Washington
> office of the National Council of Churches. The committee's
> purpose is to work for effective enforcement of the laws the
> Conference helped to get enacted. The Committee has
> recently subdivided itself into several subcommittees: on

66. J. W. Anderson touches upon this in his book *Eisenhower,
Brownell and the Congress: The Tangled Origins of the Civil Rights Bill
of 1956–1957* (University, Ala.: University of Alabama Press for The
Inter-University Case Program, 1964); and see Daniel Berman's *A Bill
Becomes A Law*, 2nd ed. (New York: Macmillan Co., 1966) for coverage
of the 1960 and 1964 Civil Rights Acts.

Housing, Employment, Education, Health & Welfare. The reorganization was a response to the difficulty of the oversight task. Committee members do compliance work in addition to their regular work for the organizations they represent in Washington.[67]

Though looking impressive on paper, the Leadership Conference has a small staff and no set budget. Moreover, it depends on voluntary contributions from its members—which are not tax deductible.[68] An illustration of how the Conference operates occurred when Roy Wilkins, its chairman, and Arnold Aronson, its secretary, met with President-elect Kennedy at the New York Carlyle Hotel in January 1961 to press for a comprehensive Executive order on civil rights. Wilkins recalled that:

Our contention was that he had the power to issue the Executive order. We felt that a piecemeal approach wouldn't get anywhere. We tried to sell Kennedy that he had the power. He said we should talk to Sorensen, if Sorensen thought it was okay we can prepare a memo. He would make no commitments, but did not dismiss it.[69]

They presented the memorandum to Theodore Sorensen, President Kennedy's Legal Counsel, in March of that year. Sorensen requested more detailed information, which was prepared by J. Francis Polhaus and two aides during the following three months.[70] The result of this labor, *Fed-*

---

67. Letter to the writer, August 11, 1969.

68. Interview with Arnold Aronson in New York on July 23, 1969, hereinafter cited as Arnold Aronson Interview. Mr. Aronson has a full-time position with the National Jewish Advisory Relations Council.

69. Roy Wilkins Interview.

70. Polhaus is both special consultant to the Conference and Legal Counsel to the Washington office of NAACP.

erally Supported Discrimination, was formally submitted to the President, and then printed and widely distributed to many Kennedy administrators.[71] Mr. Wilkins believes that it was the basis for the Civil Rights Act of 1964.[72]

Civil rights groups also used the mass media to prod the Chief Executive into a desired course of action. Roy Wilkins, for example, told the press in May, 1961, that President Kennedy was wrong in not asking for civil rights legislation at that time. He stated that the President's "decision to leave this sorry legislative history undisturbed constitutes an offering of a cactus bouquet to Negro parents and their children on the seventh anniversary next Wednesday of the Supreme Court school desegregation ruling."[73]

Consultation between individual civil rights leaders and the Chief Executive, another avenue of influence, has taken place more often with Presidents Kennedy and Johnson than with Eisenhower.[74] Arnold Aronson, a veteran of many civil rights campaigns, said that

> the Democratic Administrations had a better relationship [with civil rights groups] because we have much of the same constituencies. . . . Presidents have consulted with individual civil rights leaders on a personal basis, for ex-

---

71. (New York: Leadership Conference on Civil Rights, 1961). Funds for its publication were provided by the NAACP, the United Automobile Workers of America, and the United Steel Workers of America—all members of the Leadership Conference. The pamphlet's 61 pages include: recommendations for, the basis for, and precedents for Executive action; and examples of federally supported discrimination in military affairs, education, employment, housing, health services, and agriculture.

72. Roy Wilkins Interview.

73. *New York Times,* May 11, 1961.

74. Wilkins said that he had had little contact with President Eisenhower. Roy Wilkins Interview.

ample, Johnson consulted with Young, Wilkins, etc., the way Eisenhower never did, but on a personal level, not on an institutional level that gets down to the bureaucracy—not down to the middle and lower bureaucracy.[75]

An example of joint collaboration occurred in 1968 when various groups comprising the Leadership Conference sent representatives to the White House to consider strategy for action in the area of open housing. The Conference people wanted a strong Executive order, in the belief that a Housing statute was impossible.[76] President Johnson, however, insisted on going through the Congressional route. A participant, John Morsell, Assistant Director of the NAACP, believed that

> Johnson wanted legislation. We thought he was ducking the order and putting it into the lap of the Legislature. There were several conferences on this at Leadership Conference. We finally went along with Johnson, but also denounced this form of action . . . Johnson made it plain this was the way he wanted it. We could doubt his strategy but not his intent.[77]

President Johnson commented on this meeting at his last news conference. His words give insight into his conception of office:

> I met with 35 civil rights leaders, all of whom were advocating open housing by Executive order. When I told them we could not do it that way, we don't make laws by

---

75. Arnold Aronson Interview.

76. Interview with John Morsell in New York on July 10, 1969, hereafter cited as John Morsell Interview. Clarence Mitchell, however, agreed with the President in his desire for a Congressional law.

77. *Ibid.*

Executive order in this country, and as a product of the Hill, one who has spent 32 years in the House and in the Senate, I didn't think we could make an act stand up and be effective over the long pull of history if we did not have the Congress embrace it.[78]

Civil rights groups, when united, constituted a powerful army, able to push through the omnibus bill of 1964, the comprehensive Voting Rights bill of 1965, and the Housing bill of 1968. Their success in denying Clement F. Haynsworth, Jr. and G. Harold Carswell Supreme Court berths is another illustration of what they can do when united. They were successful, in the legislative arena, because they, in coordination with Congressional and Administration allies, made a concerted drive for their goals. A description of the collaboration that took place offers insight into the reasons for their success.

In 1964, Emanuel Celler, Chairman of the House Judiciary Committee, and his Republican counterpart, William M. McCulloch joined forces. They were aided by a 22-man steering force from the Democratic Study Group and the help of such liberal Republicans as John Lindsay, Charles McC. Mathias, and Clark MacGregor. In addition, they were in constant communication with members of the White House staff and officials in the Justice Department.[79] Principal opposition came from the Coordinating Committee for Fundamental American Freedoms, a group which received a major portion of its funds from the "Mississippi Sovereignty Commission, a state agency, partly tax-supported, created to preserve racial segrega-

78. *Weekly Compilation of Presidential Documents,* January 17, 1969, pp. 126–27.

79. See *Revolution in Civil Rights,* 3rd ed., pp. 53–60 for excellent coverage of House and Senate action.

tion," and the Southern Democrats in both Houses. More-over, in the House of Representatives "the new Southern wing of the GOP was providing some of the most effective opposition to the bill in floor debate. . . . The Southern Republicans received spotty assistance from a few North-erners."[80] Pressure for the bill was put on Congressmen by individual voters and private groups. In April, 1964, for example, 5,000 church leaders representing the three larg-est United States religions, held an interfaith rally in Washington, D.C. calling for passage of the proposed civil rights bill.[81] The labor unions in the Leadership Confer-ence also joined the drive, as Marvin Caplin pointed out:

The power of labor, in the enactment of civil rights legis-lation as well as in the enforcement of it, is impressive. Indeed, labor's role in getting new civil rights laws on the books is one of the most undisclosed and overlooked factors in written histories of such legislation. . . . The chief labor lobbyists in Washington, those working for the AFL-CIO, the ILGWU, Amalgamated Clothing Workers, Amalga-mated Butcher Workmen, UAW—men and women with excellent hill connections and great talent in approaching members, spend considerable time lobbying for civil rights bills. The Leadership Conference convenes them on civil rights issues. They then go out and work for the passage of the laws. The passage of the series of laws since 1957 is testament to their labors.[82]

Senator Jacob Javits confirmed this when he wrote that "civil rights action groups definitely did influence the pas-

80. *Ibid.*, p. 56.
81. *New York Times*, April 29, 1964.
82. Letter to the writer, August 11, 1969.

sage of civil rights acts and churches were particularly helpful too."[83]

The Voting Rights Act of 1965 was a different story, according to former Attorney General Nicholas Katzenbach. He said that civil rights groups were not so badly needed for this bill and thus had little effect on its outcome. Katzenbach said that the Justice Department "embarrassed Southerners with facts showing voting deprivation," because, he believed, Southerners were not against giving Negroes the vote, but "rather the way it was done —taking away states rights, with this clearly regional legislation."[84]

During the battle over the Housing bill of 1968, the usual coalition of civil rights forces had to match wits and resources with several opponents: the Southern bloc in Congress; a powerful real estate lobby; and other private conservative groups.[85] The three months of behind-the-scenes maneuvering that preceded passage of the bill illustrates once again the potential power of the liberals— when united. Their attempts to line up support to end a forthcoming Senate filibuster meant the difference between failure and success. An example of one such effort was a three-hour talk that Clarence Mitchell of the NAACP had with a Republican Senator on Washington's

---

83. Letter to the writer, April 11, 1968. Javits added that "with regard to enforcement, it is my understanding that specific cases of violations are brought to the attention of the Department by civil rights groups, that laxities in enforcement are brought to the attention of Congress by these same groups and that their words and suggestions are heeded." Moreover, Nicholas Katzenbach said that civil rights groups had a "big effect" on the 1964 bill. Interview.

84. Nicholas Katzenbach Interview.

85. See *Revolution in Civil Rights*, 4th ed., pp. 89–91 for a description of the maneuvering that occurred in the House and Senate.

birthday, ten days before the cloture vote. Mitchell believes that he persuaded the Senator to cast the deciding vote to end debate—the final vote being 65 to 32.[86] Another attempt to get that all-important vote occurred when Senator Jack Miller, Republican of Iowa, made a deal with Senator Edward W. Brooke, Republican of Massachusetts, in which Miller promised to cast his ballot for cloture. Senator Brooke when asked about this wrote:

> It is true that Senator Miller's vote was the decisive one in the fourth and final cloture vote. He withheld his vote during the first call of the roll while we continued discussion which had been in progress for many weeks. In the end he indicated that he would support cloture if I would vote for an amendment he wished to offer. I indicated to him that I could not work for the amendment, and would have to reserve the right to raise certain questions concerning it, but that I would pledge my vote for it . . . and, although I kept my promise to vote for it, I cannot disguise my satisfaction that the Senate did not choose to accept it. . . . Without his help, there could have been no action, much less the far-reaching legislation which was ultimately enacted.[87]

The cloture agreement was confirmed by Senator Miller who said that he cast his vote because he thought "there was a reasonable chance of effectuating a workable compromise on the underlying legislation which would enable the Federal government to make long-overdue progress on the subject of open housing."[88]

86. Interview with Clarence Mitchell, Washington Director of the NAACP in Washington, D.C. on July 18, 1969, hereafter cited as Clarence Mitchell Interview.
87. Letter to the writer, July 28, 1969.
88. Letter to the writer, July 28, 1969.

Having extricated the bill from the Senate, civil rights advocates mustered their forces to get it through the House Rules Committee, out to the House floor for a favorable vote, and to the President for his signature.

Thus, pressure exerted by united civil rights forces proved to be so overwhelming that all effective opposition gave way before it.

SUMMARY

After Reconstruction, Federal activity to bring about Negro civil rights was almost nonexistent until the middle of the twentieth century. The *Brown* school desegregation decisions and the 1957 and 1960 Civil Rights Acts, although significant, nevertheless only partially committed the Federal Government. Full Government acceptance and involvement in civil rights came about with passage of the 1964 omnibus law, the 1965 Voting Rights Act, and the Housing Act of 1968. Thus, prior to the middle of the 1960s national laws for civil rights did little to bring about political, social, and economic equality for the Negro.

During this period, pressure for and against the improvement of civil rights was intense, involving all areas of the Federal Government. The White House and Congress were the focal points for a running battle that took place between opposing factions, each determined to control the situation. Hence, a setting was created in which there was a constant exchange of pressures among the various parts of the branches of Government. It was within this hectic milieu that the Executive Branch attempted to implement Southern Negro civil rights.

UNITS OF IMPLEMENTATION

3

THE CIVIL RIGHTS DIVISION OF THE
JUSTICE DEPARTMENT: VOTING
ENFORCEMENT

THE FIRST AND THE MOST POWERFUL OF THE IMPLEMENTING units analyzed in this study,[1] the Civil Rights Division (CRD) of the Justice Department, came into being as a noncontroversial provision in the 1957 Civil Rights law.[2] Part II of that act, providing "for an additional Assistant Attorney General," is an understatement par excellence when one considers the significant role that the additional

---

1. "Powerful" in terms of its effect on other parts of the Government and the private sector. This will be established in the forthcoming text.

2. J. W. Anderson points this out in *Eisenhower, Brownell, and the Congress.* During Hearings preceding enactment of the 1957 bill, Attorney General Herbert Brownell told the House Committee on the Judiciary: "We think there should be immediate action on the bills to create the commission and to set up the new assistant attorney general. I don't see how anybody really, all things considered, would want to oppose those at the present time." U.S. Congress, 84th Cong., 2nd Sess., 1956, p. 11, quoted in Anderson, pp. 40–41.

Assistant Attorney General, and the Division he headed, played in the area of civil rights.

Its ancestry dates back to 1939 when President Roosevelt's Attorney General, Frank Murphy, created the Civil Liberties Section within the Criminal Division of the Department. This subunit, renamed Civil Rights Section, was given the responsibility 16 years later of drawing up the first civil rights law since 1875, in which it perpetuated its existence and enlarged its domain by including provision for a civil rights division.[3] Prior to the 1957 Act there had been little progress in this area, as testimony by Thurgood Marshall in 1949 indicated:

> During the period this Division has been in existence . . . the main reasons more progress has not been made are: (1) the inadequacies of the existing civil rights statutes; (2) the lack of full departmental status under an Assistant Attorney General; (3) lack of a sufficient number of agents for the Federal Bureau of Investigation; and, finally, the lack of sufficient funds to operate.[4]

The Civil Rights Division's main sponsor was Attorney General Herbert Brownell, a Republican who had represented a Manhattan district in the New York legislature. Brownell had initiated this pioneering piece of legislation almost solely on his own.[5] Moreover, because of the con-

---

3. Anderson, pp. 6, 14.

4. U.S. Congress, House, *Hearings on S. 1725 and S. 1734* before a subcommittee of the House Committee of the Judiciary, 81st Cong., 1st sess., 1949, as quoted in J. Kommers, "The Right to Vote and Its Implementation," *Notre Dame Lawyer* (June, 1964), p. 376, n. 60.

5. Anderson, pp. 5–6. President Truman also recommended this in a legislative program that he presented to Congress in 1948. Moreover, Senator Thomas Hennings's Constitutional Rights Subcommittee similarly proposed establishment of an additional Assistant Attorney General, on

troversial nature of the other parts of the bill,[6] all drafting was done in the Civil Rights Section fully isolated from any contact with members of Congress or representatives of interested lobby groups.[7] According to Anderson's account, the Attorney General's "first concern lay with the conservative Republicans in the Cabinet and on the White House staff."[8]

The first drafts, after circulation through the other parts of the Justice Department, were soon narrowed down, in effect altering the proposed power of the Federal Government to enforce civil rights.[9] However, there remained intact the simple provision which would broaden and institutionalize Frank Murphy's section on civil liberties.[10] The section had grown incrementally during two decades and had thus become somewhat of an accepted part of the political scene. In addition, its prior limited work in the area, i.e., the harm or benefits of its actions, caused no alarm to the opponents of Negro civil rights. The paragraph creating it contained no oratical declaration of human rights nor did it ordain a new Assistant Attorney

---

March 3, 1956. Pp. 12–13, 24. Anderson also reports that "three days after Christmas of 1955 . . . Brownell directed the Justice technicians to begin drafting a civil rights bill." P. 1.

6. *Ibid.*, pp. 16–17. The first two bills, as part of an original package, dealt with the general protection of all civil rights, and was an attempt to prevent coercion and intimidation in voting. The law in its final form, gave the Attorney General power to "institute for the United States, a civil action or other proper proceeding for preventive relief, including an application for a permanent or temporary injunction, restraining order, or other order. In any proceeding hereunder the United States shall be liable for costs the same as a private person." 71 Stat. 637, pt. IV, Sec. 131.

7. Anderson, p. 14.

8. *Ibid.*

9. *Ibid.*, pp. 18–19.

10. *Ibid.*, pp. 40–41.

General to solve the American dilemma. Rather, it innocuously mentioned that he "shall assist the Attorney General in the performance of his duties, and . . . shall receive compensation at the rate prescribed by law for other Assistant Attorneys General."[11] Thus, the section had evolved in a natural way to fit comfortably into its elevated position. It was able to come quietly into existence because civil rights enforcement was not yet a threat to many white Southerners. At this time, in 1957, the only other major effort in behalf of the Negro was the first Brown decision, and this had been tempered by the Supreme Court's "with all deliberate speed" holding in the second Brown case.[12]

PHILOSOPHY

The increase in public recognition of the importance of bringing about greater civil rights, and the energies expended in this direction by pressure entities, was reflected in proportionate actions by the main branches of Government and their constituent units. As the nation progressively gave the Executive Branch more power to enforce civil rights, the thinking and actions of the attorneys in the Civil Rights Division advanced from a state of inertia[13]

---

11. 71 Stat. 637, Sec. 111.

12. On December 3, 1968, in a television interview, Justice Hugo L. Black commented on the "deliberate speed" holding of 1955. He said that "looking back at it now it seems to me it's delayed the process of outlawing segregation. It seems to me, probably, with all due deference to the opinion and my brethren, all of them, that it would have been better—maybe—I don't say positively—not to have that sentence." *New York Times,* December 4, 1968.

13. Interview with St. John Barrett in Washington, D.C. on July 18, 1969, hereafter cited as St. John Barrett Interview. Barrett rose to 2nd

in the late 1950s to unprecedented activism a decade later.[14] St. John Barrett, a high-ranking member of CRD during the Eisenhower, Kennedy, and Johnson Administrations, emphasized the effect on enforcement operations when there is commitment and motivation from the top. He found that when Wilson White headed CRD, during the Eisenhower Administration, there was little activity. At that time the Division was complaint oriented, i.e., nothing was done until people sent their complaints in. This, according to Barrett, prevented CRD from being "self-starting initially." He attributed this, in part, to White's approach which he described as "completely passive, even negative." This, however, changed with White's replacement by Harold Tyler "who had a tremendous effect on the staff," and who brought John Doar in with him, who was "hard-driving, pushing."[15] When Doar came on board, during the end of the Eisenhower Administration, he saw the Civil Rights Division as "suffering from inertia . . . more likely inept." He found that the personnel there "did not know how to do it . . . they never left their desks in Washington . . . did not know what was going on in the field." He believes that when Tyler came in the "en-

Assistant Attorney General and at this writing is Deputy Legal Counsel, HEW.

14. On August 26, 1969, 75 lawyers in CRD met privately after working hours to draft a statement protesting what had appeared to them to be a softening by the Nixon Administration of enforcement of civil rights laws. The notice which called for the meeting said that "recent events have caused some of us to question the future course of law enforcement in civil rights." An attorney who attended the meeting told Fred P. Graham of the *New York Times* that "these people are here because of their social views. It's not like the Tax Division, when they have to stay a few years to get experience for private practice—these guys can leave whenever they think they aren't accomplishing anything." August 27, 1969.

15. St. John Barrett Interview.

gine was stopped," whereupon Tyler "put it into first gear."[16]

John F. Kennedy, the Democratic winner of the 1960 Presidential election, came into office with the support of a constituency that was far more desirous of White House leadership in civil rights than the electorate that ushered in his predecessor. Discounting Kennedy's personal beliefs, more was expected from him, and, theoretically at least, he had greater power. Not only did he have campaign promises to keep, but he swore to uphold the laws of the United States, which included the Civil Rights Acts of 1957 and 1960. The Justice Department—probably never so close to the President in its history because of the kinship and personality of its head lawyer—was the principal instrument through which these high expectations could be met.[17]

During the Kennedy and Johnson Administrations the philosophy of the Attorneys General and their Assistants in charge of the Civil Rights Division as to goals desired and methods of operation was, for the most part, very similar. Time and again, Robert Kennedy said that he would attempt to work through the states before commit-

---

16. John Doar Interview. Doar said that after Tyler brought him in, "the way it turned out I probably was the biggest surprise to him," inferring that he was not expected to be so much an activist as he turned out to be.

17. Burke Marshall, Assistant Attorney General, CRD, during the Kennedy Administration, pointed out that Robert Kennedy's drive and unique personality were important elements in the activist role he had in the Administration. Interview in New York on May 13, 1969, hereafter cited as Burke Marshall Interview. Moreover, Arthur Schlesinger, Jr. noted that "the Department of Justice . . . was the center of federal action and in the year of the Bay of Pigs, Laos, Berlin and test resumption, Kennedy left civil rights policy pretty much to his brother." *A Thousand Days*, p. 934.

ing the power of the Federal Government. On January 22, 1962, for example, he told a House subcommittee on Appropriations:

> In the field of civil rights the Department's basic policy is to seek effective guarantees and action from local officials and civil leaders, voluntarily and without court action where investigation has disclosed evidence of civil rights violations. This policy is proving successful and civil rights problems and difficulties generally are being resolved at the local level. . . . I feel very strongly that this problem is not going to be solved by just passing some laws. It will require some understanding. . . . We have tried to work quietly without publicity and I think this is the way it should be handled. I think the people in the communities appreciate we are not leviathans here coming in and telling them what to do.[18]

He thought that the people in the affected areas, if given the opportunity, would work out the problem. It seemed to him that

> many of these communities will take steps themselves to clear up the situation. . . . I think some laws might be helpful, but there are laws on the books now that can be enforced and that great progress can be made by good will and the Government working quietly behind the scenes, making sure we have our own house cleaned up.[19]

---

18. U.S. Congress, *Hearings*, 87th Cong., 2nd sess., pp. 7, 22.

19. *Ibid.*, p. 22. Arthur Schlesinger, Jr., wrote that "Kennedy and Marshall decided from the start that, before taking situations to the courts, they would first try to negotiate with local officials, thereby giving full respect to the federal system and full opportunity for local self-integration, where they lacked authority to initiate suits, they had ordinarily no other choice." *A Thousand Days*, p. 934.

Robert Kennedy repeated this theme in later years, in his belief that the Department of Justice should not upset the Federal system with unwarranted interference. In 1963 Attorney General Kennedy told the House Judiciary Committee:

> It has been my philosophy, since I became Attorney General, that the way to deal with this was not to have the Federal Government come into these areas and do it, but to have the local officials do it, and to get the local officials to do it, or to get people to register and vote and let them change the situation themselves. I think that was the key to it. . . . I think that in the last analysis, if we are going to have peace and harmony in the United States . . . the problem is going to have to be rectified from within. It is not going to be Washington telling people what to do.[20]

This hands-off-if-possible philosophy applied equally to legislation. In testimony for the proposed 1964 Civil Rights Act, Robert Kennedy said:

> . . . if I did not think this was the only way we could deal with this problem, I would be against this legislation. I think that every time the Federal Government passes a law in any of these areas it has its backwash and has its ill effects. And I think it is better if these matters are left to the citizens, the local communities, and to the States and that the Federal Government stay out of it.[21]

However, if Federal legislation was necessary, both Kennedy and his Assistant in charge of the Civil Rights Division, Burke Marshall, had strong feelings against a statute

---

20. U.S. Congress, *Hearings*, 88th Cong., 1st sess., Ser. No. 4, pt. IV, Executive Session, p. 2737.

21. *Ibid.*, p. 2755.

that would put too much power into the hands of the Justice Department. In accordance with this line of thought, Robert Kennedy in 1963 asked the House Judiciary Committee not to give broad injunctive power to the Attorney General in civil rights cases, because he believed that

> one result might be that State and local authorities would abdicate their law enforcement responsibilities, thereby creating a vacuum in authority which could be filled only by Federal force. This in turn—if it is to be faced squarely . . . would require creation of a national police force. . . . Obviously, the proposal injects Federal executive authority into some areas which are not its legitimate concern and vests the Attorney General with broad discretion in matters of great political and social concern.[22]

Burke Marshall confirmed this when he wrote that "Federal policy under Attorney General Kennedy has been to try to make the federal system in the voting field work by itself through local action, without federal court compulsion."[23] Moreover, he asserted that "since the beginning

---

22. *Ibid.*, pp. 2656–59. Arthur Schlesinger, Jr. observed, during his stay within the inner circles of the Kennedy Administration, that "the Department of Justice felt a responsibility to preserve an appropriate balance between national and state powers in the federal system. This feeling inclined it to question proposals that the national government be given authority to enjoin interference with constitutional protests against racial injustice." *A Thousand Days*, p. 955.

23. Marshall expounded his philosophy in his book entitled *Federalism and Civil Rights* (New York: Columbia University Press, 1964), p. 23. Moreover, in a statement presented at hearings conducted by the Civil Rights Commission in Jackson, Mississippi, on February 18, 1965, Mr. Marshall said: "We have no Federal police force empowered or equipped to provide protection or to maintain law and order on a generalized basis. And I do not believe that the situation, deplorable as it may be in many parts, warrants the departure from the historic pattern of limited Federal power that would be implied by the creation

of 1961 the Department has not brought a case or demanded voting records without first attempting to negotiate the matter with the local officials." In addition, since the autumn of 1960, according to Marshall, the bulk of the Department's work in voting has been through "recognized methods of law enforcement by federal court litigation and injunction. *No more direct controls have been sought.*"[24]

Attorney General Kennedy's successor, Nicholas Katzenbach, shared the Kennedy-Marshall philosophy of cautiously prodding the states and local areas into following the law. Katzenbach believed that "every time you displace local law and local authorities it makes the job more difficult." Moreover, he thought that "it was a failure to *make* people comply with the law," because they "had to do it on their own."[25]

The enforcement of voting rights by the Civil Rights Division gives a clear view of the philosophical approach of Justice Department officials, and the intertwining relationship of theory and application.

VOTING ENFORCEMENT

A few days before the Voting Rights Act of 1965 was

---

of a Federal force having as its purpose the maintenance of internal law and order." *Hearings, Voting* (Washington, D.C.: U.S. Commission on Civil Rights, 1965) 1:261.

24. Marshall, *Federalism and Civil Rights*, pp. 23 and 15. (Italics added)

25. Nicholas Katzenbach Interview. The writer asked Mr. Katzenbach if it were true that Robert Kennedy had made it a condition for his leaving the Department, that Johnson appoint Katzenbach as his successor. Katzenbach replied that if Kennedy did say that, it was very nice, but he thought that such action could "have hurt more than it helped." He said he got the position because he had the "confidence of civil rights groups and Congress."

signed by President Johnson, a White House aide telephoned John Doar, Assistant Attorney General, CRD, and
asked him what his judgment was concerning the number
of Federal examiners that should be sent to Southern counties covered in the law. Doar, soon after, recommended
sending examiners into 20 counties, having based his decision on four factors: (1) CRD's knowledge of facts on
counties gathered from past investigations; (2) the Government's capability to send in examiners, i.e., the Civil
Service Commission's recruiting process; (3) the areas
where it was most certain that compliance would not
come about voluntarily—but where there would not be
overt defiance; and (4) the time factor, i.e., how fast it
could be done. Doar said that "we wanted to show that
the appointment of examiners was out of the realm of
politics . . . we wanted to get voluntary compliance." He
thought that the program should be administered in a way
whereby "people would say that the Department of Justice . . . was fair." Moreover, Doar described his method
of choosing counties as "rational and objective," not the
"gee whiz" way, because, he said, his staff had "to justify
our memos—we worked like hell." CRD sent the names of
the 20 chosen counties to the Attorney General, who then
"selected ten to fifteen."[26]

The use of voting examiners—how many and where they
were to be sent, was often a subject of disagreement between civil rights groups and the Justice Department, with
the Department being pressured to use more examiners.
Doar found himself faced with the question: "What was
the function of the Federal Government."[27] The consensus

26. John Doar Interview.
27. John Doar Interview.
Floyd McKissick, former Director of the Congress of Racial Equality
(CORE), said that officials at the White House had reneged on their

in the Justice Department favored a limited and select use of the examiner provision of the 1965 Act. Stephen Pollak, who replaced Doar as head of CRD in January, 1968, said that he "never considered we were given a responsibility by the law to work to promote pressures to go out and register," but rather "to make sure those who want to register, can." Pollak "made it his position to stay out of politics," because he believed that the "Nation has an important asset in a professional nonpolitical Civil Rights Division." CRD, he felt, could not be a law enforcement agency because "people with whom you deal must feel there is a certain neutrality."[28] Doar had the same view, for he thought that there was a philosophical difference in initiating registration, in that "some of us did not think it was a departmental function." He felt that CRD had no Congressional mandate or money to do that type

promise to civil rights leaders that the "day after the Act was signed they would send in registrars en masse." McKissick said that his group was "constantly in touch with the Civil Rights Division," sending them telegrams and letters, asking for more registrars. He felt he was "always bogged down by red tape in Justice," having sent "request after request" with little result. Interview in New York on July 30, 1969, hereafter cited as Floyd McKissick Interview. Another example of pressure activity in this area occurred in September 1965 when Wiley Branton, Executive Director of the President's Council on Equal Opportunity, helped organize a private boatride down the Potomac whereby Vice President Humphrey had an informal meeting with many civil rights leaders. Some leaders in attendance were: John Morsell of NAACP, Wiley Branton, Clarence Mitchell, Martin Luther King of the Southern Christian Leadership Conference, Whitney Young, and Arnold Aronson. During the meeting, Clarence Mitchell attempted to persuade the Vice President to get Johnson and Katzenbach to send more voting examiners. Interview with Wiley Branton in Washington, D.C., on July 17, 1969, hereafter cited as Wiley Branton Interview; and Clarence Mitchell Interview; and John Morsell Interview.

28. Interview with Stephen Pollak in Washington, D.C. on July 16, 1969, hereafter cited as Stephen Pollak Interview.

of job. Moreover, Doar envisaged that type of activism as being the wrong approach, because, in his opinion, "you have to develop push and drive from the grass roots"— organization must be built from there. He had found that "when the Federal Government builds and takes over, when it leaves the whole thing caves in," because of lack of "indigenous strength."[29]

Similarly, Attorney General Katzenbach did not believe it was the Department's duty actively to get potential voters to register. He had the Department cooperate with civil rights groups by finding out where they were conducting their voter registration drive so that the Justice Department could send examiners in "if the case warranted it." However, Katzenbach had found that "this was not always necessary" because "following our philosophy we tried to send examiners only if the areas did not follow the law."[30]

Ramsey Clark, last of the Kennedy-Johnson Attorneys General, appears to have been more of an activist than either Robert Kennedy or Nicholas Katzenbach, his two immediate predecessors.[31] Katzenbach's theory of govern-

---

29. John Doar Interview.
30. Nicholas Katzenbach Interview.
31. Clark personally viewed himself as being more of an activist than his predecessor, Nicholas Katzenbach. Ramsey Clark Interview. Stephen Pollak, head of CRD under Clark, saw him, "of all who headed the Department," as "probably . . . [the] most forward." In Pollak's opinion, Clark was also more activist than Doar and "less troubled in having Justice more allied with Black interests." Stephen Pollak Interview. Clarence Mitchell thought that Clark was "the best of the three," having "had the greatest amount of personal concern—a deep sense of commitment." Mitchell said that Clark had "literally spent hours with him on things—not only matters of seeking what was legal, but what was right." Mitchell recalled that Robert Kennedy and Nicholas Katzenbach were both concerned, "but not being from the South, tended to believe Southern executives too much; for example, in the Meredith case really believed

ment did not have much persuasiveness with him, because Clark believed that "people have to exercise their rights," and that the Justice Department had the "responsibility, leadership in a sense, to bring awareness to people." He thought there was the "need to work with blacks—who were conditioned over the years," and believed it was the Government's "responsibility to get them to come forth and vote." In doing so, he thought that "affirmative action was necessary—persuasion, encouragement of Black leadership." Yet Clark was in agreement with Kennedy, Marshall, Katzenbach, Doar, and Pollak in his view that "government can't directly go out and get the voters to the polls," an activity which he thought "was the work of voter registration groups," and others.[32] He said that when he was Attorney General the Department supported groups like the Voter Education Project and had attempted to "get local people to encourage registration." Moreover, he said that he would have appointed a "big batch of examiners" to "keep momentum going," but although he "was ready to go for examiners everywhere" he found that they were not needed everywhere, and that it was "just wasteful" to send them to a place where only "two people a day registered," and where he could not "justify keeping an office open."[33]

Governor Barnett when he told them he would obey the law. Clark would not have believed this." "Katzenbach," Mitchell further added, "was more realistic than Bobby but did not have the first-hand experience that Clark had nor the power that Bobby had," while Robert Kennedy "had no real powers under Johnson." Clarence Mitchell Interview.

32. Ramsey Clark Interview. In Clark's opinion, Katzenbach believed that the Department's "ultimate purpose is to secure voting registration within the Federal framework. Use examiners only if essential," because "if you use too much of Federal force the state system would not operate on its own," and "you would displant or supplant it."

33. *Ibid.* Statistically, as of December 31, 1967, examiners had been

John N. Mitchell, President Nixon's Attorney General, approached the Voting Rights law in a somewhat different fashion. In a statement made before a House Judiciary subcommittee hearing looking into the proposed extension of the 1965 Act, Mr. Mitchell said:

> Our bill would maintain the authority of the 1965 Voting Rights Act for the Attorney General to send examiners and observers into the seven Southern states. But it would extend this authority to all states and counties where the Attorney General had received any complaints of possible violations of the 15th Amendment rights.
>
> Under the 1965 act, the Attorney General is required to go to court to request voting examiners and observers in non-Southern states. Under our bill, he has the authority to send the observers and examiners any place without first applying to the court.[34]

---

sent to 58 counties in five Southern states, where they listed as eligible to vote 158,094 persons, which included 150,767 nonwhites and 7,327 whites (U.S. Civil Service Commission, Memorandum on Voting Rights Program, January 1968). In addition, according to the Civil Rights Commission, there were 185 other eligible counties and parishes which had not been designated for examiners (76 in Georgia, 16 in Mississippi, 32 in Alabama, 25 in South Carolina, 27 in North Carolina, and 9 in Louisiana). Moreover, the Voter Education Project (VEP) of the Southern Regional Council issued a report, on July 1966, "The Effects of Federal Examiners and Organized Registration Campaigns on Negro Voter Registration," showing the following figures:

	Alabama	Miss.	S.C.
Federal Examiners and VEP	69.5	51.7	67.0
Federal Examiners Only	63.7	41.2	71.4
VEP Only	57.6	34.9	51.6
Neither	45.4	24.2	48.8

Statistics from Civil Rights Commission, *Political Participation, Voting Act of 1965*, pp. 154–56.

34. *New York Times*, July 2, 1969. Representative William M. McCulloch, Republican of Ohio and ranking minority member of the House Judiciary Committee, opposed the Administration's bill because he believed it "creates a remedy for which there is no wrong and leaves

He had told the subcommittee earlier that "while Congress may have had sufficient reason to pass regional legislation in the 1965 act, I do not believe that this justification exists any longer," for "*I cannot support what amounts to regional legislation.*"[35]

During a comprehensive exclusive interview with *U.S. News & World Report*, Mitchell clearly stated a basic part of his philosophy concerning civil rights enforcement:

> *Question*: You've been in office now for six months. What do you think are the significant changes, if any, in the policy and attitude of the Justice Department today as compared with the previous Administration?
>
> *Mitchell*: . . . I think the approach to our civil rights problems is different in concept of execution, perhaps, as distinguished from the ultimate goals that we're looking for. I think the Civil Rights Division as it existed prior to the time we came in had the same goals, but I think that they went about it as more of an adversary-proceeding operation than we have. We've tried, particularly in school desegregation, to get compliance out of voluntary procedures.[36]

---

grievous wrongs without adequate remedy. . . . That is not the kind of civil rights legislation that gives hope to black America. It is the kind of civil rights legislation that is favored by Attorney General Summer of Mississippi . . . [and] opposed by the Leadership Conference on Civil Rights and by the Civil Rights Commission." *New York Times*, July 2, 1969.

35. *New York Times*, June 27, 1969. (Italics added) An experienced civil rights worker, Marvin Caplin, Director of the Washington Office of the Leadership Conference on Civil Rights has found that "under U.S. Attorney General John Mitchell and Assistant Attorney General Jerris Leonard, civil rights enforcement gets little assistance. We fear the worst here. We think these men—Mitchell particularly—are ready to sabotage the program—through indifference, through insufficient effort, through ignorance of what terrible consequences can follow relaxation of enforcement." Letter to the writer, August 11, 1969.

36. August 18, 1969, p. 53.

This emphasis on bringing about compliance voluntarily had been spelled out in an earlier HEW-Justice joint statement in which Mitchell and HEW Secretary Robert H. Finch stated:

> Our aim is to educate, not to punish; to stimulate real progress, not to strike a pose; to induce compliance rather than compel submission.

Moreover, as in the Administration approach to the Voting Rights Act, Mitchell and Finch stated their determination to stay away from regional legislation. They further said:

> The implications of the Brown decisions are national in scope. The problem of racially separate schools is a national problem . . . and we are determined that the law of the land will be upheld; and that the Federal role in upholding that law, and in providing equal and constantly improving educational opportunities for all, will be firmly exercised *with an even hand.*[37]

Thus, the approaches of Justice Department administrators as to choice of goals and methods to achieve chosen objectives was based in large part on individual and group philosophies. The methods of operation of the Civil Rights Division, therefore, was a natural consequence of the perspectives of its policy makers.

METHODS OF OPERATION

Prior to the Civil Rights Act of 1957 there had been little activity in the Justice Department for the protection

---

37. *New York Times,* July 4, 1969. (Italics added)

of Negro rights, and not much of an increase in case load in the final years of the Eisenhower Administration.[38] In June, 1960, Assistant Attorney General Harold Tyler told a Senate Appropriations Committee that the Civil Rights Division had filed but five cases from the time of passage of the 1957 Act.[39] Theodore Sorensen had written that "beginning in 1961, more than three dozen [cases] were initiated and won in the next three years, with dozens of others in process."[40] Moreover, the Civil Rights Division received 665 complaints in fiscal year 1960 compared to 162 complaints the year before.[41] In its *Annual Report* for 1965, the Justice Department pointed out that "since its inception the major portion of the Division's activity has been directed toward enforcement of the right to vote," and although "additional duties placed upon the Division by the 1964 Act have brought about greater activity in non-voting areas, especially in school desegregation . . . *nevertheless, the workload continues to consist primarily of voting matters.*"[42]

38. See Robert K. Carr, *Federal Protection of Civil Rights: Quest for a Sword* (Ithaca, N.Y.: Cornell University Press, 1947); Anderson, *Eisenhower, Brownell, and the Congress*, pp. 6–11; and Marshall, *Federalism and Civil Rights*, p. 7.

39. U.S. Congress, Senate, Committee on Appropriations, *Hearings*, 86th Cong., 2nd sess., p. 393.

40. *Kennedy*, p. 479.

41. U.S. Department of Justice, *Annual Report of the Attorney General of the United States, for the Fiscal Year ended June 30, 1961* (Washington, D.C.: Government Printing Office, 1961), p. 197. In his book *A Thousand Days*, Arthur Schlesinger, Jr. stated that by the middle of 1963 Kennedy and Marshall filed 42 suits and "in behind-the-scenes effort . . . the administration, with helpful assistance from the Taconic Foundation and collaboration from the Southern Regional Council, persuaded the leading Negro organizations to undertake a drive which in 1963 registered a considerable number of Negro voters across the South." P. 955.

42. U.S. Department of Justice, *Annual Report of the Attorney Gen-*

However, despite the progressive extension of Federal authority in the voting area—by means of the 1957, 1960, and 1964 Acts, little was actually accomplished in the deep South until the 1965 Voting Rights Act. This was frankly stated by Attorney General Nicholas Katzenbach in testimony he gave before a House Judiciary subcommittee in March, 1965, in which he said:

> What has been the effect of these statutes? It is easy to measure. In Alabama, the number of Negroes registered to vote has increased by 5.2 percent between 1958 and 1964. . . . In Mississippi, the number of Negroes registered to vote has increased at an even slower rate. . . . In 1954, about 4.4 percent of the eligible Negroes were registered; today we estimate the figure at about 6.4 percent. . . . And in Louisiana, Negro registration has not increased at all, or if at all, imperceptibly. . . . The lesson is plain. *The three present statutes have had only minimal effect. They have been too slow.*[43]

Negro registration was accelerated after passage of the 1965 Voting Rights Act. By spring 1968 the percentage of

---

eral of the United States, for the Fiscal Year ended June 30, 1965 (Washington, D.C.: Government Printing Office, 1965), p. 170. (Italics added) Schlesinger states that "the Department gave first priority . . . to voting rights. . . . Concentration on the right to vote, in short, seemed the best available means of carrying the mind of the white South." *A Thousand Days*, p. 935. Sorenson concurs in this, and further states that Kennedy "was convinced that enfranchising the Negroes in the South . . . could in time dramatically alter the intransigence of Southern political leaders on all other civil rights measures, shift the balance of political power in several states, and immunize Southern politics from the demagogue whose only campaign cry was 'Nigger!' " *Kennedy*, p. 478. Moreover, Assistant Attorney General Stephen Pollak said that voting was the *"sine qua non*—a basic right to achieve other rights." Interview.

43. U.S. Congress, House, Committee on the Judiciary, Subcommittee No. 5, 89th Cong., 1st sess., Serial No. 2, p. 4 (Italics added)

Negroes registered in the 11 deep Southern states rose 14 percent since November, 1964, permitting 636,563 more Negroes the right to vote. Specifically, the percentages rose 28.6 percent in Alabama, 53.1 percent in Mississippi, and 26.9 percent in Louisiana, allowing 428,613 more Negroes the right to vote in those three states alone.[44]

Implementation in school desegregation began, for the most part, when the Justice Department was empowered by the 1964 Civil Rights Act to act. Because of this statute, according to an official Justice Department publication, "increasing emphasis was placed on school desegregation matters during fiscal 1965. Three portions of the Act— Title IV, Title VI, and Title IX, added greatly to the Division's responsibilities in this field," which had been "limited to the enforcement of court orders and *amicus* participation."[45] Moreover, major enforcement efforts to end discrimination in employment have been recent, as indicated in a statement that Assistant Attorney General

44. Statistics in *Revolution in Civil Rights*, 4th ed., p. 115.

45. *Annual Report of the Attorney General, for the Fiscal Year ended June 30, 1965*, p. 175. In 1965 school desegregation was the second most active field of law enforcement by CRD, which participated in six times as many school cases than the year before. *Annual Report of the Attorney General, for the Fiscal Year ended June 30, 1966*, p. 183. In June, 1965, during hearings, Katzenbach pledged a full-scale attack against segregated schools. This was launched that year with the Department filing or intervening in 44 school desegregation suits under the 1964 Act, compared to 7 such suits the year before. Justice Department statement, U.S. Congress, House, Committee on Appropriations, before a subcommittee of the Committee on Appropriations, 90th Cong., 1st sess., pt. 1, 1967, p. 354. The Department stated that two basic needs governed its school litigation program after the 1964 Act: (1) ". . . secure recognition of *Brown* v. *Board of Education* as the law in school systems throughout the South" and (2) . . . use federal court litigation to support the school desegregation program of the Department of Health, Education and Welfare under Title VI of the 1964 Act." *Annual Report of the Attorney General for the Fiscal Year ended June 30, 1967*, pp. 173–75.

Pollak made before a Senate Appropriations Committee in June 1968. He said:

> the cases that we have brought in recent years have been primarily public accommodations and school suits . . . this year we have been devoting a major share of our attention to Title VII—fair employment. We have brought, to my knowledge . . . through June 30, 1968, 23 cases under that title in fiscal year 1968. . . . In fiscal year 1967 we brought a total of 144 cases.[46]

In another area, housing, efforts are in the beginning stages, with the first Justice Department suit filed on July 14, 1969.[47]

A generally practiced rule in the Civil Rights Division called for Justice Department personnel to attempt to bring about compliance with the laws by persuasion if

---

46. Address at Emancipation Day Ceremonies, Mobile, Alabama, January 5, 1969, Department of Justice *Release*, p. 7. Mr. Pollak told the writer that in reality, employment did not have top priority in 1968, but that CRD was able to devote more time to it because "now in 1968 it was possible to move commitment of forces on employment," allowing it to get a larger degree of attention. Stephen Pollak Interview. Moreover, Ramsey Clark said: "We made it a high priority" in the "late fall of 1966." Interview.

Furthermore, it appears that the Nixon Administration is continuing to give this area high priority. A White House source told the *New York Times* that Nixon believed that such traditional civil rights activities as open housing and voting rights were less significant in the long run than efforts to open up the job market to minorities. Another high Administration official said in an interview that there might be "justifiable criticism of the Nixon Administration on school desegregation, but I'm confident we're going to go farther in this Administration than did any other on job equality." He added: "Look at what's happening now in Chicago, Pittsburgh, Boston and Philadelphia, the big thrust now is not schools, but jobs." September 24, 1969.

47. This occurred in Chicago, Ill., against a brokerage firm accused of discriminating against Negroes. *New York Times*, July 15, 1969.

possible. This was emphasized by Burke Marshall in a statement prepared for a Congressional hearing, in which he said:

> The Civil Rights Division, pursuant to a policy established by the Attorney General, files no legal action under the Civil Rights Act . . . to compel the production of Federal election records, without giving the State and local authorities full notice and opportunity to avoid recourse to litigation by corrective measures at the State and local level.

Upon further questioning, Marshall explained the preliminary steps that the Department usually took before they engaged in formal court actions:

> if we receive a complaint or if we have some other reason to believe a Federal statute is being violated, we do in fact call it to the attention of the local people where there is some action they can take to correct the situation themselves, but before that is done we go through the investigative process. I, personally, get deeply involved in discussions and conversations with the local people, and if I do not do it personally some lawyer from my Division does it. . . . So in terms of my time and the time of the lawyers, these matters that are resolved without court action take a great deal of time.[48]

The Attorney General, moreover, fully concurred with this method, as Robert Kennedy told the Senate Judiciary Committee in 1963:

> legal actions should be the last resort. In every civil rights

---

48. U.S. Congress, House, Committee on Appropriations, *Hearings* before a subcommittee of the Committee on Appropriations, 87th Cong., 2nd sess., 1962, pp. 89, 95 respectively.

situation, our consistent policy in this administration has been to seek voluntary local action first, through negotiation and persuasion. . . . The same policy has been followed even more successfully in the field of transportation, where we have dealt with air, bus, and rail facilities, and in education.[49]

This informal type of implementation apparently remains as a basic part of the Civil Rights Division arsenal, for President Nixon's CRD chief, Jerris Leonard, stated that the Administration would adopt "a sympathetic approach" to all the parties who are concerned with school desegregation matters. He called upon lawyers in his Division to achieve integration through "persuasion and leadership, backed by the use of Federal coercion when it is needed."[50]

In addition, Justice Department officials, following this flexible approach, were reluctant to be forced—by legislative enactment—to use coercive methods. The Kennedy Administration's view on fund-withholding from segregated institutions was stated by Burke Marshall in testimony before a House subcommittee on Education and Labor. Marshall said:

Unless no other course is available . . . I question whether the withholding of funds is best adapted to achieving the desired result. . . . Where possible, we favor the positive, direct approach of a desegregation suit to a withdrawal of funds.[51]

49. U.S. Congress, Senate, Committee on the Judiciary, *Hearings*, 88th Cong., 1st sess., 1963, p. 103.

50. *New York Times*, September 22, 1969.

51. U.S. Congress, House, Committee on Education and Labor, *Hearings* before a subcommittee on Integration in Federal and Public Education, Committee on Education and Labor, 87th Cong., 2nd sess., 1962, p. 601.

His words were not heeded, for Congress, in Title VI of the 1964 Civil Rights Act, prohibited the Federal Government from giving funds to racially discriminating recipients. Nevertheless, the Justice Department continued to show great reluctance to use this method, as evidenced by a policy statement issued by Attorney General Katzenbach on December 27, 1965. Katzenbach, acting as coordinator for all Title VI enforcement activities, reminded the heads of 21 departments and agencies concerned that

> title VI requires that a concerted effort be made to persuade any noncomplying applicant or recipient voluntarily to comply with Title VI. Efforts to secure voluntary compliance should be undertaken at the outset in every noncompliance situation and should be pursued through each stage of enforcement action.[52]

The Justice Department, continuing this line of thought under the Republican Nixon Administration, has indicated a similar disinclination to use the fund-withholding weapon. Attorney General John Mitchell and HEW Secretary Robert Finch said in a joint statement relating to public school desegregation that they would aim "to minimize the number of cases in which it becomes necessary

52. *Guidelines for the Enforcement of Title VI, Civil Rights Act of 1964*, in *Compliance Officers Manual for Title VI, Act of 1964* (Washington, D.C.: U.S. Government Printing Office for the U.S. Civil Rights Commission, 1966), p. 32.

In an Address given in 1966, Attorney General Katzenbach said: "The Department of Justice takes no pride in the fact that it has had to originate or to intervene in large numbers of school desegregation suits over the years. The 22 suits which the Department has brought this year derive from the unfortunate failure of the normal processes of political and community adjustment." "Law Day Celebration and Banquet," University of S. Carolina Law School, April 28, 1968, Columbia, South Carolina, Department of Justice *Release*, p. 7.

to employ the particular remedy of a cut-off of Federal funds, recognizing that the burden of this cutoff falls nearly always on those the act was intended to help, the children of the poor and the black."[53] Shortly thereafter, on September 26, 1969, the President directly stated his viewpoint. Nixon said:

> I do not consider that it is a victory for integration when the Federal Government cuts off funds for a school and thereby, for both black and white students in that school, denies them the education they should have. . . . I believe, therefore, that that particular device should be used, as we are currently using it, only when it is absolutely necessary for the purpose of achieving our objective of desegregated education.
>
> We are for it but we are going to avoid both extremes.[54]

Thus, Nixon's reluctance to use Executive force to execute the civil rights laws is not unique, for this attitude was shared by former Presidents. It was an avowed policy, for example, during the Kennedy and Johnson Administrations not to become active participants in voter registration drives, but rather to let private groups handle that kind of activity.[55] Attorney General Katzenbach expressed the belief that

53. *New York Times,* July 4, 1969.

54. News conference on September 26, 1969, *New York Times,* September 27, 1969.

55. Stephen Pollak said that Attorney General Kennedy and Burke Marshall tried to get private support to get out the vote, but would not use CRD for this type of activity. Interview. This was confirmed by Roy Wilkins, who recalled that in some counties the Government was unable to get people to register even though examiners were sent in. Thus, he said, the "NAACP agreed to keep tabs with the Justice Department where registrars were going in, and cooperate with local NAACP affiliates to get registration." Interview.

the key to this kind of success is not examiners alone, but
also the local momentum.

. . . for decades, no Negro had ever registered to vote in
either Madison or East Carroll Parish. But because of
registration drives generated by CORE in Madison Parish
and by local Negro leaders in East Carroll, Negroes began
to brave the registrars' offices.[56]

Similarly, John Doar feared that the "public would believe that the Federal examiners are a substitute for active
local organizations" in accomplishing registration. This,
he wrote, could be "counterproductive as far as bringing
Negroes out of the caste system and making them visible
participants in our political life." Doar thought that "a
political organization at the local level is needed and the
designation of examiners alone and the subsequent registration of the Negro electorate by the Federal Govern-

56. Speech before the National Press Club in Washington, D.C. on
October 21, 1965, Department of Justice *Release*. Several months later,
on February 28, 1966, Katzenbach told civil rights leaders that private
organizations, rather than the Federal Government, had the responsibility for getting voters registered. He said that "the most important
generating factor is local organization. . . . Counties which have extensive
Negro registration, whether by local officials or by Federal examiners
are counties in which registration campaigns have been conducted. In
counties without such campaigns, even the presence of examiners has
been of limited gain." *New York Times,* March 1, 1966. John Doar said
that the Civil Rights Commission wanted the Justice Department and
the Civil Service Commission to mobilize the registrars, start registration
drives, and conduct other such operations, but Doar would have no part
of that. Interview.
Concerning school desegregation, Katzenbach believed that it was a
question of finding parents, under the freedom of choice policy, who
wanted to send their children to white schools. "We need large numbers
of Negro students to go. . . . It is hard to get the Negro parents to send
their kids to white schools. . . . It is up to civil rights groups to get them
to do this . . . it was fine to cooperate with them," but "it was not the
job of our lawyers to go out." Nicholas Katzenbach Interview.

ment cannot achieve this."[57] Theoretically, Ramsey Clark did not share this view, but in practice he believed that "Government can't directly go out and get the voters to the polls . . . that was the work of voter registration groups."[58]

CIVIL RIGHTS DIVISION STAFF

As greater compliance was brought about in the area of voting rights, more and more Civil Rights Division energy was expended in the enforcement of laws in other spheres of racial discrimination. Most staff efforts, however, throughout the history of the Division, have been concentrated in the Southern states. Civil Rights Division activity in other sections of the nation has been a relatively recent occurrence.[59] Moreover, compared to other

---

57. Memorandum dated January 12, 1967, from John Doar to Ramsey Clark, as quoted in Civil Rights Commission, *Political Participation*, p. 156.

58. Ramsey Clark Interview.

59. After a comprehensive study, the Civil Rights Commission reported that "prior to the 1967 reorganization of the Civil Rights Division, 40 attorneys were assigned to the Southeastern and Southwestern Sections which included Mississippi, Alabama, Louisiana, Georgia, Florida, and South Carolina. As of March 13, 1968, 27 attorneys were assigned to the new Southern Section, which includes Mississippi, Alabama, Louisiana, Florida, and Georgia. South Carolina, along with North Carolina and Virginia, was placed in the new Eastern Section to which 11 attorneys were assigned. In addition, other attorneys in the Planning and Coordination Office and in the Title VI unit also deal with Southern problems as part of their regular duties. Where responsibilities under the Voting Rights Act in connection with elections have made heavy demands on manpower, the Assistant Attorney General has called on attorneys assigned to sections with responsibilities for States outside the South." Letter from Stephen J. Pollak to William L. Taylor, March 13, 1968, as cited in Civil Rights Commission, *Political Participation*, p. 169, n. 91. Concerning CRD activity in other parts of the nation, the Government

divisions within the Justice Department, CRD has had a small staff.[60] John Doar felt that he never had to ask for a larger staff because he thought "it was administratively feasible to expand at 15 percent to 25 percent per year." He thought it was "hard to expand much faster."[61] On the other hand, Katzenbach, Clark, Marshall, and Pollak all believed that they could have used more men.[62] Pollak told an Alabama audience on January 5, 1969, that "the Civil Rights Division does not have the resources to do the whole job. We have 105 attorneys, one-half an attorney for each one million United States citizens." Moreover, he thought that "the commitment of all our personnel in one state would be insufficient to insure full enforcement of all the civil rights in that state, just as I am sure that the commitment of all our personnel to

filed its first Northern school desegregation case on July 8, 1968, in an attempt to get a suburban Chicago school district to desegregate its faculties and student bodies. *New York Times,* July 9, 1968. Exactly one year later the Justice Department warned the school board of Waterbury, Connecticut that it must take immediate action to correct racial imbalance in its schools or be the subject of the first school desegregation suit ever filed by the Government in the northeastern states. The letter, signed by Jerris Leonard, chief of CRD, had followed a formal investigation. *New York Times,* July 9, 1969. After several months, the Justice Department officially filed suit to bring Waterbury into compliance. *New York Times,* October 15, 1969.

60. From approximately 1,000 lawyers in the Justice Department (excluding U.S. Attorneys) the Civil Rights Division, for fiscal year 1958 to 1969, increased from 18 to 105 attorneys. The following statistics are derived from the *Annual Reports of the Attorney General* and official figures given by Justice Department officials at Appropriations and other hearings: 1958 (18); 1959 (29); 1960 (29); 1961 (35); 1962 (40); 1963 (48); 1964 (72); 1965 (72); 1966 (86); 1967 (86); 1968 (105); 1969 (105).

61. John Doar Interview.

62. Based on interviews with: Nicholas Katzenbach, Ramsey Clark, Burke Marshall, and Stephen Pollak.

enforce one of these laws nationwide would still be inadequate."[63] This statement, made by a member of the Johnson Administration, offers an interesting comparison to a remark made by Jerris Leonard—Pollak's counterpart in the Republican Nixon Administration. Leonard, speaking about a possible order by the Supreme Court which would direct the immediate desegregation of schools throughout the South, said that "if the Court were to order instant integration nothing would change. Somebody would have to enforce that order. There just are not enough bodies and people" in the Civil Rights Division "to enforce that kind of a decision."[64] Ramsey Clark, similarly, had told the Senate Appropriations Committee in June 1968 that the Justice Department had

> a responsibility to enforce the laws. Our ability to do so is limited by inadequate manpower. If we had that manpower we could better enforce the laws, and secure trials. Most cases as a practical matter don't go to trial anyway.[65]

As a general rule, civil rights cases were prepared and presented in court solely by CRD lawyers, the Department making very little use of the United States Attorneys who were based in the South. Nicholas Katzenbach said that the U.S. Attorneys were usually present in court because "they were needed to show that the law had to be obeyed. Their presence helped in the courtroom." But, they were not asked to take the cases, because, Katzenbach believed, they would be too greatly exposed, having had their

63. Emancipation Day Ceremonies, Mobile, Alabama, Department of Justice Release.

64. New York Times, September 30, 1969.

65. U.S. Congress, Senate, Hearings before the Senate Appropriations Committee, 90th Cong., 2nd sess., 1969, p. 734.

homes and families in the area in which they served. Moreover, he felt, they had other duties, and their "strong defense of civil rights cases would render them ineffective" in these areas.[66] Ramsey Clark confirmed this, saying that the U.S. Attorneys "are confirmed by the Senate and nominated by Senators," and we "can't then show up these Southern Senators."[67] Moreover, John Doar said that they were not used because they "did not have it in their gut" to do the job.[68]

Furthermore, the relatively few Negro attorneys in the Division did not, for the most part, directly participate in Southern courtroom litigation. Burke Marshall believed that a Black lawyer would have had a difficult time before a white Southern jury. Moreover, he said, it was difficult to find Negro attorneys.[69] The Department, according to Ramsey Clark, "tried very hard to recruit Black attorneys . . . but they are few and far between . . . hard to find . . . there are less today than in 1948." However, Clark also believed that it would have been difficult for a Black lawyer to try a Southern civil rights case.[70] Katzenbach felt the same way, and further recalled that Robert Kennedy

66. Nicholas Katzenbach Interview.

67. Ramsey Clark Interview.

68. John Doar Interview.

69. Burke Marshall Interview. At a Senate Appropriation Committee hearing in 1964, Marshall said that there were four Negro attorneys, out of 40, in the Civil Rights Division, and that "none of the people who work in the Civil Rights Division or in the Department of Justice was hired either because he was white or because he was Negro." He further stated that there were, as of June 30, 1963, two Negro U.S. Attorneys and 38 assistant U.S. Attorneys. U.S. Congress, Senate, 88th Cong., 2nd sess., pp. 1107–8. Ramsey Clark, interviewed in July, 1969, thought that the Department had approximately 70 Negro attorneys. Interview.

70. Ramsey Clark Interview.

got many Negroes into the Department as a "show for civil rights groups."[71]

An intangible but highly significant factor that aided the Civil Rights Division in its enforcement work was the pride and *esprit de corps* that existed.[72] Ramsey Clark remembered the Division as being a very intense place— the most active part of the Department, which "attracted concerned people who were committed." Clark found that these men were not triggered from outside pressure but rather from internal pressure "generated from the commitment of people," because the Civil Rights Division was "not a steppingstone to a lucrative law practice." He noted

---

71. Nicholas Katzenbach Interview. However, Jack Greenberg, Director-Counsel of the NAACP Legal Defense and Educational Fund, and Norman C. Amaker, his first Assistant Counsel, both emphatically disagreed with the above-stated Justice Department belief that Black lawyers would not be so effective as white lawyers in the South. Greenberg said that 95 percent of his organization's cases were handled by Negro attorneys—"white lawyers almost invariably won't take cases . . . maybe 5 to 10 white lawyers who will take cases," in the entire South. Norman Amaker, a Negro, who has filed and tried "hundreds of cases in the South—more than any single man," said that the "most effective lawyers have been local Black lawyers," and that from his personal experience Southern judges are more pleased to see Black lawyers because the judges feel that Black attorneys are fighting for their own cause, while white attorneys are resented. Interviews with Jack Greenberg in New York on July 3, 1969, hereafter cited as Jack Greenberg Interview; and with Norman Amaker in New York on July 3, 1969, hereafter cited as Norman Amaker Interview.

72. This feeling was easily detected by the writer and directly stated in interviews with Justice Department officials. Moreover, it was reflected in a meeting held on August 26, 1969, in which 75 CRD lawyers drafted a statement protesting what appeared to them to be a softening by the Nixon Administration of civil rights enforcement. *New York Times,* August 27, 1969. Furthermore, Ramsey Clark said that there was a "romance of civil rights" on the part of new recruits during the early years—1961 to 1966. Interview.

that there was not much difference in CRD staff under Nixon, in that 99 percent of the people are the same as served under Johnson.[73] Moreover, Stephen Pollak has observed that "policy comes from the bottom up . . . until policy is changed." As Assistant Attorney General, Pollak found that "line officials continue to apply prior policy . . . developing and proposing to the Assistant Attorney General proposed lawsuits."[74]

Thus, the strong traditions of the Department, the common legal backgrounds of its members, and the sense of mission of many attorneys in the Civil Rights Division had helped make CRD an organization that was able to work in unison.

THE CIVIL RIGHTS DIVISION AND PRESSURE ENTITIES

The Civil Rights Division was influenced by and in turn exerted pressure on other pressure entities. The Justice Department's relations with the White House, Congress, other parts of the bureaucracy, and formal interest groups offers insight into its operations as a civil rights implementing unit.

During the Kennedy and Johnson years in office, the formulation and implementation of civil rights policy was, in most instances, left to the Justice Department, which had a great deal of autonomy in its choice of methods and designation of time tables. Arthur Schlesinger, Jr., during his stay at the White House, observed that President

---

73. Ramsey Clark Interview. President Nixon's Attorney General, John Mitchell, has not made any sweeping personnel changes. He has retained 3 of the 8 Assistant Attorneys General and added but 50 new Republican faces on a staff of approximately 1,000 attorneys. *New York Times,* July 28, 1969.

74. Stephen Pollak Interview.

Kennedy "left civil rights policy pretty much to his brother."[75] Nicholas Katzenbach recalls that President Johnson took his advice on civil rights and that White House aide Joseph Califano, who was Johnson's liaison man with the Justice Department, was not very familiar with the area and thus depended on Katzenbach and John Doar for what amounted to policy decisions. According to Katzenbach, Califano "asked our advice and took our views as his. He was very careful."[76] This was confirmed by Stephen Pollak who said that "most civil rights policy came out of the Department . . . they looked to us . . . had confidence in us."[77] Moreover, John Doar recalled that shortly before the President signed the 1965 Voting Rights bill, the White House asked Doar to determine criteria for the use of voting examiners. His judgment as to the number of examiners to be used, counties that they were to be used in, and the speed in which the Act could be enforced, were fully accepted by President Johnson.[78]

President Nixon also appears to have great confidence in his Attorney General, for according to Warren Weaver, Jr., a political analyst for the *New York Times*, many in the Capitol view John Mitchell "as a figure of preeminent power and influence in the new Administration," a man who had a great deal to say about the appointment of Chief Justice Warren Burger, the proposed Voting Rights Act extension, and the Administration's school desegregation policies.[79]

During the Johnson Administration, the Justice Department often acted as a political buffer for the President,

75. *A Thousand Days*, p. 934.
76. Nicholas Katzenbach Interview.
77. Stephen Pollak Interview.
78. John Doar Interview.
79. *New York Times*, July 28, 1969.

deflecting the attacks of Congressmen, interest groups, and bureaucratic agencies. For example, Nicholas Katzenbach said that Presidential aide Joseph Califano would send incoming civil rights complaints directly to the Justice Department, thus allowing the President to tell complainers that he "can't bend Katzenbach." Moreover, Katzenbach believed that he was able to resist pressure, because he had the backing of the President in their mutually advantageous relationship. He thought it was a basic part of his responsibility as Attorney General to "take the heat off the President . . . to keep the President out of fire."[80] Thus, because of this working relationship, many officials in the Department of Justice during the Kennedy and Johnson Administration enjoyed a high degree of political insulation. They were afforded the luxury of not having to accede to many pressures exerted by various interest entities.[81] This may have led officials in the Justice Department to neglect the civil rights groups, because the Department's relations with them was somewhat strained until Ramsey Clark assumed office in early 1967, and brought about a *rapprochement*. Clark made a special effort to build better relations between the Justice Department, the Civil Rights Commission, and civil rights groups. He recalls that the Department's "posture with civil rights groups was not good . . . they thought we were conservative . . . lawyers inhibited by *stare decisis*."[82]

Generally speaking, there was little pressure on voting rights, according to Nicholas Katzenbach, but there was

---

80. Nicholas Katzenbach Interview.

81. This statement is based on interviews with Nicholas Katzenbach, Ramsey Clark, John Doar, and Stephen Pollak, who all said that they felt little pressure—especially from formal civil rights groups.

82. Ramsey Clark Interview.

"of course pressure from Negro groups down South," who always wanted more examiners. He felt the Department could "cope with that." He found that most of the pressure that did come was from the New York delegation in the House of Representatives.

However, in the area of school desegregation, liberals pressed to get enforcement efforts accelerated. Moreover, according to Katzenbach, the NAACP Legal Defense and Educational Fund had an effect on the Department's actions, because when the Fund opened Southern cases it aroused public opinion which, at times, prompted the Justice Department to enter the case.[83] This was confirmed by Jack Greenberg, Director-Counsel of the Fund, who said that on occasion he was asked by Burke Marshall to initiate a case, after which the Justice Department would enter, finding it politically easier at that stage.[84]

Ramsey Clark and John Doar, like Katzenbach, said they *felt* little pressure to move faster or slow down. Clark recalled that there was "not as much pressure as you would think for speeding up," in voting and school desegregation. However, he found that the Leadership Conference on Civil Rights put pressure on Congress and Congress in turn tried to influence the Justice Department.[85] Clark's Assistant Attorney General in charge of CRD, Stephen Pollak, said he did not feel external pressure but rather "internal pressure," i.e., self-pressure. Pollak said that "you would find out where you were by how you did in the court cases . . . if your positions were being accepted in Congress . . . and if your positions were accepted by large groups in the country." Moreover, he be-

83. Nicholas Katzenbach Interview.
84. Jack Greenberg Interview.
85. Ramsey Clark Interview.

lieved that "you would see things were going well if the local officials were complying by law and if the Negroes were turned out . . . but you could not guide yourself by any single group."[86]

The solidification of relations that Ramsey Clark brought about between his department and civil rights groups appears to be short-lived under the Nixon Administration. The Director of the Washington office of the Leadership Conference on Civil Rights, Marvin Caplan, believes that

> under U.S. Attorney General John Mitchell and Assistant Attorney General Jerris Leonard, civil rights enforcement gets little assistance. We fear the worst here. We think these men—Mitchell particularly—are ready to sabotage the program—through indifference, through insufficient effort, through ignorance of what terrible consequences can follow relaxation of enforcement.[87]

In addition, the NAACP Legal Defense and Educational Fund in August, 1969, broke a 15-year partnership with the Justice Department when it asked a Federal court in Mississippi to change the status of the Federal Government from a fellow plaintiff to a defendant in a pending school desegregation case.[88]

Congressional pressure, however, had a greater effect on the operations of the Civil Rights Division than pressure exerted from interest groups in the private sector. The Senate and the House of Representatives wielded significant power through their use of the swords of appropriation and investigation. All aspects of CRD's operations

---

86. Stephen Pollak Interview.
87. Letter to the writer, August 11, 1969.
88. *New York Times,* August 26, 1969.

were delved into and questioned—especially by the Southern Congressmen. Burke Marshall recalled that Representative Rooney, of the House subcommittee which had jurisdiction over Justice Department appropriations, cut down CRD allocations one year because he did not like Marshall's answers.[89] At a Senate Appropriations Committee hearing in 1968, Senator Allen J. Ellender of Louisiana told a Justice Department representative that "you had better make a better case than you have if you expect this committee to approve the money you are requesting, particularly in view of the fact that the House has denied it."[90]

In dealing with Congress, the Kennedy and Johnson Administrations, according to Nicholas Katzenbach, always attempted to secure bipartisan support fully aware that they would need sufficient votes to break a potential Senate filibuster. However, he believed that the "problem was not with Southern segregationists but with Southern moderates—white representatives who were far more moderate than areas they came from. These were the guys who had the problems, who were getting hurt." Katzenbach said that the Administration needed and thus tried not to hurt such men as Lister Hill of Alabama and John J. Sparkman, both Senators from Alabama.[91] Ramsey Clark also recognized the power of those who controlled the committees of Congress and found, in his experience, that a committee's actions will often be a reflection of the philosophy of its chairman.[92]

---

89. Burke Marshall Interview.
90. U.S. Congress, Senate, *Hearings* before the Senate Appropriations Committee, 90th Cong., 2nd sess., p. 874.
91. Nicholas Katzenbach Interview.
92. Ramsey Clark Interview.

Justice Department preparation for Congressional hearings took an inordinately large amount of time and effort, for according to CRD official St. John Barrett, "any factual inquiry creates pressures . . . you must explain what you are doing, what your representative said you would do."[93] From 1963 to 1967, for example, the Attorney General annually appeared before Congressional committees an average of 31 times.[94] Ramsey Clark believes that these appearances took time from enforcement work, and that it was the intention of some Congressmen to keep the Department from devoting more time to implementing the civil rights laws.[95]

Southern representatives, at such hearings, were always concerned about the enforcement philosophy of Justice Department officials. The following colloquy between Senator Strom Thurmond of South Carolina and Ramsey Clark of Texas, at the latter's confirmation hearing, illustrates this point:

> *Thurmond*: . . . some people from the South feel that in order to keep the people of the Nation thinking they are not prejudiced, they have to lean over and be biased against the South. Now, I want to know, do you feel like you can be fair to the South and fair to all parts of this Nation. . . . You do not carry any presumption around you that you feel you are guilty of something, do you, and you've got to prove you are not, because you are from the South?
>
> *Clark*: I would hope not, Senator. I love the South. Two

---

93. St. John Barrett Interview.

94. Moreover, other officials in the Justice Department made many appearances before various Congressional committees: 105 times (1963); 214 times (1964); 84 times (1965); 182 times (1966); 88 times (1967). Statistics are from *Reports of the Attorney General,* 1963–1967.

95. Ramsey Clark Interview.

of my grandparents came from Mississippi, two from Texas; both of my parents were born in Texas. . . . I love the South and its people.[96]

An interesting comparison to the Thurmond-Clark preceding dialogue is the exchange that took place in 1969 between Senator Philip A. Hart, a liberal Democrat from Michigan, and Jerris Leonard, nominee for Assistant Attorney General, Civil Rights Division:

> *Hart*: . . . the Department of Justice, primarily your Division, does have responsibility for the coordination under the executive order of all those activities involved in title 6 of the Civil Rights Law of 1964. There are always pressures when any community's Federal funds are shut off. . . I would hope that you would recognize the clear intention of Congress in the 1964 act and resist pressure from whatever source it came. Can we count on that?
>
> *Leonard*: Senator, I would think it would be part of my obligation to resist pressures not only in that area but in any area. To the extent that I am able, I will certainly do that.[97]

In another sphere, the Federal courts, the personalities and holdings of Federal justices were always important factors considered by the Justice Department in the development of strategy. Harry Golden, having interviewed high Justice Department officials, found out that President Kennedy "received a weekly report on the progress," of Federal court cases, "and these reports assured him that he would win the struggle everywhere in the South by the

---

96. U.S. Congress, Senate, *Hearings* before the Senate Committee on the Judiciary, 90th Cong., 1st sess., March 2, 1967, p. 9. The office was that of Attorney General.

97. U.S. Congress, Senate, *Hearings* before the Senate Committee on the Judiciary, 91st Cong., 1st sess., June 29, 1969, p. 46.

end of 1968." Moreover, Golden was told that "President Kennedy's concern was the speed with which Attorney General Robert F. Kennedy and Assistant Attorney General Burke Marshall could get their cases through the federal district courts into the circuit . . . courts."[98]

Judicial appointments were, according to Arthur Schlesinger, Jr., "a recurring negotiation between Justice and the White House. James Eastland of Mississippi, the chairman of the Senate Judiciary Committee, had his own views about judges, especially in the South." Thus, Schlesinger wrote,

> in an effort to placate Eastland, and in preparation for Eastland's asquiescence in the appointment of Thurgood Marshall of the National Association of Colored People, to the Second Circuit Court, the Attorney General recommended the appointment early in 1961 of Harold Cox and J. Robert Elliott to district court judgeships in Mississippi and Alabama.[99]

However, according to statements made by former Attorneys General Nicholas Katzenbach and Ramsey Clark, Senator Eastland was no real threat. Katzenbach recalled that they did not fear him in making appointments outside of Eastland's home state, Mississippi. Ramsey Clark, similarly, had "no feeling that he held us back."[100]

Not only was the Justice Department dependent on the Federal courts, but the judiciary also needed the sword of the Executive, as evidenced by events in Little Rock, Arkansas, and Oxford, Mississippi. Assistant Attorney Gen-

---

98. *Mr. Kennedy and the Negroes* (Greenwich, Conn.: Fawcett Publications, 1964), p. 131.

99. *A Thousand Days,* pp. 697–98.

100. Nicholas Katzenbach Interview; Ramsey Clark Interview.

eral Jerris Leonard put it bluntly when he stated that even
if the Supreme Court ordered instant school integration
"nothing would change. Somebody would have to enforce
that order."[101] Ramsey Clark also alluded to this practical
fact when he testified before a Senate Appropriations
Committee in June 1968. Referring to a Supreme Court
ruling on discrimination in housing, and the 1968 Housing
Act, he said:

> In the argument before the Supreme Court, the Department
> of Justice advised the Court that even if it held with the
> petitioner in that case, the civil rights legislation would still
> be necessary because it has the effective sanctions that are
> needed to enforce the rule of law. The mere recognition of
> the right by the Supreme Court without adequate sanctions,
> without enforcing tools, would not bring about the purpose
> of the law which is to achieve for every citizen the right
> that is theirs.[102]

In relation to other Federal civil rights enforcement
units, the Justice Department was a moderating force.[103]
Moreover, the Department became the final resting place
of units of implementation that were considered expend-
able or obstructive to the fulfillment of CRD's functions.
The President's Council on Equal Oppportunity, for example, was abolished and its Title VI coordination functions were given to the Attorney General; and the Community Relations Service was transferred to the Justice
Department, because, according to Katzenbach, the De-

---

101. *New York Times,* September 30, 1969.

102. U.S. Congress, Senate, *Hearing* before the Senate Appropriations
Committee, 90th Cong., 2nd sess., p. 732.

103. This will be demonstrated in following chapters.

partment wanted to get the Service out of the South where "they were getting in the way."[104]

SUMMARY

The auspicious inception of the Civil Rights Division, and its continued existence in an indigenous and complementary environment—the Justice Department—gave it strength for its operations. CRD was a natural part of the Justice Department, and it considered itself (and was thought of by others) a permanent unit with select duties prescribed by law.

Its philosophy, throughout its existence, has called for nondramatic, steady progress, using as few forceful means as possible. Litigation has always been its forte, to be carefully and selectively applied when less formal methods of compliance prove to be ineffective. Moreover, the close communication that has usually existed between the White House and the Justice Department has added to CRD's staying power, and has, in effect, allowed it to assume first place among the other civil rights enforcement units. Thus, the Civil Rights Division has grown in influence and responsibilities, while several other units responsible for civil rights implementation have either dwindled in power or disappeared.

---

104. Nicholas Katzenbach Interview. See chapters 5 and 6 for details.

4

THE DEPARTMENT OF HEALTH, EDUCATION AND WELFARE; PUBLIC SCHOOL DESEGREGATION

I. UNITED STATES OFFICE OF EDUCATION: EQUAL
EDUCATIONAL OPPORTUNITIES PROGRAM (EEOP)

THE UNITED STATES COMMISSIONER OF EDUCATION AND THE Attorney General were specifically empowered in Title IV of the 1964 Civil Rights Act to use their offices to help bring about desegregation of public schools.[1] Prior to this Act the Departments of Justice, and Health, Education and Welfare did little to effectuate the *Brown* school desegregation decisions. The percentage of black students attending schools with white students at the time of the 1964 statute was approximately one percent, a figure indicative of the lack of progress made.[2] However, Congress

---

1. 78 Stat. 241–68. Approved July 2, 1964.
2. This figure is for the 11 Southern states of the old Confederacy: Alabama, Arkansas, Florida, Georgia, Louisiana, Mississippi, North Caro-

now stated that students were to be assigned "to public schools and within such schools without regard to their race, color, religion, or national origin."[3] The U.S. Commissioner of Education was now given major administrative legal responsibility for this task. Some of the enforcement tools given him by the 1964 law included authorization: to render technical assistance; to set up training institutes; or to make grants in order to assist in bringing about public school desegregation.[4] However, use of the grant provision was restricted, for according to Title VI of the same law, "each Federal department and agency which is empowered to extend Federal financial assistance to any program or activity by way of grant, loan, or contract" is prohibited from giving such funds to a recipient who discriminates because of a person's race, color, or national origin.[5] Many people at HEW, however, neither wanted nor were prepared for this provision.

Philosophy of the Department

As early as February 1962, HEW Secretary Abraham Ribicoff said:

I think it would be a tragedy for education if we insisted that we solve every problem facing this country on the back of education, because this would do no good for education and wouldn't solve the problems of segregation. If we have a problem of civil rights, we are going to have to solve it

---

lina, South Carolina, Tennessee, Texas, and Virginia. Cited in U.S. Commission on Civil Rights, *Southern School Desegregation, 1966–67* (Washington, D.C.: U.S. Government Printing Office, July 1967), p. 5.

3. 78 Stat. 246, Title IV, sec. 401.

4. *Ibid.*, sec. 403–5.

5. 78 Stat. 252–53.

on its own and not try to solve it by stopping the progress of education and the betterment of our schools.[6]

Rather than this, Ribicoff said, he favored an approach "of careful review and quiet action."[7] When asked by a House subcommittee why his department continued to give money to segregated schools after the *Brown* decisions, Secretary Ribicoff said:

> Congressmen, you people control the purse strings. You vote the impacted money in Congress. You vote us the money and say, "Give it out." As far as I am concerned, our department listens to the voice and the instructions of the Congress of the United States . . . this is a congressional problem and not an administrative problem. You can determine under what conditions the money is paid out.[8]

Similarly, during the same hearings, Sterling McMurrin, Commissioner of Education, said that in his view, the enforcement of the National Defense Act, and its non-discrimination provisions, was basically the province of the courts. The Office of Education, he believed, was not directed by Congress to take the initiative in this area, and such being the case, has "attempted to administer the act in such a way as to carry the benefits of the act to the largest possible number of people in spite of the existence of segregation and . . . felt that in doing this . . . [was] carrying out the intent of the Congress."[9]

---

6. Stated in interview on February 19, 1962, on NBC television program "Meet the Press," as quoted in U.S. Congress, House, Committee on Education and Labor, *Hearings* of subcommittee on Integration in Federally Assisted Public Education Programs, 87th Cong., 2nd sess., 1962, p. 58.

7. *Hearings, Ibid.*

8. *Ibid.*, p. 21.

9. *Ibid.*, p. 68.

This approach was continued by Ribicoff's successor, Anthony Celebreeze, who admitted "that in the nine years since the Supreme Court has ruled, there hasn't been compliance. . . ." He also did not want blanket authority to cut off Federal funds, but rather suggested to a House Judiciary subcommittee an approach by which his men

> judge, as we sit down with the school officials, whether they are really making a diligent effort, what their problems are and how we can work out their problems. Now, that may take six months or a year, but at least we would be actively engaged in it.[10]

Celebreeze's unrealistic timetable as well as his inadequate personnel estimates for future enforcement were illustrative of HEW's inexperience in this area. He anticipated, for example, that he would be able to meet the needs for technical assistance to desegregating schools by increasing Office of Education staff "to about ten more people in 1964 and possibly 15 to 20 people in 1965."[11] Neither did he, his staff, or President Kennedy consider Title VI, the cut-off provision in the 1964 Act, as a key part of the bill, for HEW was not involved in the preliminary discussions or the drafting of this title—a part of the 1963 bill that they would be called upon to administer.[12]

---

10. U.S. Congress, House, Committee on the Judiciary, *Hearings* before Judiciary subcommittee No. 5, Series No. 4, pt. II, 88th Cong., 1st sess., 1963, p. 1548.

11. *Ibid.,* p. 1528.

12. Gary Orfield wrote in his fine work, *The Reconstruction of Southern Education* (New York: John Wiley & Sons, 1969) that Lee White, Kennedy Presidential aide, told him in a private interview held on June 21, 1967, that the Administration did not view Title VI as a "make or break item," but rather as something "kind of tucked away among

Thus, President Johnson, in signing the Civil Rights Act on July 4, 1964, put legal responsibility for public school desegregation into the hands of a staff that was few in number, lacking in experience, and philosophically unsuited for this type of program. The Office of Education neither desired nor expected what turned out to be the burdensome task of implementing the education part of Title VI.[13]

The law had little effect on the 1964-65 school year, because officials held off most desegregation efforts during the summer of 1964 while they waited for the President to issue uniform, government-wide Title VI implementation regulations.[14] There was some activity, however, emanating from Secretary Celebreeze's office, where James M. Quigley, Assistant Secretary of HEW, was given joint responsibility with the Office of Education for civil rights enforcement. During the last half of 1964, Quigley attempted to prod segregated Southern school districts, often one at a time, into compliance. In addition to Quigley's district-by-district personal negotiations, he and David Seeley (assistant to Commissioner of Education Francis Keppel) visited many Southern educators in an

some giants." Orfield states that had Kennedy lived, Title VI "was one of the segments of the bill that might possibly have been traded to the South for an end to the Senate filibuster." P. 39. Moreover, Orfield discovered that the people at the Office of Education, in their mistaken belief that Title VI would never remain in the bill, assumed "no significant role in drafting the legislation." P. 60. This was confirmed by former U.S. Commissioner of Education Francis Keppel who said that his role in bringing about Title VI was negligible in that he had "very little to do with the actual language." Interview in New York on July 31, 1969, hereafter cited as Francis Keppel Interview.

13. The Bureau of the Budget underestimated the nature of the job in the belief that existing staff could adequately handle Title VI responsibilities. Orfield, p. 64.

14. *Ibid.*

attempt to create favorable conditions for school desegregation.[15] Implementation efforts during these months were exploratory probes on the part of the compliance people at HEW in their efforts to prepare for future operations.[16] Not only was this a new and untried area for them, but it was a task that many in the Office of Education preferred not to have. Commissioner Keppel found that he had "inherited a sleepy Office of Education . . . not taking much initiative in civil rights."[17] Furthermore, he believed, there should have been more time for adequate preparation—"we need a real warmup, a careful study." Keppel found himself with "a last minute staff," and an unenthusiastic department secretary—Anthony Celebreeze, who "was not a starter . . . not an activist." Keppel recalls, for example, Celebreeze telling him on various occasions to "stop using the word 'busing!' "[18]

However, soon after President Johnson approved Government-wide Title VI compliance regulations on December 3, 1964, implementation efforts at the Office of Education began in earnest.[19] The Regulations, although

15. Interview with David Seeley, Director of the Equal Educational Opportunities Program, USOE, HEW, in New York on July 24, 1969, hereafter cited as David Seeley Interview. One of these meetings was sponsored by the U.S. Civil Rights Commission and took place in Atlanta. Quigley told the gathering of 800 Southerners, and various officials from nine Federal agencies, that "we're here to help you . . . to work with you. We do not come with all the answers." *New York Times*, April 15, 1965.

16. Orfield points out that "during the summer there was not a single person in the Office of Education devoting full time to what was soon to become the Office's most visible responsibility." P. 65.

17. Francis Keppel Interview.

18. Francis Keppel Interview. This view of Celebreeze was shared by David Seeley; David Seeley Interview.

19. *Federal Register,* Title 45, Subtitle A. The Regulations took effect one month later on January 3, 1965.

not stating in specific detail what was expected of the Southern school districts, provided a frame of reference for the enforcement personnel at the Office of Education and gave them something tangible to begin operations with. One part of the Regulations, for example, described how elementary and secondary schools or school systems could satisfy the nondiscrimination requirements of the 1964 Act. Other pertinent sections dealt with administrative activities involving: the preparation and availability of compliance information on the part of both Federal departments and fund recipients; procedures for effecting compliance, including the termination of or refusal to grant Federal financial assistance; and factors involving the holding of hearings.[20]

The Regulations with accompanying instructions were mailed to school districts in late December, 1964, by a group headed by David Seeley. On January 3, 1965, Seeley was officially named director of a newly created USOE compliance unit—the Equal Educational Opportunities Program (EEOP).

Inception of EEOP

Seeley, a young lawyer, had been offered the position after Commissioner Keppel failed to get an experienced educator to join his staff.[21] Seeley freely acknowledged

---

20. Moreover, the Regulations stated that a public elementary or secondary school would be eligible for financial assistance under Title VI if it met one of the following three conditions: (1) filed an assurance of compliance; (2) was subject to a final Federal court order for the desegregation of its schools (and promised to obey it); or (3) submitted a plan to the Commissioner of Education which he found acceptable. *Ibid.*, Section 80.4.

21. Francis Keppel Interview and David Seeley Interview.

that he was "too inexperienced for the job."[22] Thus, on January 3, 1965, Seeley and a "grab-bag staff" began an attempt to desegregate the school systems of the South.[23] The innumerable obstacles that were present at EEOP's inception proved, for the most part, to be insurmountable. The Program was limited by a small, inexperienced staff, an unseasoned director, a hazy mandate, and limited funds. In addition, it was in a locale—the Office of Education, which found this type of activity distasteful.[24] The head of the Department of HEW, moreover, did not like forceful displays of activism, preferring a more gradual and peaceful type of operation.[25]

In view of these unfavorable conditions, how could this array of conscientious men hope to change an entrenched system? David Seeley, cognizant of the crippling limitations, was careful not to reveal his unit's weaknesses to

22. David Seeley Interview. His work record is as follows: Teaching Fellow in Education, Harvard Graduate School of Education, September 1960 to January 1961); Administrative Assistant, Harvard-Lexington Summer School, Harvard University (June 1961 to August 1961); Director of Program of Teacher Training in Ibadan, Nigeria—a program for training Peace Corps volunteers assigned as secondary school teachers in Nigeria (August 1961 to July 1962); Special Assistant to the U.S. Commissioner of Education, U.S. Office of Education (June 1963 to February 1966).

23. Seeley used this description. Interview.

24. Seeley said that most of the USOE personnel were from the South and, in his opinion, "many seemed segregationists . . . or not in sympathy in a moral sense." Interview. Others involved with USOE stress the point that the people in charge of its many programs had considered Title VI implementation duties an unwanted task. Interview with Ruby Martin, Director, Office for Civil Rights, HEW, in Washington, D.C., on July 17, 1969; and Interview (telephone) with F. Peter Libassi, who preceded Mrs. Martin as Director, Office for Civil Rights, HEW, from Washington, D.C., on September 9, 1969.

25. David Seeley Interview. Seeley found that Celebreeze "wanted to stay clear of controversy."

Southern school officials. Armed with Titles IV and VI of the 1964 Civil Rights Act, and the official implementing Regulations, he proceeded to play out what he called a "big bluff game."[26]

Methods of Operation

Early in 1965 the people in EEOP realized that the existing Regulations did not offer sufficient guidance for the Southern school districts to develop unitary systems of education. Conscious of the forthcoming fall school term, Seeley and his consultants proceeded to develop a more explicit set of instructions to guide the confused Southern school districts. These instructions, prepared solely by EEOP staff without the aid or the approval of the Secretary of HEW, the White House, or the Department of Justice, were unofficially floated in a March, 1965, *Saturday Review* article written by EEOP consultant, Professor G. W. Foster, Jr.[27] Soon after publication, thousands of reprints were sent to Southern school officials. Still encountering no opposition, Seeley and his staff then converted this basic data into official guidelines for school desegregation.[28] These Guidelines, the first of several to be issued, set up minimum standards which a desegregating school had to meet before it was eligible to receive Federal funds. Basically, its provisions stated that: a school system desegregating for the first time had to show

26. *Ibid.*

27. March 20, 1965, p. 60. Foster, a law professor at the University of Wisconsin, was a part-time consultant to EEOP. David Seeley Interview.

28. David Seeley and David Barus joint interview, in New York on July 24, 1969, hereafter cited as Seeley-Barus Interview. Barus was Seeley's Acting Program Deputy and, in Barus's words, "chief full-time legal consultant."

a good faith start by desegregating at least four grades in the fall of 1965; all twelve grades had to be desegregated by the target date of fall, 1967; faculties had to be desegregated, but not necessarily during the first year; and, similar to the Regulations, school districts were permitted to desegregate in a variety of ways, which included use of free choice and attendance zone plans. Furthermore, a district could qualify for Federal financial assistance if it met one of the conditions specified in the compliance Regulations.[29]

The Guidelines, based on the 1964 Civil Rights Act, the HEW Regulations, and the most advanced Federal court decisions, were, according to Seeley, rather conservative, and not at the time taken seriously by school districts in the South. Much of their content was taken out of court orders, EEOP being a "hop, skip and a jump ahead of them," trying "to judge what would be acceptable."[30] Holdings of the Federal courts, especially the Fourth and Fifth Circuits, were vitally important elements in the Program's operations. Commissioner Keppel thought that it was important to keep the Executive and Judicial branches "on parallel tracks running at about the same speed," because, he believed, "if the Executive Branch had different standards than the courts there would be loss of confidence . . . in the minds of the people." Keppel did not want to see the populace "play one off against the other." Thus, he said, the first data on his desk in the morning were judgments from the United States Court of Appeals for the Fifth Circuit.[31]

---

29. See n. 20 above. The Guidelines were officially entitled "General Statement of Policies Under Title VI of the Civil Rights Act of 1964 Respecting Desegregation of Elementary and Secondary Schools."

30. David Seeley Interview.

31. Francis Keppel Interview.

Time after time, the Fifth Circuit Court of Appeals stepped in to give the Federal school desegregation effort a boost.[32] In the *Singleton* case, for example, the court upheld the school desegregation Guidelines and the Commissioner's right to issue them. Judge John M. Wisdom, speaking for the court, said:

> We attach great weight to the standards established by the Office of Education. The judiciary has of course functions and duties distinct from those of the executive department, but in carrying out a national policy the three departments of government are united by a common objective. There should be close correlation, therefore, between the judiciary's standards in enforcing the national policy requiring desegregation of public schools and the executive department's standards in administering this policy. Absent legal questions, the United States Office of Education is better qualified than the courts and is the more appropriate federal body to weigh administrative difficulties inherent in school desegregation plans.[33]

The following year, on December 29, 1966, the Fifth Circuit once again buttressed EEOP's sagging program by declaring in the *Jefferson County* case that it fully accepted HEW's second set (revised) of guidelines. Once again, Judge Wisdom, speaking for the three-man court, stated:

---

32. Francis Keppel was told by Chief Justice Earl Warren that the judges on the Fifth Circuit were doing a courageous job. Warren proceeded to list them "up and down the line," speaking of social and economic damage that they had incurred because of their actions. Francis Keppel Interview. See Jack W. Peltason, *Fifty-Eight Lonely Men* (New York: Harcourt, Brace and World, 1961).

33. *Singleton* v. *Jackson Municipal Separate School District*, 348 F. 2d 729 (5th Cir. 1965).

We hold that H.E.W.'s standards are substantially the same as this court's standards. They are required by the Constitution, and as we construe them, are within the scope of the Civil Rights Act of 1964.

Going further, he said that the

only school desegregation plan that meets institutional standards is one that works. . . . But helping public schools to meet that test, by assisting the courts in their independent evaluation of school desegregation plans, and by . . . simplifying the process of desegregation, the H.E.W. guidelines offer new hope to Negro schoolchildren long denied their constitutional rights. . . . When desegregation plans do not meet minimum standards, the school authorities should ask H.E.W. for assistance, and District Courts should invite H.E.W. to assist.[34]

Moreover, the court looked askance at so-called "freedom of choice" plans, noting that "this method of desegregation is better suited than any other to preserve the essentials of the dual school system while giving paper compliance with the duty to desegregate."[35]

The compliance people at HEW were reinvigorated now that they had the support of the Fifth Circuit—a

34. *United States* v. *Jefferson County Board of Education*, 372 F. 2d 836 (5th Cir. 1966), affirmed on rehearing *en banc* C.A. No. 23345, 5th Cir., March 29, 1967.

35. *Ibid.* Moreover, following the Supreme Court's October, 1969, edict that ended the 1955 "with all deliberate speed" doctrine, the Fifth Circuit on December 1, 1969, ordered 16 school districts in six Southern states to have integrated school systems ready for full operation by the fall of 1970. The court's 13 judges, sitting *en banc,* said that the Supreme Court's decision "supervened all existing authority to the contrary," and "sent the doctrine of deliberate speed to its final resting place." *New York Times,* December 2, 1969.

court of appeals for the six Southern states of Alabama, Florida, Georgia, Louisiana, Mississippi, and Texas. An official at HEW stated a few days after the *Jefferson County* holding that as long as the fight was being waged by the Office of Education alone, there were "many people who persuaded themselves that we would either abandon the field or be defeated. Now we have backing in the courts."[36]

However, even with court backing, EEOP still had to spend a great deal of its time defending its actions. The Guidelines, revised and reissued on March 7, 1966, were constantly attacked by people in all segments of Southern society. Opponents especially focused on the newly enunciated HEW percentage guide for school desegregation. This guide established standards for what the Commissioner of Education considered an adequate annual increase in the percentage of students transferring from segregated schools.[37] In addition, the new Guidelines called for significant progress in the desegregation of teachers and staff. In effect, this meant that EEOP was

---

36. *New York Times,* December 31, 1966.

37. The 1966 Guidelines were officially entitled "Revised Statement of Policies for School Desegregation Plans Under Title VI of the Civil Rights Act of 1964," in *Federal Register,* Title 45, pt. 181. The most controversial and hotly debated part of the Revised Guidelines, Section 181.54, stated that "the Commissioner will, in general, be guided by the following criteria in scheduling free choice plans for review:

(1) If a significant percentage of the students, such as 8 percent or 9 percent, transferred from segregated schools for the 1965–66 school year, total transfers on the order of at least twice that percentage would normally be expected.

(2) If a smaller percentage of the students, such as 4 percent or 5 percent, transferred from segregated schools for the 1965–66 school year, a substantial increase in transfers would normally be expected, such as would bring the total at at least triple the percentage for the 1965–66 school year."

beginning to bear down in its efforts, for prior to the revised Guidelines there was little more than paper compliance.[38] Commissioner of Education Harold Howe (Keppel's successor) readily admitted this when he told a House Appropriations subcommittee in March, 1966:

> the revised guidelines make an important administrative change. This past year much of our effort and that of local school officials was expended in negotiating desegregation plans for individual school districts. This proved to be a truly monumental task. And in the end the effort did not achieve one of its main purposes. Very few of the school districts made any real efforts to devise plans which would desegregate their school systems more effectively in the

---

38. David Seeley Interview. Seeley also said that the Revised Guidelines were "purposely written to have the effect to pressure districts," and at the same time to protect the Government from legal challenge. That is why, he said, "we could not be specific. . . . We wanted to have a tool . . . a defensibly hazy one." Thus, in his application of "psychological pressure" he "deliberately made them hazy." Ramsey Clark believes that "the reason people were against the Guidelines is that they worked." He thought that the percentages were needed, because the "rate of progress was too slow," without them, "prolonging their agony." Clark felt that "the longer it took the worse it was—once they did it they would see that it wasn't so bad." He realized that the South would "try to slow down wherever they could," but they would nevertheless just have "to get in and swim," after which they would "accept it more readily." Ramsey Clark Interview.

Furthermore, according to Seeley, the Justice Department toned the 1966 Guidelines down because they were "very nervous about the percentages." David Seeley Interview. This was confirmed by Nicholas Katzenbach who said he advised HEW not to use the percentages. Katzenbach had personally spoken to Secretary John Gardner suggesting that HEW drop the percentage guide, but Gardner refused. Katzenbach did not insist, but he believes that he "could have stopped them—after all the President threw the whole thing into my hands." He said that "Gardner would have caved in if I strongly insisted," and the "President would have backed me." Instead, Justice "eased down" what HEW had originally wanted to do. Nicholas Katzenbach Interview.

light of their individual circumstances; rather they almost invariably required the Federal Government to prescribe the minimum plan that would be acceptable.

This year the emphasis will be shifted from negotiation to performance.[39]

However, pressure against the percentages soon grew so intense that HEW Secretary John Gardner felt obliged to send an explanatory letter, on April 9, 1966, to members of Congress and state governors. He said, in part:

We have received a number of inquiries about our revised school desegregation guidelines, some of which reflect a misunderstanding of their purpose and intent. . . . The guidelines do not, as some have assumed, require the instantaneous desegregation of the faculty in every school building in every district. Nor do they prescribe rigid means. They provide considerable flexibility as to how a district might undertake faculty desegregation.

In relation to the percentages, Gardner wrote that

some have contended that this portion of the guidelines imposes a formula of "racial balance." This contention misconceives the purpose of the percentages. . . . In seeking appropriate criteria to guide us in review of free choice plans, we have adopted the objective criteria applied by the Courts in similar situations. One such criterion is the distribution of students by race in the various schools of a system after the students made their choices. . . . With more than 2,000 separate districts to consider, such percentages

39. U.S. Congress, Senate, Committee on Appropriations, *Hearings* before a subcommittee of the Committee on Appropriations for Labor, Health, Education and Welfare, 89th Cong., 2nd sess., 1966, pt. 1, p. 288.

are thus an administrative guide which helps us to determine those districts requiring further review.[40]

Thus, even though EEOP accelerated operations, it was never able to fully get off the ground, because it was constantly stymied by a myriad of forces. Throughout its 28-month existence, it was not only engaged in a running battle with the opponents of civil rights, but Seeley's group also had to contend with: the demands of civil rights entities; the inquiries of Congressmen who were concerned about efficient methods of administration; differences of opinion with the Justice Department; and the watchful eye of the White House.

Pressure Exerted on EEOP

The continuous defiance of the South had the greatest effect on EEOP's performance, because pressure from all segments of the Southern states was continuous and intense. This was especially the situation, according to Seeley, after EEOP began pressing for real compliance. He found that the "calculated push" of the South was a real threat to the Program's operations and a determining factor in his disinclination to go North, for he believed that "if pressure came from the North also, we would not have survived."[41]

Moreover, the staff at EEOP spent a great deal of time defending their program before Congressional committees,

---

40. Cited in U.S. Congress, Senate, Committee on Labor and Public Welfare, *Hearings* before a subcommittee of the Committee on Labor and Public Welfare for Education, Labor and Public Welfare, 89th Cong., 2nd sess., 1966, pt. 5, 1966, pp. 2045–47. Gardner was aided in drafting the letter by Justice Department officials, Nicholas Katzenbach, John Doar, and David Filvaroff. John Doar Interview.

41. Seeley and Barus Interview.

where their appropriation requests were always reduced, their leaders continually harassed, and their methods opposed. They were subjected to a constant barrage of opposition which came principally—though not entirely—from the Southern members of Congress.[42] A case in point occurred at an October, 1966, Senate Appropriations Committee hearing in which Senator John L. McClellan, Democrat of Arkansas, told an HEW official that he was going to vote "for as little appropriation as I can." His committee shortly thereafter backed the House of Representatives in reducing the Office of Education's Title IV funds from $11.1 million to $8 million.[43] This was not unusual, for appropriations allocated for the civil rights educational activities of the Office of Education annually averaged, from 1965 through 1968, $8 million. In 1968, for example, USOE asked for $30 million and was given $10 million. During appropriations hearings for fiscal year 1969, Commissioner Howe had to explain why Congress should give his office more funds in view of the fact that the Bureau of the Budget had cut his initial estimate. Representative John J. Rooney, Democrat of New York, asked him about this:

> *Rooney*: What are you really figuring it at this year? What do you suppose whoever the genius is down in the Bureau of the Budget has in mind when he cuts you from 25 to 14, or approximately 15?
>
> *Howe*: I expect he had in mind that that is about what you might give us.[44]

---

42. Seeley and Barus Interview.

43. *New York Times*, October 14, 1966.

44. U.S. Congress, House, Committtee on Appropriations, *Hearings* before a subcommittee of the Committee on Appropriations, Departments of State, Justice, Commerce and Related Agencies, 90th Cong., 2nd sess., 1968, p. 995.

Southern members of Congress, moreover, directly pressured the House Appropriations Committee in an attempt to get it to reduce HEW's appropriations. On April 10, 1967, for example, a petition of protest bearing the signatures of more than sixty Southern representatives was sent to this committee. It said, in part:

> We, the undersigned, respectfully submit that the Department of Education, [sic] by refusing to approve the operation of certain schools, school districts, and other educational institutions, is thereby using force to require such schools . . . to make assignments based on race of students and faculty, contrary to the Civil Rights Act of 1964. . . .
>
> We therefore urge your Committee to take appropriate action to see that funds are not made available for a continuation of such policies. . . .[45]

Alabama Governor George Wallace had similarly once stated, at a specially convened conference of Southern governors and Congressmen, that he would work for integration flexibility through Senator Lister Hill, chairman of a Senate Appropriations subcommittee which had jurisdiction over HEW.[46]

In addition, Southern Congressmen periodically tried to demean Commissioner Harold Howe by referring to him as "commissar," and by demanding that he be fired. Watkins Abbitt, Democrat of Virginia, for example, said on the House floor that Howe was "well on his way to wrecking public education," and that the Office of Educa-

---

45. Cited in U.S. Congress, House, Committee on Appropriations, *Hearings* before a subcommittee of the Committee on Appropriations, Departments of Labor and Health, Education and Welfare, 90th Cong., 1st sess., 1967, pt. 6, pp. 23–24.

46. *New York Times,* May 19, 1965.

tion was attempting "to coerce and blackmail public school officials into submitting to guidelines far more stringent and objectionable than was ever contemplated by the Congress when the law was enacted."[47]

However, there was also pressure from proponents of civil rights to accelerate the desegregation of public schools. Their power was not comparable to the tremendous thrust of the senior Southern Congressmen, one reason being that civil rights groups and liberal members of Congress worked sporadically to counter opposition.[48] One of these occasions occurred when Emanuel Celler, a civil rights proponent and chairman of the House Judiciary Committee, used his prestige and power to prevent Howard W. Smith, Southern chairman of the House Rules Committee, from conducting hearings on the controversial activities of the Office of Education. Testifying before the Rules Committee on September 29, 1966, Celler asserted: "We have jurisdiction. We will carry out the jurisdiction expeditiously and satisfactorily to everybody and I do not think anything more is necessary."[49] But this type of defense generally came only in emergencies. According to Francis Keppel, the people at EEOP would have been "happy to get more pressure on the liberal side," because "there was always more pressure from the South than from the liberals." He thought that liberal help could have been an important boost for Seeley's staff in its negotiations with Southern school officials. Positive and continuous pressure did come from the Civil Rights Commission

---

47. U.S. Congress, House, 89th Cong., 2nd sess., October 6, 1966, *Congressional Record* 112:25574–75.

48. Seeley and Barus Interview; Peter Libassi Interview.

49. U.S. Congress, House, Rules Committee, "Policies and Guidelines for School Desegregation," 89th Cong., 2nd sess., 1966, p. 18.

which, Keppel said, "kept pushing everybody—thank God for them."[50]

EEOP's relations with other governmental units, however, was never close. It did not, for example, enjoy a close working relationship with its sister enforcer, the Civil Rights Division of the Justice Department. To a certain extent, at various times, there was a mutual feeling of distrust that existed between the two units, which had probably developed as a result of their differing philosophies and methods. The Civil Rights Division, a veteran in this area, believed that its tried and tested litigative methods were best suited to bring about public school desegregation. Nicholas Katzenbach felt that "part of the problem was that . . . the Office of Education did not know the area that well—had a lot to learn," wherein the Justice Department "had a lot of experience in education." He recalled that the Justice Department was "always holding them back."[51] Thinking the same way as Katzenbach on this issue, John Doar found that "Seeley's efforts were counter-productive. We went slower, but more sure-footed, steady progress" was made. Doar felt that Seeley "fell back completely."[52]

The people at EEOP had similar feelings about the attorneys at the Justice Department. Francis Keppel said that he "never did feel that Justice was particularly activist." He viewed Attorney General Katzenbach as being "much less emotionally identified than Bobby [Kennedy]."[53] David Seeley thought that those over at the

50. Francis Keppel Interview.
51. Nicholas Ketzenbach Interview.
52. John Doar Interview.
53. Francis Keppel Interview.

Justice Department were too careful, and too often acted as a brake on the activities of his office.[54]

Thus, each unit went its own way during most of 1965, EEOP trying to implement the laws administratively, and CRD enforcing the laws through the process of litigation. There were few interdepartmental meetings until late in 1965, when F. Peter Libassi, appointed assistant for civil rights to HEW Secretary Gardner, purposely worked to create a stronger relationship.[55]

White House relations with EEOP were cordial, but never close. Seeley's office was generally given a wide rein so long as the job was proceeding smoothly and the Administration was not being embarrassed. President Johnson, according to Seeley, always supported EEOP on the controversial school desegregation Guidelines. Seeley said that "Johnson was good on this. . . . He never intimated that they wanted us to ease up on standards."[56] However, neither did the President throw the full weight of his office behind the efforts of EEOP. Seeley believes that the program would have had "less trouble if the Administration, Justice and Humphrey would have made clear to the South that we meant business." Seeley wanted the President to call a conference of Southern governors and Senators, but Johnson declined.[57] During times of extreme pressure, President Johnson did step in either to publicly state his support for the unit under fire or to extricate his Administration from a politically damaging situation. This type of activity took place when the President felt it was

54. David Seeley Interview.
55. Interview with St. John Barrett; Interview with F. Peter Libassi.
56. David Seeley Interview.
57. *Ibid.*

necessary to support the school desegregation Guidelines. The topic was brought up at a Presidential News Conference which took place on September 30, 1966. President Johnson was asked:

> *Question*: . . . I wonder if you could give us your views in light of the congressional discussions of the school guidelines and hospital desegregation . . . on the adequacies of the existing guidelines, whether your policies will be modified?
>
> *President*: My views are principally the views that have been stated by the Secretary of Health, Education and Welfare . . . that it is our intention to execute and enforce the law as passed by the Congress and carry out the intention of the Congress.
>
> We are doing that as interpreted by the Secretary of Health, Education and Welfare and the Attorney General.[58]

On the other hand, when EEOP was having great administrative difficulty, during the summer of 1965, processing incoming school desegregation plans, the President entered the picture, because "there was great pressure to get them accepted."[59] At that time, the Southern school districts were preparing for a fall term and still had not received approval from the Office of Education to go ahead. Johnson told Keppel that he wanted people to work around the clock processing the 1,000 outstanding plans.[60] In addition, the President publicly stated on August 31 that

a staff of 117 men and women in the U.S. Office of Educa-

58. *Public Papers of the Presidents,* Lyndon B. Johnson, 1966, pt. II, pp. 1106–7.
59. Francis Keppel Interview.
60. Seeley and Barus Interview.

tion, working around the clock and over weekends, is assisting local school districts in achieving acceptable plans.

. . . I have directed the Office of Education to stand ready day and night to work toward solutions in the remaining communities which have not submitted plans or whose plans have not yet been accepted.[61]

To meet this Presidential command, the Office of Education co-opted people from other areas of HEW, and was further aided by 30 lawyers sent from the Justice Department. The total processing job took two to three months with two shifts working from nine in the morning until nine at night seven days a week. Moreover, Seeley sent a detailed nightly tabulation to White House liaison men Joseph Califano, Douglas Cater, and Bufford Ellington. These reports depicted the status of all the school districts in the Southern states and indicated the type of response from each, i.e., if they submitted a plan, were involved in negotiations, the acceptability of the plan and the stage of negotiations, or if they were rejected and were put into the hardcore column. After September a weekly report replaced the daily tabulation sent to the White House.[62]

This crackdown by the President was minor compared to his intervention following EEOP's mishandling of a situation that involved deferment of school funds to Chicago's schools. Essentially, on October 1, 1965, Keppel and Seeley (without adequate legal evidence) notified Illinois Superintendent of Public Instruction Ray Page that a forthcoming $32.5 million grant for ESEA Title I funds would be withheld because preliminary checks indicated

61. *Public Papers of the Presidents*, Lyndon B. Johnson, 1965, p. 185.
62. Seeley and Barus Interview.

that there had been noncompliance with Title VI of the 1964 Act. Commissioner Keppel recalled that "the reason I wanted fund deferral . . . is that I thought Willis was going to spread the Title I money evenly and not put it where it was needed—for the poor, for the black kids."[63] The deferral action—the first of its kind outside the South, was not discussed beforehand with the Secretary of HEW or with attorneys in the Justice Department. Moreover, though Keppel telephoned a Presidential aide telling him about the forthcoming action, "it was not a good check . . . the man did not get a straight enough judgment . . . the issue was not presented clearly enough."[64] Seeley admits that it was a "complete bungling on our part."[65] Shortly thereafter, Mayor Richard Daley, Democratic leader of Chicago, let Johnson know of his displeasure. The President, upon being told that EEOP could not support its deferral action in the courts, sent HEW Undersecretary Wilbur Cohen to Chicago to work it out. Johnson, according to Seeley, "did not say how to settle it, but wanted funds to flow with Chicago commitments and compromises."[66] Soon after, on October 5, an accord was reached between Cohen and Frank B. Whiston, president of the Chicago Board of Education, in which it was agreed that in return for HEW's release of the funds, Whiston would

63. Francis Keppel Interview. Benjamin Willis was the Superintendent of Chicago's public schools.

Title I of the Elementary and Secondary Education Act of 1965 authorized the Commissioner of Education to provide aid to educationally deprived children through state educational agencies. This was HEW's "carrot," in that first year funding for Title I was in excess of $1 billion.

64. *Ibid.*

65. David Seeley Interview.

66. David Seeley Interview.

within 60 days "examine the validity of any complaints" and take "appropriate action . . . if any is called for."[67]

The ramifications of the Chicago incident were harmful for the school desegregation effort. It helped bring about the departures of Francis Keppel and James Quigley, and, in Seeley's opinion, "hurt our bluff, our psychological program." He thought that "each time something like this happened we had to back off."[68] According to Elaine Heffernan, a person who was close to the action at HEW as Peter Libassi's aide, Chicago was a "debacle" which created a credibility gap. She believed that the incident "gave out a message to politicians all over the country that political pressure pays off."[69]

Another result of the Chicago affair was the hiring of F. Peter Libassi as Special Assistant for civil rights to HEW Secretary John Gardner. A major part of Libassi's job was to take care of relations with the White House. He was, according to Elaine Heffernan, to "sell the White House, prepare the White House, convince them," so that Gardner could get their confidence back. She said that Gardner thought this was necessary because "Chicago made the White House skeptical of HEW's skill . . . there was now a lack of confidence." Thus, anytime anything concerning civil rights implementation was planned, the

67. As quoted in Elizabeth B. Drew, "Education's Billion-Dollar Baby," *The Atlantic Monthly* (July, 1966), p. 42.

68. David Seeley Interview.

69. Interview with Elaine Heffernan in Washington, D.C., on July 17, 1969, hereafter cited as Elaine Heffernan Interview. Miss Heffernan was Peter Libassi's personal secretary when he had positions at CRC and HEW. She is, at the time of writing, a staff assistant in the Office for Civil Rights, HEW. Much of the writer's insight into the Office for Civil Rights stems from the extensive interview with Miss Heffernan.

White House was notified with weekly memoranda sent to Lee White (Douglas Cater when White left), Joseph Califano, and John Doar. In the beginning, according to Miss Heffernan, Libassi "reported to the White House almost every time he turned around, ascertaining that there were no similar Chicago problems." Moreover, the Department spent a significant amount of time during 1966 studying how they could legally cut off funds to Chicago. They could not, however, develop sufficient legal evidence to justify taking Chicago to a hearing. Thus, Chicago, Illinois, remained a "thorn in the side of Gardner," who kept asking Libassi . . . 'what are we going to do about Chicago, what are we going to do about Chicago.' "[70]

But Libassi's main efforts were directed toward cultivating a good relationship with the White House. For example, all orders to terminate funds to schools practicing racial discrimination were first sent to the White House. This was done regularly in a systematic attempt to convince the President and his advisers of the reliability of HEW. It apparently worked, because Miss Heffernan often heard Libassi say: "I got everything I really wanted at the White House in all my years at HEW."[71]

However, Seeley's group, located in the Office of Education, was not so fortunate, because it was only a matter of time until the House Appropriations Committee followed through on its 1966 *command* to Gardner to place all civil rights enforcement activities in his office. John Fogarty, chairman of the House Appropriations subcommittee that had jurisdiction over HEW, told the members of the House of Representatives on May 4, 1966, that

---

70. Elaine Heffernan Interview.
71. Elaine Heffernan Interview.

HEW's spending for civil rights activities was "budgeted a great many different places in the department." The committee, he said, "deleted these every place they occurred and has consolidated all funds in the office of the secretary." In addition, the committee report filed had specifically stated that "in the opinion of the committee this work can be accomplished more effectively and efficiently by having one office responsible."[72]

The same Appropriations subcommittee followed this up one year later during hearings in which Representative Daniel Flood (who replaced the deceased Fogarty as chairman) told HEW Undersecretary Wilbur Cohen:

> It was my understanding last year that this committee directed that all civil rights enforcement funds and activities be centralized in the Office of the Secretary—period. We made no bones about that. . . . *It was not a request . . . it was a command.*[73]

Secretary Gardner acceded to the pressure, fearful that appropriations for the entire HEW program would be endangered. On May 11, 1967, he officially transferred EEOP's Title VI responsibilities to a central coordinating unit located in his office. Thereafter, this unit—the Office for Civil Rights, assumed total responsibility for the implementation of all Title VI facets of the department's civil rights program. EEOP, however, retained jurisdiction over Title IV operations, which up to that time was a

---

72. As quoted in William Steif, "The New Look in Civil Rights Enforcement," *Southern Education Report* (September, 1967), pp. 2–3.

73. U.S. Congress, House, Committee on Appropriations, *Hearings* before a subcommittee of the Committee on Appropriations, Departments of Labor and Health, Education and Welfare, 90th Cong., 1st sess., pt. 3, pp. 1276, 1279. (Italics added)

poorly funded and little-used provision of the 1964 Act.[74]

II. THE OFFICE FOR CIVIL RIGHTS

The Office for Civil Rights (OCR) was in a far better position to implement the school desegregation provisions of the 1964 Civil Rights Act when it was given that task in 1967 than was EEOP two years earlier. At the time of its establishment, EEOP found itself in an alien environment—the Office of Education, with inadequate resources. Its plight was further compounded by an inexperienced staff which attempted by trial and error to muddle through a heretofore uncharted course. In addition, it was in a department that was headed by a secretary, Anthony Celebreeze, who played a passive civil rights role in which he did little to motivate his compliance people.

The Office for Civil Rights, on the other hand, put in the office of the secretary, was under the protective wing of a man, John Gardner, who was known to be sympathetic to the civil rights cause, and who enjoyed the respect of the President.[75] Moreover, OCR's staff, headed by F. Peter Libassi, had the advantage of profiting from the mistakes of EEOP, its predecessor.

Philosophy
Philosophically, Libassi and his staff were more pragmatic about their work in comparison to the emotionally involved people who operated EEOP. Though equally committed to the civil rights cause, Libassi's office went about their task cautiously, carefully preparing for each new step. OCR, moreover, was responsible under Title VI

74. David Seeley Interview.
75. Elaine Heffernan Interview.

for the desegregation of all recipient institutions which received funds from any of the health, education, or welfare divisions of the Department. This, in effect, gave Libassi's office a wider responsibility than its predecessor had, for EEOP concentrated its efforts in one area—the desegregation of public schools. OCR had to balance many things, and according to Elaine Heffernan "this makes a difference." She noted that at EEOP

> everything was subordinated to school desegregation—including Title VI implementation as a Departmental whole. At OCR, there was no freedom to subordinate anything. Title VI implementation was the job, and all the elements had to be fitted together in a manner conducive to getting the job done. Title VI implementation came first; to the extent that it included school desegregation, fine. But where school desegregation did not come . . . implementation had to continue.[76]

Libassi's pragmatism was reflected in the efficient, objective manner in which he conducted everyday operations, and in his attempt to buttress OCR by solidifying relations with the White House and the Department of Justice. He and Gardner, as previously mentioned, continually worked to regain the confidence of the White House. They knew that HEW's efforts in the controversial civil rights area would be handicapped without the support of the President. Equally important for a sound and safe implementation program was a close working relationship with the Justice Department, which had been designated, in September 1965, coordinator of all Title VI enforcement activities. Libassi did not want to expose

---

76. Elaine Heffernan Interview.

OCR's flanks and possibly suffer the same hardships that EEOP had when it had unilaterally issued the Guidelines and amateurishly withheld Chicago school funds.

Relationship With the Justice Department

Libassi needed the legal support of the Justice Department to guide the Office for Civil Rights past the many obstacles that had led to the downfall of EEOP. According to one participant, Libassi

> knew the program must come under attack. He knew that unless it was *legally* irreproachable, it could not be politically defensible. . . . In this light, Justice backing became *strategically* important to HEW. . . .
>
> How could HEW have survived three Congressional attacks on the revised Guidelines as illegal unless the Attorney General was ready to defend their legality?

Thus, OCR

> needed to be able to get Katzenbach or Clark or a representative to write to or testify before a Congressman on issues like faculty desegregation. Without this we would have appeared to be out on a limb and the President would have been powerless to help us except by a suicidal gesture. At such Congressional investigatory squeezes . . . we did not need LBJ, we needed his Attorney General.[77]

The need for this legal backstop was satisfied with the establishment of a very close working relationship between the two organizations. The relationship was one of two-way consultation in which both units sought each other's advice and exchanged information. There were,

---

77. Elaine Heffernan Interview.

according to Elaine Heffernan, constant telephone calls and meetings between Libassi and Assistant Attorney General John Doar, among others in the Justice Department. Moreover, the staffs in the respective departments had frequent contacts in which they handled preliminary or procedural matters. In addition, there was a steady exchange of written data in the form of informational notices, HEW statistical reports, and drafts of proposed policies and letters.[78]

This association, which had its beginnings in early 1966, was of equal benefit to the Justice Department, which was also involved in school desegregation. Under Title IV of the 1964 Civil Rights Act, the Attorney General was authorized to institute civil actions in Federal courts in order to achieve desegregation in public education. This meant that the Civil Rights Division would not only be involved in its own litigation efforts, but would also have to defend the actions of the HEW unit of implementation. Thus, the attorneys at the Justice Department did not want a recurrence of the mishaps that took place when EEOP was responsible for Title VI enforcement. John Doar viewed HEW-Justice programs as being two engines of an airplane which he believed should be kept synchronized. He wanted to keep the thrust of the HEW-Justice engines "at about the same horsepower," which would prevent one engine from pulling off because it was too "revved up." Using this approach, Doar thought that the Administration would get "compliance and not defiance."[79]

From the time of the Chicago mishap in September, 1965, officials in the Departments of HEW and Justice have attempted to mutually align their enforcement ac-

78. Elaine Heffernan Interview.
79. John Doar Interview.

tivities. Attorney General Nicholas Katzenbach, for example, told a Texas audience on September 30, 1965, that "the Department of Justice this year began a major effort to complement the efforts of the Office of Education."[80] Similarly, Secretary John Gardner told a House Appropriations subcommittee in March 1967 that HEW based its actions

> on careful examination not only of the legislation and the legislative history, but the court cases which must serve as our guide, and continuous checking with the Attorney General. I would find it impossible to operate on the basis of my own opinions and judgments in this.
>
> It seems to me that I must move at every step in conformity with what the Attorney General and the courts regard as appropriate.[81]

Peter Libassi, in testimony before the same committee, used the protective cloak of the Attorney General when he told Kentucky Democrat William H. Natcher:

> We have been very careful in the administration of this program which involved termination of Federal funds. Every one of these proceedings is checked with the Department of Justice. We do not initiate any case until the Department has reviewed the facts and is sure that the proceeding is consistent with the act.[82]

As Attorney General, Ramsey Clark also thought that

---

80. Address before the Rotary Club of Houston, Texas. Department of Justice *Release.*

81. U.S. Congress, House, Committee on Appropriations, *Hearings* before a subcommittee of the Committee on Appropriations, Departments of Labor and Health, Education and Welfare, 90th Cong., 1st sess., 1967, pt. 2, p. 101.

82. *Ibid.,* p. 150.

the Departments of HEW and Justice should move forward at the same speed. He believed that one of the benefits of the monthly meetings of compliance officers that he, as coordinator of Title VI, had called was that Libassi "got to see what was being done by others . . . and realized that if he got too far out in front he would be too much of a target for opponents." Clark felt that "you must move forward in a solid front."[83]

That the Departments of HEW and Justice have mutual needs and the necessity to display a united front has also been recognized in the Nixon Administration. This was illustrated in a joint statement on school desegregation made by Attorney General John Mitchell and HEW Secretary Robert Finch on July 3, 1969:

> For local and Federal authorities alike, school desegregation poses both educational and law enforcement problems. To the extent practicable, on the Federal level the law enforcement aspects will be handled by the Department of Justice in judicial proceedings affording due process of law, and the educational aspects will be administered by H.E.W. *Because they are so closely interwoven, these aspects cannot be entirely separated.* We intend to use the administrative machinery of H.E.W. in tandem with the stepped-up enforcement activities of Justice.[84]

The Office for Civil Rights, during the Administration of Lyndon Johnson, assiduously cultivated the support of the White House and the Department of Justice, and thus was in a better position to face its detractors.

---

83. Ramsey Clark Interview. See chapter 6, "The Attorney General as Coordinator" section.

84. *New York Times*, July 4, 1969. (Italics added)

Congressional Pressure

According to Commissioner of Education Harold Howe:

> The major pressures on my office came from two sources. The civil rights groups of all descriptions generally pressured us to make more stringent guidelines and to enforce them more vigorously. On the other side State school superintendents in the South, Governors of Southern States, a variety of Congressmen and Senators largely from the South in the Congress of the United States and similar elements built up pressures to water down the guidelines, to enforce them less vigorously and to scuttle Title VI of the Civil Rights Act.[85]

Congressional investigations were found by Peter Libassi to take "an inordinate amount of our time," and "did limit our implementing policy." He recalled that some Congressmen were not only "constantly trying to force us to retreat on policy," but were applying "personal pressure also" when they tried to get him fired. On the positive side, Libassi felt that Congressional investigations had "forced improvements in the administration of the program," because Congress made them "run a more efficient program," whereby "administration people did not abuse their authority." The power of Congress, recalls Libassi, "was always in the back of our minds. You knew you were going to be held accountable."[86]

---

85. Letter to the writer from Harold Howe, September 1, 1969.

86. Peter Libassi Interview. Commissioner of Education Harold Howe, for example, appeared before Congressional committees, from January through August 1966, a total of 20 times, during which he prepared testimony on 14 occasions and accompanied the Secretary of HEW on the other 6. During the same period other people on his staff appeared before Congressional committees either as primary or supporting witnesses 52 times. U.S. Congress, House, *Hearings* before the Special sub-

Congressional pressure was steady and intense, and thus affected the operations of the Office for Civil Rights. According to Elaine Heffernan, Libassi's staff found it extremely difficult to control the pressures, because

> they were always ahead of us. We were always reacting, responding . . . never got the initiative after we took it once in March 1966 and kept it briefly for about three to four months. . . . By July and August 1966 . . . the paper tiger was unmasked as a real threat to segregation. From then on, it was controversy all the way, with attack after attack.

Miss Heffernan found that the effect of this barrage was that

> it exhausted us. It did not so much require us to "soften" any given policy already formulated, that is to say, it never compelled us to betray our policies, but it did shrink away the base for our action. As time passed, we had steadily less room, fewer options . . . also pressures affected our energy and mentality.[87]

Some support for desegregation efforts came from various proponents of civil rights, but hardly enough to offset the opposition forces. One active participant observed that "pressures pro at least helped to counter those con so that we came out sort of 70 percent con and 30 percent pro . . . which is better than 100 percent con."[88] The lack of consistent liberal power was sorrowfully admitted by

---

committee of the Committee on Education and Labor, 89th Cong., 2nd sess., 1966, pp. 279–80.

87. Elaine Heffernan Interview.
88. Elaine Heffernan Interview.

Marvin Caplin, Director of the Washington office of the Leadership Conference on Civil Rights, who found that "one trouble is that we tend to deal with each new crisis as it appears, instead of trying to forestall crisis by continuous action. But we simply do not have the staff or resources for that. Hence, the weaknesses in enforcement."[89]

White House Relations

One sector, however, that gave little trouble to OCR was the White House. The consensus of opinion of those who were involved in school desegregation work is that President Johnson and his staff never attempted to make them slow down their activities. Derrick Bell, for example, who was special assistant to Libassi and who had been hired to legally guide OCR in its dealings with the Legal Counsel at HEW and the attorneys at the Justice Department, had found that OCR's notices of enforcement activities to the White House "seldom resulted in requests that we not take action, although on occasion we were requested to delay for a week or two contemplating enforcement action to permit a key appropriation or other important bill to get through."[90] Elaine Heffernan recalled that the White House, also the subject of great pressure, "bore up very well." OCR, she noted, "heard from them constantly, of course, but never did we hear, 'just don't do it, period.'" She found that OCR's "dealings with the White House were not in the nature of a response to pressure, except in the sense that we and the White House were together in being pressured by someone else."[91] Libassi, nevertheless, felt that he had to go about his work

89. Letter to the writer, August 11, 1969.
90. Letter to the writer, September 24, 1969.
91. Elaine Heffernan Interview.

very carefully, for he knew that "every decision was going to be within the newspapers within 24 hours," and that Southern opponents upon finding fault would "get in touch with the White House and they with us."[92] OCR, thus, had to be very careful in their methods of operation.

Methods of Operation

Though never secure, OCR was, compared to EEOP, better able to use its energies to bring about public school desegregation. David Seeley's trail-blazing operation at EEOP suffered chronic administrative weaknesses which in part resulted from an early underestimation of the nature of the job. John Gardner recognized this when he said:

> My predecessors vastly underestimated what it took to cope with 2,000 districts. They provided a set of guidelines that did *not* prove to be strong. So when I came in, we reorganized.[93]

Moreover, the crisis atmosphere that pervaded compliance activities at EEOP was not conducive to the creation of sound administrative methods. There were few written instructions for the staff, no fixed way to handle complaints, and general uncertainty as to the legality of certain compliance procedures. Seeley was asked about this during Congressional hearings held in December 1966, at which time he described how his staff handled complaints that came in after school districts had filed assurances of compliance:

> Typically, the complaint does not give us enough detail

92. Peter Libassi Interview.
93. As quoted in Robert G. Sherrill, "Guidelines to Frustration," *The Nation* (January 16, 1967), p. 70.

to know whether it has substance. The first step is that you go back to the complainant. If the complaint seems to have substance, then it will follow any of a number of courses: either a visit to the school district, if that seems appropriate, or a letter asking the school district to give us its side of the story, or in some cases more recently we have discussed the matter with the State department of education. . . .

There is no fixed pattern for handling the complaint. We do whatever seems appropriate in the particular case.[94]

Commissioner Howe was asked, during the same hearings, how the Office of Education determined the point at which a school system was considered completely desegregated. He replied:

We have no such criteria that we can apply. It is not stated in the guidelines; it is not stated in public policy anywhere that I know. We have no guidance from the Congress or the courts in this area, so I would hesitate to describe such a situation.[95]

Additional aspects relating to the organizational inadequacy of EEOP came to view in the following colloquy that William C. Cramer, Republican of Florida, had with David Seeley and Harold Howe:

Cramer: Do you have a memorandum of instructions for the staff people who visit the respective school boards upon which they can advise the school boards as to what pro-

---

94. U.S. Congress, House, Committee of the Judiciary, *Hearings* before a Special subcommittee on Civil Rights of the Committee of the Judiciary, Guidelines for School Desegregation, 89th Cong., 2nd sess., 1966, p. 130. (Italics added)

95. *Ibid.*, p. 39.

cedure will be followed and what their rights are relating to deferrals?

Seeley: Not as yet. . . .

Cramer: Did the Commissioner indicate that there were some interoffice communications or letters relating to this subject?

Howe: I simply suggested that there might be. I do not know of any. I wondered whether Mr. Seeley did.[96]

When Seeley was asked about the type of instructions that were given to his staff, he said:

Most of the instructions . . . were verbal in the sense that we did have a series of training programs, each of them lasting a week, at the beginning of the summer, through which all of the staff members passed. Although this included some written materials, most of the discussion was verbal. We have had at least one written memorandum, perhaps more . . . in which the staff was informed in written form of their instructions.[97]

Moreover, because of an inadequate number of personnel, EEOP's follow-up program was totally deficient—a condition shared, to a lesser extent, by OCR.[98] Seeley admitted before a House Judiciary subcommittee in Decem-

96. *Ibid.,* p. 46.

97. *Ibid.,* p. 67.

98. In February 1969, OCR had more enforcement employees working on Northern school desegregation than on Southern—52 and 51 respectively. Moreover, it was reported that President Johnson, in the last months of his Administration denied a budget request that would have increased OCR's staff from 300 to 600. *New York Times,* February 23, 1969. In addition, OCR Director Ruby Martin said that school districts under court order were desegregating painfully slowly because there is "no machinery now in existence for monitoring compliance with court orders for school desegregation." *New York Times,* January 17, 1969.

ber 1966 that "frankly, we have not really had the opportunity as yet to go back to the States to see how they are doing with these commitments."[99] This was again disclosed several months later when Secretary Gardner told the Senate Appropriations Committee:

> Title VI regulations, as approved by the President, require on-site visits to verify assurances of compliance. Although assurances have been received from all agencies and institutions receiving assistance, *we have not had the manpower to visit more than a fraction.*[100]

Following HEW findings, announced in November, 1969, that there was misuse of Federal funds in Mississippi schools, Commissioner of Education James E. Allen, Jr. said that a 15-man intradepartmental panel had been named to study the operations of Title I of the Elementary and Secondary Education Act of 1965.[101] In announcing this nationwide investigation, Dr. Allen said: "We now have had four years' experience with this billion dollar program. I feel that we should take a hard look at it not only to tighten the management but also to strengthen its educational impact."[102] *New York Times* civil rights analyst John Herbers wrote that "officials in the agency have conceded privately that there have been flagrant abuses of the funds."[103]

---

99. *Hearings,* p. 132, n. 97.

100. U.S. Congress, Senate, Appropriations Committee, *Hearings,* Departments of Labor and Health, Education and Welfare, 90th Cong., 1st sess., 1967, p. 681. (Italics added)

101. *New York Times,* November 26, 1969.

102. *Ibid.,* November 27, 1969.

103. *Ibid.* It was also reported that on November 7 the NAACP Legal Defense and Educational Fund, Inc., and the Washington Research Project of the Southern Center for Studies in Public Policy charged

Thus, from the time that HEW was given responsibility for public school desegregation in the summer of 1964 to the Nixon Administration, it has had to overcome great obstacles. When the Office for Civil Rights assumed EEOP's Title VI duties in 1967 it inherited a chronically disabled operation, which was in dire need of organizational revamping. Libassi's philosophical and procedural approach differed from Seeley's in many respects. Seeley envisaged the compliance operation as a "bluff game" in which EEOP purposely made its standards hazy in order to gain the initiative by throwing the Southern school districts off balance. This was coupled with a threat strategy in which EEOP tried to "cajole" the districts into compliance.[104] Libassi, on the other hand, in his belief that threats should be minimized, prohibited his staff from threatening things that they could not follow through with. According to Elaine Heffernan, Libassi's standing rule was: "Say only what you mean and mean what you say." She observed that

after centralization, from 1967 through 1968, OCR ran pretty much on the Libassi strategy. OCR levelled with State and local school officials. Compliance negotiations continued, but the manners were different: less obvious advocacy by staff of desegregation; more impersonal concentration on ways and means and on the legal obligations faced by the Department under Title VI and by the school officials under case law.

---

after a six-month study that Title I funds had been "wasted, diverted or otherwise misused by state and local authorities."

104. Seeley told Gene Roberts of the *New York Times*: "We stay away from ordering anyone to do anything, but we do cajole. It is better to cajole a school district, than just to cut off its funds." October 17, 1966.

Whereas in 1966, EEOP staff conveyed the impression that they were *enforcing* the guidelines, in 1967 and 1968, OCR staff tried to make clear that they were seeking voluntary compliance with a Federal statute, as directed by that law and by Presidential Regulation.[105]

Libassi's new approach, combined with administrative reorganization that progressively converted the program into more of a decentralized national operation, helped bring about an increase in the percentage of black and white children attending the same schools in the South.[106] The school desegregation percentages rose from 2.25 percent in the 1964-65 school year, to 6 percent in 1965-66, 12.5 percent in 1966-67, 13.9 percent in 1967-68, 20.3 percent in 1968-69, and approximately 33 to 40 percent in the 1969-70 school year.[107]

The Nixon Administration appears also to disfavor the application of forceful methods, for, among other reasons, fear af alienating a politically lucrative South.[108] This es-

---

105. Elaine Heffernan Interview.

106. OCR's field to headquarters personnel ratio eventually became approximately one-third at headquarters (in Washington), to two-thirds in the field, which had the effect of regionalizing the compliance operation. Moreover, National guidelines were published in March 1968 which apply to schools in both North and South. Elaine Heffernan Interview.

107. Statistics derived from: U.S. Commission on Civil Rights, *Southern School Desegregation, 1966–67*, pp. 5–9; *New York Times*, January 17 and September 14, 1969; and Elaine Heffernan Interview. Figures are for the 11 Southern states of the Old Confederacy. See above, chapter 1, note 1.

108. Roy Reed of the *New York Times*, basing his judgment on reports from 11 Southern states, believes that if President Nixon "is pursuing his much-discussed Southern strategy—an effort, officially discounted, to build a winning constituency out of the South, the Midwest, and the West, while ignoring the big Northeastern urban states—he is making headway." Reed found that "Republican officials throughout the South consider Mr. Agnew the leader in the drive to expand Republican strength

sentially pragmatic approach has found expression in the words and actions of high officials in the Nixon Cabinet. Former HEW Secretary Robert Finch, for example, stated in February 1969 that he wanted to introduce a more reasonable method of obtaining compliance in Southern school districts, and thus "get away from the cop mentality." He felt that in the past some people were "overzealous, going into some of these districts and saying: 'You're going to integrate and the hell with trying to keep an education system open.'" Finch believes that school segregation cases should be decided on a district-by-dis-

---

in the South." Moreover, "the Nixon Administration has showered attention on the South this year. Cabinet and sub-Cabinet officials have made dozens of visits, and the President has been to the region three times." *New York Times,* December 7, 1969.

The change in the Southern political scene was borne out by Gallup surveys in which voting adults in the South were asked: "If the election for Congress were being held today, which party would you like to see win in this Congressional district—the Democratic party or the Republican party?" The inroads made by the Republican party in terms of voting strength are indicated by the following responses:

	Rep.	Dem.
Jan.–Feb. '70	39%	61%
Jan. '66	29	71
Feb. '62	23	77
Feb. '58	23	77
Feb. '54	22	78

This growth in voter allegiance is also reflected in the number of seats won in the South by the two major parties in the last four off-year Congressional elections:

	Rep.	Dem.
1966	28	91
1962	18	101
1958	14	105
1954	9	111

(*New York Times,* March 8, 1970)

trict basis in an attempt to keep as many schools open as possible. In his mind "the worst thing you can do is just lopping funds and closing down schools."[109] He elaborated on this theme one month later when he was asked in a personal interview whether his opinions represented a change from the views of his predecessors. Finch replied:

> I feel that I have a commitment to try to resolve it the best way I can. It's a political question, and essentially I'm a political animal. We're trying to achieve a result that will halt deliberate efforts to discriminate. At the same time, we intend to do our best to sustain the schools and keep them open.
> . . . You can't do it with a sledge hammer, and you can't do it overnight—without tearing a community to pieces.[110]

This philosophy was again revealed in an important HEW-Justice joint statement made on July 3, 1969, in which Finch and Mitchell said that their "aim is to educate, not to punish; to stimulate real progress, not to strike a pose; to induce compliance rather than compel submission." They planned to avoid the "confusion" that they believed had surrounded the guidelines, and were thus "jointly announcing new, coordinated procedures, not new 'guidelines.'" Moreover, they asserted their determination to view the situation as a national predicament, because

> the implications of the *Brown* decisions are national in scope. The problem of racially separate schools is a national problem, and we intend to approach enforcement by coordinated administrative action and court litigation.[111]

109. *New York Times*, February 11, 1969.
110. *U.S. News & World Report*, March 10, 1969, p. 46.
111. *New York Times*, July 4, 1969.

Furthermore, they stated that the Administration, while seeking bona fide desegregation and not accepting unworkable "freedom of choice" plans, would "achieve full compliance with the law in a manner that provides the most progress with the least disruption and friction." Finch and Mitchell planned to do this by using "the administrative machinery of H.E.W. in tandem with the stepped-up enforcement activities of Justice, and to draw on H.E.W. for more assistance by professional educators as provided for under Title IV of the 1964 act." In addition, they felt that an effective desegregation program should have enough flexibility to give the enforcers room for experimentation. Therefore, they stated:

> it is not our purpose here to lay down a single arbitrary date by which the desegregation process should be completed in all districts, or to lay down a single, arbitrary system by which it should be achieved.
> A policy requiring all school districts, regardless of the difficulties they face, to complete desegregation by the same terminal date is too rigid to be either workable or equitable. This is reflected in the history of the "guidelines."[112]

Shortly thereafter, this approach was applied when the Departments of HEW and Justice asked the United States Court of Appeals for the Fifth Circuit to grant a desegregation delay for 33 Mississippi school districts. The Fifth Circuit granted a stay, but was subsequently reversed when the United States Supreme Court held, on October 29, 1969, that "continued operation of segregated schools under a standard of allowing 'all deliberate speed' for desegregation is no longer constitutionally permissible." The eight Justices unanimously stated that "under explicit

112. *Ibid.*

holdings of this Court, the obligation of every school district is to terminate dual school systems at once and to operate now and hereafter only unitary schools."[113]

The following day brought reactions from the Nixon Administration. The President issued a prepared statement in which he said:

> The Supreme Court has spoken decisively on the timing of school desegregation. There are, of course, practical and human problems involved. With all of us working together in full respect for the law, I am confident we can overcome these problems.
>
> I intend to use the leadership resources of the executive branch of government to assist in every possible way in doing so. I call upon all citizens, and particularly those in leadership positions, to work together in seeking solutions for these problems in accordance with the mandate of the Court.[114]

In a separate statement, Attorney General John Mitchell said that the Justice Department intended "to bring every available resource to bear" on the problem and to "enforce the mandates issued by the courts pursuant to the Supreme Court decisions."[115] HEW Secretary Robert Finch

---

113. *New York Times,* October 30, 1969. *Beatrice Alexander, et al., petrs.* v. *Holmes County Board of Education, et al.*

114. *New York Times,* October 31, 1969.

115. *Ibid.* However, many staff members of HEW's Office for Civil Rights found Administration enforcement wanting. Shortly after the forced resignation of HEW Office for Civil Rights chief Leon E. Panetta on February 17, 1970 (reportedly for his strict enforcement views) members of his office wrote the President a letter in which they called upon Nixon to exercise "the strong moral leadership that we feel is now essential to avoid a reversal of the nation's longstanding commitment to equal opportunity." Moreover, Paul M. Rilling, HEW director of the six-state Southern region, in charge of enforcing Title VI of the Civil Rights

asserted that "by the language of the decision itself, neither the courts nor this department should tolerate any further delays in abolishing the vestiges of the dual system."[116]

During the following weeks HEW issued a policy statement specifying how it was going to accelerate school desegregation in the South,[117] and the Fifth Circuit Court of Appeals gave the affected 33 Mississippi School districts until December 31, 1969, to implement workable desegregation plans.[118] Once again, the judiciary had come to the aid of the school desegregation program.

Act, resigned on March 3 stating that "this Administration will not enforce Title VI with vigor and consistency." He said that "the failure of will of this Administration may be encouraging another round of massive resistance tactics on the part of Deep South segregationists." *New York Times*, March 4, 1970.

Dr. James E. Allen, Jr., Nixon's Commissioner of Education, was forced to resign on June 10, 1970, apparently because of his desire to stringently enforce the school desegregation laws. At a news conference held shortly after his resignation, Dr. Allen stated: "The Administration's concern is with meeting the minimum requirements of the Civil Rights Act. My commitment is that desegregation is a basic education necessity, and that the Administration should take more steps to accomplish it." *New York Times*, June 12, 1970.

Bishop Stephen G. Spottswood, chairman of the board of directors of the NAACP told that organization's annual convention: "For the first time since Woodrow Wilson, we have a national Administration that can be rightly characterized as anti-Negro.

This is the first time since 1920 that the national Administration has made it a matter of calculated policy to work against the needs and aspirations of the largest minority of its citizens." *New York Times*, June 30, 1970.

116. *New York Times*, October 31, 1969.

117. *New York Times*, November 15, 1969. HEW said that its negotiations with 112 Southern school districts would be "immediately affected" by the Supreme Court decision. Many of these districts were told that they would have their funds cut off if they did not comply.

118. *New York Times*, November 7, 1969. Three weeks later the Fifth Circuit ordered 16 other school districts in 6 Southern states to have

SUMMARY

There were two basic units in the Department of Health, Education and Welfare which had alternate (at times simultaneous) responsibility for public school desegregation. The Equal Educational Opportunities Program—the initial enforcement unit, began operations plagued by an inhospitable locale, insufficient resources, and an inexperienced staff. EEOP fell easy prey to its powerful opponents while it simultaneously attempted to get recalcitrant Southern school districts to desegregate, and strove to put its own home in order.

Its successor, the Office for Civil Rights, had more favorable conditions in which to conduct its operations. It had been financially and emotionally shielded by a civil rights minded department head, who had seen fit to place it within the confines of his office. Moreover, OCR, directed by an astute administrator, repaired the fragmented relationship that EEOP had with the White House and the Justice Department, and was thus better able to implement the law.

---

integrated school systems by the fall of 1970. *New York Times,* December 2, 1969. See above, n. 35.

John Herbers reports that "of the 4,000 school districts in the South and border states, about 3,000 have been legally desegregated. About 390 districts, including most of the major cities, are under Federal Court order and are thus in some stage of desegregation. About 120 districts, mostly rural ones, have had their Federal funds terminated for failure to desegregate. The remaining districts—approximately 500—are in some stage of desegregation under Title VI of the 1964 Act, which carries cutoff penalties." *New York Times,* October 30, 1969.

5

THE COMMUNITY RELATIONS SERVICE:
IMPLEMENTATION BY CONCILIATION
AND MEDIATION

ISAIAH'S ADVICE IN ECCLESIASTES, "COME NOW, AND LET US reason together," was an oft-quoted philosophical staple in the life of Lyndon Baines Johnson. In the 1957 civil rights debates he expressed this line of thought by suggesting the creation of a community relations service.[1] Once again, in 1959, Senate majority leader Johnson formally proposed the establishment of this type of mechanism, but was rebuffed when the Congress failed to incorporate it into the 1960 Civil Rights Act.[2] With the backing of Vice President Johnson, John Kennedy included provision for the Community Relations Service (CRS) in his second Civil Rights Message of June 20,

---

1. *New York Times,* January 21, 1959, as cited by George Sulzner, III, "The United States Commission on Civil Rights: A Study of Incrementalism in Policy-Making" (unpublished Ph.D. dissertation, University of Michigan, 1967), p. 142, n. 18.

2. *Ibid.*

1963.[3] Though it was not made part of the bill approved by the House Judiciary Committee, it did find its way into what became the omnibus Civil Rights Act of 1964 when it was accepted as a House amendment on February 10, 1964.[4]

INCEPTION, AND LOCATION IN THE
DEPARTMENT OF COMMERCE

Conditions at the time of the Service's inception were somewhat unfavorable considering the lukewarm approval given by civil rights entities, and the mixed reception by Southern members of Congress. A charter member of the Service, Roger Wilkins, said that when CRS "first started, people at the Civil Rights Commission were offended" by the creation of it, because some people at the Commission wanted to run action programs, which was not in their charter. This, at times, led to jurisdictional disputes, and, according to Wilkins, "some of our guys stepped on their toes." He specifically recalled seeing a "head-on collision" between Calvin Kytle (second director of CRS) and William L. Taylor (staff director of the Commission), at a Budget Bureau meeting. Wilkins said that this state of strained relations continued for two and one-half years,

---

3. Theodore Sorensen wrote that "with the backing of the Vice President, a Community Relations Service had been added to work quietly with local communities in search of progress." *Kennedy*, p. 496.

4. *Congressional Quarterly* states that "a similar provision had appeared in the original Administration civil rights bill, except that the Administration had not recommended placing it within the Commerce Department and suggested no ceiling on the size of the staff. *Revolution in Civil Rights*, 1965 ed., p. 50.

until he, as new director of the Service in 1966, tried to make peace.[5]

Moreover, many believed that the Service was a mechanism that was favored by the South. Nicholas Katzenbach considered it a "sop" for the Southerners, and Roger Wilkins thought it was a move to "pacify the South."[6] Furthermore, while it is true that CRS was amended to the 1964 Civil Rights bill on the motion of South Carolina Democrat Robert T. Ashmore,[7] it was also severely criticized by South Carolina Senator Strom Thurmond.[8] In addition, the Service's first director was a man who served as Governor of Florida from 1954 to 1960—LeRoy Collins.[9]

Added to CRS's birth defects were the narrow power entrusted to it, the limited funds given it, and the foreign locale that it was placed in. The Commerce Department, its first abode, turned out to be an uninterested host. Attorney General Katzenbach told a Senate subcommittee of the Committee on Government Operations that CRS was placed in the Commerce Department primarily to help enforce the public accommodations provision of the 1964 Civil Rights Act. Katzenbach said that

the Service was placed in the Department of Commerce, on

5. Interview with Roger Wilkins, former director of CRS, in New York on August 6 and August 13, 1969, hereafter cited as Roger Wilkins Interview.

6. Nicholas Katzenbach Interview; Roger Wilkins Interview.

7. *Revolution in Civil Rights*, 1965 ed., p. 50.

8. At Senate Commerce Committee confirmation hearings for designated CRS director LeRoy Collins, Thurmond made highly critical remarks about CRS and Collins. Accompanying Collins and speaking in his behalf were two men who had voted against the 1964 Civil Rights bill—Florida Senators Spessard L. Holland and George A. Smathers. *New York Times*, July 8, 1964.

9. For some time prior to his official designation, Collins was known to be Johnson's choice. *Ibid.*, July 4, 1964.

the recommendation of President Kennedy and Attorney General Kennedy primarily because it was then thought that its concern would relate largely, if not exclusively, to the business community.

Hundreds of angry demonstrations, spreading from Birmingham across the South, concentrated public anxiety on the public accommodations section. Under the circumstances, we believed . . . that the business community of the South offered the best rallying point for an effective force in support of law. . . . And it seemed eminent good sense to enlist the support of the Commerce Department, headed by a distinguished former Governor of North Carolina, to seek the spirit of compliance.[10]

Whatever the logical reasons for the Service's placement within the Commerce Department, Roger Wilkins found that CRS had poor relations with Commerce, with his group feeling like a "misfit." He said, for example, that the Service received neither overt aid nor sympathy from departmental officials on budgetary matters. Moreover, according to Wilkins, Secretary John Connors "didn't know about civil rights," thus creating a situation in which "I had to explain all about it when I had a problem—he was concerned about the gold drain."[11]

PHILOSOPHY

The manner in which CRS officials interpreted the

---

10. Statement before the Senate subcommittee on Executive Reorganization of the Senate Committee on Government Operations, March 3, 1966. Department of Justice *Release*.

11. Roger Wilkins Interview. Wilkins was assistant director of CRS for Community Action, from October 1964 to December 1965 at which time he was appointed director. He remained at that post until the end of the Johnson Administration.

statute that established the Service had a great effect on its operations. The law, Title X of the 1964 Act, said, in part, that the Service's function shall be

> to provide assistance to communities and persons therein in resolving disputes, disagreements, or difficulties relating to discriminatory practices based on race, color, or national origin, which impair the rights of persons in such communities under the Constitution or laws of the United States or which affect or may affect interstate commerce. The Service may offer its services in cases of such disputes, disagreements, or difficulties whenever, in its judgment, peaceful relations among the citizens of the community involved are threatened thereby, and it may offer its services either upon its own motion or upon the request of an appropriate State or local official or other interested person.[12]

In most instances this mandate was understood by the first two directors of the Service, LeRoy Collins and Calvin Kytle, as calling for a fire-fighting type of operation.[13] Collins, after eight months in office, believed that his job was to "help put out fires which flare up in human relations and, if possible, to prevent such fires from breaking out in the first place."[14] Calvin Kytle, when deputy director of the Service told a House subcommittee in March 1965: "You can think of our conciliation unit as I described it as a fire-fighting unit, and I think it would be proper to think of one other unit in our service, the com-

---

12. 78 Stat. 267, section 1002.

13. Roger Wilkins Interview. Kytle, born in South Carolina, was Collins's deputy until Collins was elevated to Undersecretary of Commerce in June 1965 at which time Kytle was appointed acting director of CRS. He served until December of that year, never being given permanent status.

14. *New York Times*, February 4, 1965.

munity action section, as a fire-prevention unit."[15] However, Roger Wilkins, assistant director in charge of the
Community Action section of the Service under Collins
and Kytle, strongly opposed what he considered an organization "set up to stop racial crises," and which moved
"when the Negroes march." Wilkins said that everyone in
CRS understood what was intended as the task of the
Service, which was to wait "in Washington for the news
ticker to say Negroes are marching." He disagreed with
the Collins-Kytle approach and tried to persuade them to
use the Service as more of a preventive unit. His efforts
were in vain, because both Collins and Kytle interpreted
Title X as permitting them to handle *crisis* situations.[16]
Their methods of operation reflected this view.

METHODS OF OPERATION

During their two-year stay at the Commerce Department, the small staff constituting CRS had attempted to
conciliate many types of racial disputes.[17] They concentrated their efforts, for the most part, in the South.[18] The
Service did, however, handle several cases elsewhere, and
was able to institute at least one major preventive type of

15. U.S. Congress, House, Committee on Appropriations, *Hearings*
before a subcommittee of the Committee on Appropriations, 89th Cong.,
1st sess., 1965, p. 85.

16. Roger Wilkins Interview.

17. Some of the categories were: public accommodations, school
desegregation, public facilities, housing and real estate, community tension, and employment and labor practices.

18. At House appropriations hearings held in 1966 Roger Wilkins
said that "with the limited resources available . . . it has been necessary
to concentrate our efforts on southern cities." U.S. Congress, House,
Committee on Appropriations, *Hearings* before a subcommittee of the
Committee on Appropriations, 89th Cong., 2nd sess., p. 422.

program in the North.[19] Their source of complaints, in general, according to Congressional testimony of Roger Wilkins, was: newspapers, the news ticker, the National Citizens Committee on Community Relations, private organizations, human relations commissions, civil rights groups, and public officials.[20] Their basic methods of operation were described by Calvin Kytle to a House Appropriations subcommittee, using a prototype community as an illustration. Kytle said that the Service generally followed six steps when it entered a community:

(1) Fact finding for the development of a full picture of the community situation.

(2) Field work in the community and the surrounding area conducted by full-time staff members and by contract conciliators.

(3) Assessment and staff planning in Washington.

(4) Liaison with local officials and Federal agencies.

(5) Continuous liaison by telephone on a round-the-clock basis with a wide range of persons in the community.

(6) Assisting the community not only in conciliation efforts but also in long-range community planning and development activities.[21]

Other specific examples of the Service's activities were pin-

---

19. Roger Wilkins Interview. Wilkins said that his first entering wedge into the ghetto areas of the North came about when he and two other CRS officials devised a project in which the Service would coordinate Federal programs in what turned out to be nine Northern cities. The plan was presented to Vice President Humphrey's Council on Equal Opportunity early in 1965, and, being approved, was used during the summer of 1965.

20. *Hearings.* See above, p. 439, n. 18.

21. U.S. Congress, House, Committee on Appropriations, *Hearings* before a subcommittee of the Committee on Appropriations, 89th Cong., 1st sess., 1965, p. 76.

pointed by Kytle. Because they give a clear view of the
Service's scope and methods, these examples are worth
stating in detail:

Place: Deep southern rural community.

Complaint: Negroes boycotting high school in protest of:
(a) loss of accreditation, (b) condemned buildings, (c) insufficient heating, (d) lack of equipment, (e) need of text-
books, (f) segregated schools. Three hundred eighty-nine
students and parents jailed; vandalism of grocery stores; 25
automobile windows smashed and a complete breakdown
of communications between Negroes and whites.

CRS goal: To establish communications between groups;
work out agreement with school board for correction of
deficiencies at Negro high school; help community develop
plan for desegregation of school; seek release of persons
from jail; get pupils back to school; encourage steps toward
a biracial committee.

Procedure: Four conciliators, working a total of over 10
weeks, met with elected officials, businessmen, school board
officials, Negro parents, students and civil rights groups
(including the one that filed desegregation suit during this
period). Negotiated agreement satisfactory to both sides.
Established biracial committee and had all persons released
from jail.

Results: Reduced community tension; board of education
submitted plan for school desegregation to HEW; students
released from jail and returned to school; needed repairs
initiated; school reaccredited; meeting arranged for involvement of Federal agencies in obtaining Federal programs for
the community. . . .

Place: Southern coastal city.

Complaint: White mobs roaming beaches, streets, and
residential areas; assaulting Negroes, destroying property.

CRS goal: To cooperate with Federal, State and local officials in the restoration of law and order; to focus attention
of both races on the need to resolve their differences and
to build a better community.

Procedure: Five conciliators, working over a 3-month
period, conferred with local leaders, analyzed sociological
data. . . .

Results: Biracial meetings have begun. Mob violence
under control. Efforts under way to desegregate hospital
and to employ more Negro policemen. Important religious
and business leaders cooperating. White power structure
persuaded to provide police protection for large meetings
held by Negroes in formerly all-white restaurants.

Status: Active.[22]

Kytle also related an incident to the House subcommittee that was reminiscent of Lyndon Johnson's "let us reason together" approach. He described a situation in which
the Service

brought the leaders of the white community together in
the same room, across the same table, with the leaders of
the Negro community, and for the first time, perhaps for
the first time since Reconstruction itself, a meaningful
dialog went on between white leaders and Negro leaders
. . . and it was the first time in a long, long while that there
had been any man to man, face to face, confrontation in a
rational way.[23]

Kytle, at the time deputy director of CRS, later told the
Congressmen that "our faith is in the fact that if you can
finally get people together to sit down rationally and talk

---

22. *Ibid.*, pp. 90–92.
23. *Ibid.*, p. 75.

with one another, something good will come out of it."[24]

Two years after it was established the Community Relations Service had its third director, Roger Wilkins, and was in the process of being transferred to the Justice Department for the officially announced reason of streamlining the civil rights enforcement program.[25] In a statement to the Senate subcommittee on Executive Reorganization on March 3, 1966, Attorney General Katzenbach spoke in favor of the proposed transfer. He said that the Service

> should be associated with that department of the government with basic and comprehensive responsibility for racial problems . . ; the Attorney General is the one officer of the government who is preoccupied daily with civil rights relating to every level and to every part of the nation . . ; as time has gone on, the operations of the Community Relations Service have had steadily decreasing relevance to the dominant concerns of the Department of Commerce . . ; the expanding range of the Service's activities has brought it more and more often into areas in which the Department of Justice has a direct enforcement responsibility . . . the subject matter, the essential human problems and many of the organizations we deal with are, more often than not,

24. *Ibid.,* p. 89.
25. President Johnson, in his reorganization message to Congress, said that "placing the Community Relations Service within the Justice Department will enhance the ability of the Justice Department to mediate and conciliate and will insure that the Federal Government speaks with a unified voice in those tense situations where the good offices of the Federal Government are called upon to assist." *Congressional Record* 112:2822, February 10, 1966.

the same. . . . No other Department has as natural a need for the Community Relations Service as does the Department of Justice.[26]

Katzenbach later told a House subcommittee that the proposed transfer was "designed to help the government achieve greater coordination and effectiveness in its civil rights activities," and "if both the Department and the Service are to use their complementary expertise most creatively, flexibly, and effectively, this transfer must be approved."[27] However, these statements were merely rhetoric for Congressional consumption. Mr. Katzenbach said in a private interview several years later that the real reason that the Justice Department wanted CRS in its domain was that "they were starting trouble down South . . . getting in the way." He said that he thought it was necessary to get them out of the South into the North where the activists did you no harm. In his opinion, the Service "messed you up down South" with their urging civil rights groups and others to do things.[28] Ramsey Clark concurred with Katzenbach's statement that the Justice Department wanted CRS transferred so that they could have greater

---

26. Senate subcommittee of the Committee on Government Operations. Department of Justice *Release*.

27. House subcommittee on Reorganization of the Committee on Government Operations, March 18, 1966. Department of Justice *Release*.

28. Nicholas Katzenbach Interview. Stephen Pollak also felt that when CRS was in the Commerce Department it had been a "pain in the neck." Interview.

Legally, transfer required tacit approval of both houses of Congress during the 60-day period following the President's reorganization message. During this period, Senator Javits, Republican of New York, led a move to block the transfer in the Senate, but his proposal was defeated 42 to 32. Moreover, Katzenbach said that Senator Robert Kennedy supported the transfer at the Congressional hearings because of Kennedy's trust and personal relationship with him. Nicholas Katzenbach Interview.

control of the Service's activities. He said that LeRoy Collins had created problems in Selma, Montgomery, and Watts by his unpredictable and unsettling actions.[29] Moreover, when Roger Wilkins, an assistant director of the Service, first learned of the proposed transfer, he stoically accepted the situation, because he "did not think the Service was a big enough issue to fight the President—it was an experimental thing."[30] However, in the ensuing months he became an ardent advocate of the transfer as illustrated in his testimony before the Senate Commerce Committee:

> It seems to me that if this agency is in the Department of Justice, and if I, as Director, report to the Attorney General, the activities and efforts which we undertake will be much more effective, because they will be much better coordinated with the other civil rights activities in the Federal Government including the Title VI activities which is also the responsibility of the Attorney General to coordinate. . . . It seems to me that for the sake of coordination, for the sake of streamlining, for the sake of more effective activity it is appropriate for this to go into the Department of Justice where I believe it will operate very well.
>
> All of my dealings with the Attorney General and his principal assistants have led me to conclude that they support us very strongly. With that kind of support I think that we will be very effective in the Department of Justice.[31]

---

29. Ramsey Clark Interview. As an example of this, Clark said that while Justice Department people were working on a case in the South, they saw Collins, a representative of the Federal Government, talking to Martin Luther King as he was marching in a demonstration.

30. Roger Wilkins Interview.

31. U.S. Congress, Senate, Confirmation *Hearings* before the Senate Commerce Committee, 89th Cong., 2nd sess., January 25, 1966, p. 11. For the post of CRS director.

What happened during those months to change the mind of Roger Wilkins? Once again, as with Katzenbach's public and private statements, a Government official's public testimony and private views were not the same. Wilkins said in an interview that after the transfer was proposed in September 1965 he decided that he would resign as soon as it was effectuated. But in December of that year, acting CRS director Calvin Kytle suddenly resigned, whereupon Deputy Attorney General Ramsey Clark, who was in charge of the transfer operation, asked Wilkins to go to Justice as director of the Service. Wilkins trusted and liked Clark, and thus when Clark told him that "he would be the guy who would be boss" over Wilkins, he "became an advocate of the change."[32]

Moreover, tied in with the transfer were promises of a larger budget and staff for the Service and an Assistant Attorney Generalship for its director. This would, in effect, put CRS on a par with the Civil Rights Division.[33] Thus Wilkins believed that the transfer would not only give him the opportunity to go North where he could "affect the equality of life of the guy on 117th Street and Lenox Avenue," but also the chance to get a high position in the councils of Justice "where the civil rights action was, where policy was made." He saw such a position in the Justice Department as "a critical and vital role" for the black man in Government—"even if the Service did nothing there," because it would permit him to be on the scene in day-to-day relationships with key decision-makers. He

32. Roger Wilkins Interview. His trust in Clark, he said, began in the summer of 1965 when Clark headed a team of investigators looking into the cause of the Watts riot. Wilkins said that Clark met black leaders and "dealt with them in a beautiful way."

33. Katzenbach stated this in his testimony to a Senate subcommittee on Government Operations. See above, n. 26.

could then help "to influence and shape their policies—on the spot."[34]

After Wilkins's agreement for the transfer was secured, opposition within Congress was easily quelled and acquiescent support from the major civil rights groups was obtained, thus permitting the Community Relations Service to become part of the Department of Justice.[35]

Once out of the Commerce Department, CRS was turned toward the North.[36] Wilkins wanted to put his men into areas where they would remain, and, in a catalytic way, help organize blacks—"show them how to get money from the Government." He wanted his men to assume the role of "advocates of the poor."[37] However, he needed

---

34. Roger Wilkins Interview.

35. Senator Javits told the Senate that civil rights groups had originally opposed the transfer but had been reversed at White House conferences. He said that an "unparalleled lobbying campaign—conducted at the highest levels" had taken place. *New York Times,* April 7, 1966.

New York Times civil rights specialist John Herbers reported that the President in a White House meeting with Martin Luther King, Roy Wilkins, Whitney Young, Floyd McKissick, Joseph L. Rauh, and others, persuaded them to back him on the transfer. *New York Times,* March 24, 1966.

Clarence Mitchell said that "we took the position that it ought to be an independent agency, but after meeting with Katzenbach where he explained why he thought it might be better in Justice, we agreed." Interview.

John Morsell, Assistant Director of NAACP, said that "we registered our objections . . . but we felt that the Service would have greater independence—freedom of action in Justice," where it "would truly be a strong force." He added, however, "but we knew it would become submerged." Interview.

Calvin Kytle was reportedly against the move, and considered it "unwise." *New York Times,* December 15, 1965. And CRS staff said they were appalled at "being placed under a bunch of lawyers." *New York Times,* October 17, 1965.

36. Nicholas Katzenbach Interview.

37. Roger Wilkins Interview. He said that he wanted to help or-

funds to properly staff such an operation, which Congress
was not inclined to appropriate.

Wilkins found that Representative John J. Rooney,
chairman of the House Appropriations subcommittee that
had jurisdiction over the Service, "liked me, but not the
program."[38] An illustration of Congressional control of the
Service's purse strings, when it was in the Department of
Commerce, occurred during an appropriation hearing in
1965 when Rooney told deputy director Kytle: "Mr.
Kytle, any time anybody comes here and does not want
to fully discuss things with us, that is the end of the money.
We do not have any problems in this regard."[39] On another
occasion, after the Service had been transferred to the
Justice Department, Senator Jacob Javits advised Attorney General Ramsey Clark at a Congressional hearing
that it would be better for the Service to concentrate its
operations at a few select points rather than to spread
itself out thin in many cities.[40] Clark and Wilkins apparently accepted this "advice" because one year later a
CRS official read the following statement to the Senate
Appropriations Committee:

> In accordance with the suggestions made by members
> of the Committee at the time of our hearings last year, we

ganize and support black institutions and "put pressure on white institutions."

In interviews with the writer, Roy Wilkins, Clarence Mitchell, and
John Morsell all agreed that communication with CRS director Roger
Wilkins was smoother than with LeRoy Collins or Calvin Kytle.

38. Roger Wilkins Interview.

39. U.S. Congress, House, Committee on Appropriations, *Hearings*
before a subcommittee of the Committee on Appropriations, 89th Cong.,
1st sess., 1965, p. 88.

40. U.S. Congress, Senate, Senate Appropriations Committee, *Hearings*, 90th Cong., 1st sess., 1967, p. 850.

re-evaluated our proposal made at that time to extend continuing service to 87 cities. We were persuaded by the
arguments for a more concentrated service in few cities and
therefore have limited the continuing program to 35 cities.
. . . Another question raised by the Committee concerned the
number of regional offices—we had proposed six. Further
study of this led to the conclusion that in fiscal year 1968
we should only establish three regional offices outside of
Washington.[41]

Congress's tight control of the Service's finances affected
its operations. Roger Wilkins told a House Appropriations
subcommittee in 1966 that he could not get away from a
crisis type of operation and do preventive work in the
large Northern urban centers because "with our present
resources it is not possible to do this pre-crisis work in
northern and western cities and still continue to deal with
crisis situations."[42] Even though the Service's budget and
staff grew in the Justice Department, it still never had
enough personnel to do the kind of work that Wilkins envisaged for it.[43] Moreover, the move to Justice had an
unsettling effect on staff members in both organizations
because they had to accept a *fait accompli* thrust upon
them by the President.[44] Ramsey Clark recalled that it
was a "gloomy day when they came in," there being appre-

41. U.S. Congress, Senate, Senate Appropriations Committee, *Hearings*, 90th Cong., 2nd sess., 1968, p. 890.

42. U.S. Congress, House, Committee on Appropriations, *Hearings*
before a subcommittee of the Committee on Appropriations, 89th Cong.,
2nd sess., 1966, p. 425.

43. CRS's permanent staff on board (professional and clerical) grew
from approximately 38 in 1965 to 100 in fiscal year 1968.

44. President Johnson's announcement on September 24, 1965, that
he was going to coordinate civil rights functions, caught almost everyone
by surprise. Ramsey Clark Interview.

hension in both groups. He said that people in CRS told him that they feared they would be too close to the litigation process which would possibly compromise their methods of operation. Moreover, Clark believed that the "people in CRS feared that I was too close to Wilkins . . . they were worried."[45]

It appears, for the most part, that initial CRS staff fears that they would be swallowed up by the Justice Department were well founded; more so under Katzenbach and Doar than when Clark and Pollak were in charge. Roger Wilkins, when in the Department of Justice, admittedly had poor relations with Attorney General Katzenbach, whom he felt "did not pay attention to us." He said that "Katzenbach and Doar were not with me or the Service," not having faith in CRS ability. Moreover, Wilkins found that Katzenbach did not use the Service very much in the South, because "he had more faith in the Civil Rights Division." Nor did the Attorney General use his new Assistant Attorney General, Wilkins, to represent him on committees pertaining to civil rights matters, but instead preferred to use John Doar, whom "he had confidence in." Furthermore, the Service's relationship with the widely respected Civil Rights Division was cordial but never close. Wilkins said that they "always intended to cooperate, but never got around to it." Moreover, he always checked with Clark and Katzenbach before he sent his men into an area, because he said:

By and large my philosophy was when there was the

45. Ramsey Clark Interview. Moreover, Clark said that the Service's transfer to Justice "created an awkward posture," when one considers the litigation work of Justice and the statutory secrecy of the Service. He thought that a far better place for CRS would have been in the Department of Housing and Urban Development.

possibility of litigation I would pull my guys off. . . . I didn't want to mess up a lawsuit; and when our guys saw potential litigation we talked to Doar, etc., to see if Justice wanted to handle the case.[46]

The Service's role in the Justice Department broadened when Ramsey Clark assumed command in late 1966. Both Clark and Wilkins disliked the "fireman" approach to civil rights problems, and thus endeavored to get the Service further involved in preventive operations. Clark said that when the Service was at the Justice Department there "was a conscious effort to develop a theory of purpose," for it. Clark, when Attorney General, believed that CRS could not spread itself out too thin, because "to handle the whole nation it would take 10,000 people." Thus, he readily agreed with Senator Javits's advice to concentrate the Service's limited resources in one area, where Clark thought it could "make itself felt."[47] Moreover, he supported Wilkins's theory of going "for the jugular," which meant reaching people through the mass media and human relations commissions. Clark believed that, in this respect, the Community Relations Service helped advance civil rights, because they worked with the networks and the soul stations, and "helped mature the media . . . who [as a result] were not as haphazard in covering" racial events. He described the Service as being "our eyes and ears."[48]

Concomitant with the rapport that existed between

46. Roger Wilkins Interview.

47. Ramsey Clark Interview. He said that a major project took place in Washington, D.C.

48. *Ibid.* Wilkins said that he eventually replaced John Doar as Justice's civil rights representative on many committees. Roger Wilkins Interview.

Clark and Wilkins was an improvement in the Service's working relationship with the Civil Rights Division. This occurred, according to Wilkins, primarily because Stephen Pollak replaced John Doar as head of the Division. Wilkins felt that Pollak understood the problem better, and had "respect for my guys." This was demonstrated, he said, by Pollak's practice of having his men brief "us on what they were doing," and by having his section heads work with their counterparts in the Service.[49]

It remains to be seen what the role of the Community Relations Service will be under the Nixon Administration, but statements made by Attorney General John Mitchell seem to indicate a return to the "fireman" approach. Mitchell, when asked if he thought that the Federal Government should have task forces to deal with big-city riots, replied:

The Federal Government does have plans and programs for these areas. We have our community-relations service [sic] in the Department of Justice. When there are indications of trouble, we put their personnel into the field to work with the local group—whether they be minority groups or whatever—and the local law-enforcement agencies to try to cool the situation so that you do not have major riots or disturbances.[50]

SUMMARY

The Community Relations Service's ability to meet its legal civil rights responsibilities was impaired by several factors: (1) lack of support at the time of its inception; (2) placement in an unfamiliar environment; (3) nar-

---

49. Roger Wilkins Interview.

50. Personal interview with *U.S. News & World Report,* August 18, 1969, p. 50.

rowly interpreted duties; and (4) low morale within its ranks, caused in part by its lack of prestige.[51] This chronic condition that had existed during its two-year stay in the Commerce Department did not immediately improve upon the Service's transfer to the Justice Department in 1966. The transfer—a move designed to get CRS out of the South, left the Service dependent on the Attorney General to determine the type of activities it would engage in. CRS did little under Katzenbach, but enlarged its sphere of operations under Clark—who was known to be more of a civil rights activist. Its future under the Attorney Generalship of John Mitchell looks dismal.

---

51. Wilkins felt that "all had disdain" for the Service, because "we had no philosophy and no purpose." He said that Ramsey Clark and Andrew Brimmer (Assistant Secretary for Economic Affairs, Department of Commerce) had told him that they did not have much faith in the Service. Moreover, Wilkins felt that "civil rights groups did not take us seriously." Roger Wilkins Interview.

6

EXECUTIVE COORDINATION

EXECUTIVE UNITS OF IMPLEMENTATION HAVE BEEN EXAM-
ined, in the last three chapters, through use of a concep-
tual approach that was presented in the earlier part of this
study.[1] These implementation units were viewed as pressure entities that had developed individual life styles as
the result of such factors as: inception conditions; the
locale they were placed in; their philosophy concerning
goals and methods; actual methods of operation; and the
type of relations that they had with other entities, such
as the White House and Congress.

This chapter will examine the efforts that were made
to coordinate the civil rights activities engaged in by the
enforcement units and other parts of the Executive
Branch. This is essential for a full understanding of the
Federal Government's role in civil rights enforcement
because coordination is a basic requirement for any administrative program, especially one that was as all en-

---

1. See chapter 1.

compassing and far reaching as the program dealt with in this study.

Prior to the formation, in 1961, of President Kennedy's Subcabinet Committee on Civil Rights, there was no formal coordinating unit in this area.[2]

THE SUBCABINET COMMITTEE ON CIVIL RIGHTS

The Subcabinet Committee had William Taylor of the Civil Rights Commission as its secretary, and was composed of senior staff members (assistant secretaries and executive assistants) from 17 departments and agencies who had been "assigned responsibility for equal employment opportunity and other civil rights functions."[3] Their monthly meetings were usually well-attended conferences (30 to 40 people), with full agendas prepared by CRC

---

2. Earlier administrations had people whose duties included the area of minority problems. For example, President Franklin Roosevelt gave these duties to his wife, James Rowe, and David Niles; President Truman had David Niles and Philleo Nash; President Eisenhower had Maxwell Rabb; President Kennedy had Harris Wofford and Lee White, among others; and President Johnson has used Hubert Humphrey, Lee White, Joseph Califano, and Nicholas Katzenbach, among others. See Richard P. Longakers *The Presidency and Individual Liberties* (Ithaca, N.Y.: Cornell University Press, 1961).

There also existed at the same time as the Subcabinet Committee a small ad hoc committee that met "frequently and informally to discuss ongoing programs and propose solutions for the emergencies of the moment." For the short amount of time that it was in operation it also assisted Kennedy civil rights aide Harris Wofford "in the many tactical and administrative problems on which he advised the President and his chief lieutenants. . . ." Harold Fleming, "The Federal Executive and Civil Rights: 1961–1965," *Daedalus* (Fall, 1965), p. 926.

3. Fleming, *ibid.* Donald F. Sullivan, having personally interviewed Wofford, concurs in the details relating to the Subcabinet group. "The Civil Rights Programs of the Kennedy Administration" (unpublished Ph.D. dissertation, University of Oklahoma, 1965), p. 208.

staff.[4] Topics covered during their meetings were primarily related to civil rights problems within the Federal Government, i.e., subjects like departmental hiring policies and discriminatory practices within the various agencies.[5] They met regularly in 1961 and part of 1962 under the chairmanship of Harris Wofford, White House Special Assistant for civil rights, but began to be phased out when Lee White replaced Wofford in the spring of 1962.[6] They met infrequently in 1963 and by 1964 the Subcabinet Committee "existed more on paper than in fact."[7]

Its effectiveness, according to several people who had participated in its meetings, was limited. Ramsey Clark found that the gatherings were, for the most part, a "waste of time," and John Doar felt that not much was accomplished.[8] CRC assistant staff director F. Peter Libassi thought that the meetings were too "large and unwieldy" for really serious coordination work, but were "all right to raise issues," and good as a "quick communication unit to get information from the White House to all agencies."[9]

---

4. Fleming, *ibid.*

5. Peter Libassi Interview. Libassi had quite an amazing employment record during the Kennedy and Johnson Administrations. He was assistant staff director, CRC; did staff work for the Subcabinet Committee; was an important staff member of the President's Committee on Equal Opportunity; was Special Assistant for civil rights to HEW Secretary John Gardner; and was director of the Office for Civil Rights, HEW.

6. Sulllivan, "The Civil Rights Programs of the Kennedy Administration," p. 208. Fleming, "The Federal Executive and Civil Rights," pp. 926–27. Libassi said that the Subcommittee was able to meet more frequently when Wofford was in charge because he, unlike Lee White, had this as his sole duty. Peter Libassi Interview.

7. Fleming, *ibid.*, p. 927.

8. Ramsey Clark Interview; John Doar Interview.

9. Peter Libassi Interview. In February, 1970, President Nixon established a Cabinet-level committee which would, according to its chairman Vice President Spiro Agnew, attempt to guide Southern school districts

Another central unit of coordination was established by President Johnson on February 5, 1965, and was officially called the President's Council on Equal Opportunity.[10]

THE PRESIDENT'S COUNCIL ON EQUAL OPPORTUNITY

Johnson had acted on the recommendation of Vice President-elect Hubert Humphrey, who had suggested this move to the President in January in a report entitled, "On the Coordination of Civil Rights Activities in the Federal Government." Humphrey stated in the report that the numerous programs that came into existence as a result of the 1964 Civil Rights Act had created "a problem of coordination." He felt that this necessitated the availability of "facilities for consultation and cooperation at all levels of the Federal Government, and with other public and private groups as well."[11] However, Humphrey opposed the creation of a unit that would be given power to compel agency action, but rather preferred a mechanism which would "offer leadership, support, guidance, advance planning, evaluation, and advice to foster and increase individual agency effectiveness, cooperation and coordination."[12]

This apparently set the tone for the unit, because the

---

into court-ordered integration "in the least disruptive way." Others on the committee include Attorney General John N. Mitchell, HEW Secretary Robert H. Finch and one of Nixon's top White House counselors. *New York Times,* February 2, 1970. Robert C. Mardian, general counsel of HEW, was designated as executive director. Mr. Mardian is considered to be a conservative on school desegregation matters. *New York Times,* February 21, 1970.

10. Executive Order No. 11197.
11. As quoted in *Revolution in Civil Rights,* 1965 ed., p. 75.
12. *Ibid.*

President, at the time of the Council's establishment, publicly endorsed the idea of "a comparatively simple coordinating mechanism without elaborate staff and organization. . . ." He further said that "the direct personal contact with responsible government officers which the Council will provide should prove a most effective means of insuring cooperation, coordination and harmonious working relationships."[13] This initial restriction on the role of the Council was reemphasized several months later by Vice President Humphrey, who had been chosen as its chairman. Humphrey said:

> Unless there be any doubt about it, I want it quite clear that my role of coordination is not one of administration. The responsibility for Title VI is in each agency. I'm just going to be looking over the transom. . . . I'm going to be the monitor, in a sense, hoping that we can work together cooperatively in an effort to improve the administration.[14]

Moreover, David Filvaroff, as the coordination unit's General Counsel, interpreted its function as that of en-

---

13. "Letter to the Vice President Upon Establishing the President's Council on Equal Opportunity." February 6, 1965. *Public Papers of the Presidents*, Lyndon B. Johnson, 1965, pt. I, pp. 152–53.

Several months before, on December 10, 1964, the President made the following announcement to the National Urban League's Community Action Assembly:

". . . I have asked Vice President-elect Hubert Humphrey, and he has agreed, to assume the responsibility for working with all of these groups, assisting in coordination of their efforts, and helping them to build toward an energetic pursuit of equal opportunity for all people in this Nation."

Public Papers of the Presidents, Lyndon B. Johnson, 1963–1964, pt. II, p. 1654.

14. As quoted in "Title VI of the Civil Rights Act of 1964: Implementation and Impact," *George Washington Law Review* (September 1968), p. 858, n. 123.

couraging and not forcing Federal agencies to meet their responsibilities.[15] Furthermore, officials in the Justice Department were also greatly concerned about the type of unit that would best bring about implementation of the civil rights laws. According to John Doar, there were two schools of thought, in the Justice Department and elsewhere, concerning the most efficacious way to enforce the laws. He called them the LeRoy Collins approach, and the Norbert Schlei approach.[16]

LeRoy Collins, and others who shared his views, believed that there should be a coordination czar who would be given sufficient staff and power to see that the civil rights responsibilities of Federal agencies were properly carried out. This approach called for the centralization of many aspects of civil rights enforcement in a single unit of coordination. On the other hand, those who favored the Norbert Schlei school of thought wanted a decentralized implementation process. This group, which included many in the Justice Department, believed that the Federal Government was too large for a single unit to properly coordinate. They, instead, preferred to let each individual department and agency handle its own Title VI activities, because greater expertise and knowledge could be found within them. Morover, according to this approach, conflicts between agencies relating to jurisdic-

---

15. *Ibid.*, p. 858.

16. John Doar Interview. LeRoy Collins, a former Governor of Florida, became the Community Relations Service's first director in 1964. He left that post in July 1965 to assume the duties of Undersecretary of Commerce.

Norbert A. Schlei was, during the Kennedy and Johnson Administration, Assistant Attorney General, Office of Legal Counsel. Schlei was a leading proponent for the decentralization of activities relating to civil rights implementation.

tional and other disputes would be settled in the courts.[17]

The Council on Equal Opportunity was probably a compromise between the Collins and Schlei factions. While it was authorized to act in certain areas, its initial restrictions, as stated earlier, were great. Some of the powers given to the Council as stated in the Executive Order establishing it were:

(1) Recommend to the President such policies, programs and actions as will promote the accomplishment of the purposes of the Civil Rights Acts of 1957 and 1964 and other Federal laws relating to civil rights. . . .

(2) Advise the President of inadequacies in existing Federal laws, policies, and programs relating to civil rights. . . .

(3) Recommend to the President such changes in administrative structure and relationships, including those for merger, combination, or elimination of agencies, committees, or other bodies. . . .

(4) Recommend to the President measures which will promote the coordination of Federal activities with those programs of State and local governments which promote civil rights and foster equal opportunity.

(5) Assist Federal departments and agencies to coordinate their programs and activities and to adopt consistent and uniform policies, practices, and procedures with respect to civil rights. . . .

(6) Request reports or other information from Federal departments and agencies.

(7) Consult with interested public and private groups and individuals.

(8) Convene such conferences as may promote and coordinate the activities of Federal, State, and local governments and private groups with respect to civil rights.[18]

---

17. John Doar Interview.
18. Executive Order No. 11197, *Federal Register* 30: 1721, February 9, 1965, sec. 4.

Moreover, each Federal department and agency involved in Title VI activities, had to designate an officer "of a rank not lower than Deputy Assistant Secretary or the equivalent, to oversee and coordinate the activities of such department or agency related to the purpose of this order, and to serve as liaison with the Council."[19]

Evidence indicates, however, that President Johnson was not fully in favor of this type of coordination mechanism, and had reluctantly agreed to give it a trial run. Peter Libassi, who was on part-time loan from the Civil Rights Commission to the Council, said that the new unit of coordination was Humphrey's idea. Humphrey, he said, had presented a detailed report to the President favoring the creation of the Council, but Johnson was uncertain whether another organization, in addition to the White House staff, should be created. Libassi doubts whether the President was convinced.[20] Wiley Branton, Executive Secretary of the Council, had the same feeling that "Johnson had some misgivings that he created it," because "the White House never officially announced my appointment; . . . neither did we have a staff." Branton, upset about this, told Vice President Humphrey that if Johnson had found disfavor with him personally, he would resign.[21] Branton was allowed to remain. During the eight-month

---

19. *Ibid.*, sec. 8.

20. Peter Libassi Interview. Libassi said that David Filvaroff and John Stewart (White House aide) drew up the preliminary report for Humphrey.

Burke Marshall, acting as special consultant to the President when he left the Justice Department in 1965, helped write the Executive order which created the Council. Burke Marshall Interview.

21. Interview with Wiley Branton in Washington, D.C., on July 17, 1969, hereinafter cited as Wiley Branton Interview. Branton, a Negro lawyer, had been director of the Voter Education Project in Atlanta, Georgia, and was an active member of the civil rights community.

period that the Council existed, he and Humphrey (its chairman) worked very closely, the Vice President giving Branton his daily agenda to facilitate rapid contact. Moreover, Branton said that he often saw Humphrey on matters relating to the Council as much as three or four times a day.[22]

Officially, the Council on Equal Opportunity consisted of the top officials representing 16 departments, agencies, and commissions (or their designated alternates), but in practice its operations were run by Branton, Libassi, and Filvaroff with the aid of a staff that never exceeded a dozen people. According to Branton, the Council did not need a large staff because they considered themselves a "coordinating mechanism to bring the agencies together."[23] He said that they had attempted to do this by "insisting on progress reports" concerning the civil rights activities of various agencies. Moreover, the Council helped prod departments and agencies by directing that they "act in furtherance of setting up guidelines for enforcement."[24]

22. *Ibid.*

23. *Ibid.* However, Branton said, if the Council had continued to operate, it would have hired analysts to check up on the accuracy of the reports solicited from the various agencies and departments.

24. *Ibid.* David Filvaroff summarized the accomplishments of the Council in a September 22, 1965, memorandum to Vice President Humphrey, which, in part, stated:

Education

(1) Avoided complete chaos in the handling of school desegregation under Title VI by getting HEW and the Office of Education to promulgate guidelines for submission of plans.

(2) . . . arranged for approximately 30 Justice Departent people to assist OE in examining and deciding upon [school desegregation] plans.

(3) Moved HEW to respond to complaints of firing of Negro teachers as a result of desegregation; as a result, retaliation against Negro teachers, in large measure, has been halted.

Another part of the Council's role, as envisaged by Branton, was "to work out accommodations in government" by calling the heads of disagreeing agencies or departments together so that they could resolve their differences. An illustration of this was the Council's arrangement of a meeting between Attorney General Nicholas Katzenbach and Civil Rights Commission staff director William Taylor, both of whom were engaged in a serious disagreement on the desirability of holding Commission hearings in Mississippi.[25] Branton knew that the Council had no legal enforcement power in this type of situation, but felt that it could provide the mechanism to bring altercating agencies together. Moreover, Council ma-

---

Title VI

(1) Held many meetings with Title VI agencies to assure consistency and uniformity in implementation of Title VI. . . .

(2) Arranged for a staff of Title VI Hearings Examiners from among existing agency employees and provided a special training program for them.

(3) Developed a coordinated Title VI enforcement program for medical facilities and colleges and universities. . . .

(4) Established system for continuing monitoring of Title VI action by the 22 Federal agencies with Title VI responsibilities.

Summer Tensions

(1) Established, through the Community Relations Task Force of the Council, a broad program of assistance to nine major Northern cities. . . .

Employment

(3) Developing, through Council Employment Task Force, affirmative program for Equal Employment Opportunity in half dozen key cities. Justice, EEOC, Contract Compliance, Department of Labor, Poverty Program, Commerce, all participating.

(copy of memorandum from the personal files of Wiley Branton)

25. Wiley Branton Interview. CRC was dissuaded several times from holding hearings in Mississippi because the Justice Department "feared that the hearings would stir local trouble and prejudice its own complicated litigations." Schlesinger, *A Thousand Days*, p. 951.

chinery was also used to: set the stage for preliminary discussions preceding the White House Conference on Civil Rights;[26] arrange a private meeting between the Vice President and civil rights leaders;[27] and aid the Equal Employment Opportunity Council to begin its operations.[28]

In view of the restrictions imposed at the time of its establishment, it is surprising that the Council was able to do as much as it did. Where did it get its power from? Branton believes that it was able to exert pressure on the departments and agencies because it had the support of Vice President Humphrey—"that was what gave us our club," and being the *President's* Council led others to think that they had the backing of President Johnson.[29]

In reality, the Council's relationship with the White House staff was not good. According to Branton, "they would use the Council when they wanted to and ignore it when crucial things were involved—some at the White House were not sold."[30] An example of this was the treat-

26. Wiley Branton Interview. Council money was used for this Conference. The Council received its funds, as stipulated in the Executive Order creating it, from the departments and agencies that comprised it.

27. This took place on the Presidential yacht *Honey Fitz* on September 21, 1965. See chapter 3, n. 27.

28. The Council helped find space for them, office furniture, and staff; assisted in setting up guidelines for EEOC's operation; and gave "them administrative direction to get them launched." Wiley Branton Interview.

29. *Ibid.* Branton said that two weekly reports were prepared by the Council: the first went to Humphrey and was concerned with what the Council did during the preceding week, and the second report was a draft of Council activities for the same period, which the Vice President sent to President Johnson.

The Council had little contact with the Civil Rights Division, other than some meetings with John Doar concerning school desegregation guidelines. According to Branton, "they were extremely cautious. We were demanding answers." Wiley Branton Interview.

30. Wiley Branton Interview.

ment afforded the Council when the Watts riot occurred in August 1965. Branton, on a speaking engagement in Los Angeles at the time, was directed by Vice President Humphrey to gather all relevant information in preparation for an emergency Council meeting. However, the White House interceded, canceled the Council meeting, and appointed its own team to go to Watts. Neither Branton nor a Community Relations Service official, who also happened to be in Los Angeles at the time, was used.[31]

The Watts incident was an ominous sign, in that the Council was summarily abolished one month later.[32] On September 24, 1965 President Johnson applied the *coup de grace* by means of an official reply to a Vice Presidential memorandum. Johnson said:

> I concur in your recommendations to streamline and strengthen the civil rights effort of this Administration.
>
> I share your conviction that it is of paramount importance to attach responsibility for effective civil rights programs to each and every official of the Federal government.[33]

The memorandum that Johnson referred to, made pub-

---

31. *Ibid.*

32. At the same time, President Johnson abolished the Committee on Equal Employment Opportunity, and announced his plan to transfer the Community Relations Service to the Justice Department. Branton said that he had found out about the Council's abolition on the same day that it was officially announced (September 24, 1965). He had been called to an early breakfast meeting at Humphrey's home, where Branton found that the Vice President was "terribly distressed," and just as surprised as he was. Humphrey, he said "deeply regretted the fact that the Council was being abolished." Moreover, a few hours later, while waiting at the White House to see the President, Branton saw a shocked LeRoy Collins being told about the transfer. Wiley Branton Interview.

33. Memorandum on Reassignment of Civil Rights Functions, *Public Papers of the Presidents*, Lyndon B. Johnson, 1965, p. 1017.

lic on the same day, seemed to indicate White House acceptance of the Schlei or decentralization approach. Some excerpts are revealing:

> A cardinal principle underlying these recommendations is that whenever possible operating functions should be performed by departments and agencies with clearly defined responsibilities, as distinguished from interagency committees or other interagency arrangements. . . . In short, I believe the time has now come when operating functions can and should be performed by departments and agencies with clearly defined responsibilities for the basic program, and that interagency arrangements would now only diffuse responsibility.

Then in two brief sentences, Humphrey said:

> I have examined the role of the Council and have concluded that the reasons for creating the Council no longer exist, and I recommend, therefore, that it be terminated. I am satisfied that the working relationships between departments and agencies have advanced to the point where the formal organizational structure of the Council is no longer essential and should be terminated by Executive order.[34]

Officially stated reasons for the reassignment of civil rights functions, and other reasons that many believe were not stated, leave the issue a subject of speculation. Theories concerning the Council's abolition range from its being a capricious move on the part of President Johnson, to the successful exertion of pressure by harassed departments.[35] John Doar believes that HEW's mishandling

---

34. *Ibid.*, pp. 1017–19.
35. Ramsey Clark thought that it was "a capricious move" on the

of the Chicago school fund deferral incident in September 1965 caused the White House "to decide it needed tighter control." Doar saw the Chicago affair as bringing to the surface a basic conflict that existed between the White House people who were "oversensitive to politics" (and thus wanted to protect the President politically) and people in the field—like the Civil Rights Division, who wanted "to get the job done." He believed that the President felt that it was necessary to get somebody to balance these two needs—somebody "in charge who has political antennae." Thus, according to Doar, all enforcement coordination duties were given to the Attorney General for political balancing.[36]

---

part of the President, "not for reason or substance," but for "something said or done." Interview.

Peter Libassi believes that the President was furious after the Chicago incident, and "solved this by putting all in Justice, so that no department will do anything that is illegal." Interview.

John Morsell of the NAACP believes that its abolition was the result of a "fierce argument" between Wiley Branton and Clarence Mitchell on the earlier-mentioned September 21, 1965, boatride of civil rights leaders that was hosted by Vice President Humphrey. The altercation occurred three days before the Council was abolished, and according to Morsell, "convinced Humphrey that the Council was not going to work." Moreover, Morsell said that the general feeling of civil rights groups was that they "wanted enforcement nailed down in each agency." Interview.

Roy Wilkins thought it was abolished because of pressure from the big departments. Interview.

Arnold Aronson concurs with Wilkins. Interview.

Stephen Pollak thought that the disestablishment of the Council was a result of the Chicago incident, which led the President to seek better HEW-Justice coordination and "more sturdy direction." Interview.

36. John Doar Interview. Hubert Humphrey in a revealing letter to the writer, dated May 7, 1969, said:

We found . . . that many of the decisions called for in implementing Title 6 were extremely difficult decisions and that they would not be made satisfactorily unless the individual departments were willing

But why did Vice President Humphrey recommend that "the Justice Department which has the ultimate responsibility for enforcing Title VI should be assigned the task of coordinating the Federal Government's enforcement policies in this area"?[37] The Department of Justice was probably chosen for four basic reasons: (1) it had the most experience and expertise in civil rights enforcement, its Civil Rights Division being in the field since 1957; (2) Attorney General Nicholas Katzenbach, whose philosophy was to keep the heat off the President, was trusted by Johnson; (3) the Justice Department, as the legal arm of the Government, was naturally involved in all aspects of civil rights and would be called upon to legally defend the actions of other departments; and, in the writer's opinion, (4) the Justice Department was a useful front, perhaps appearing to liberals as an affirmative central unit of coordination. But more often than not it assumed a restraining role in its interdepartmental relations.[38]

to face up to them directly. For this reason, President Johnson and I determined in the early fall of 1965 that this responsibility had to be placed directly upon the secretary of each department. For this reason, the Council on Equal Opportunity was dissolved and the Department of Justice emerged as the principal coordinator of Title 6 enforcement.

I believe this was a generally good solution to a very difficult problem. The record will show that Justice and Health, Education and Welfare did, in fact, cooperate quite closely on these problems and that significant progress was made. The respective departments did face up to their responsibilities once the burden was placed squarely on their shoulders and, to the best of my knowledge, the actions were taken in a reasonably coordinate fashion. The President backed up his Cabinet officers on these decisions, especially those dealing with the promulgation of guidelines for school desegregation. Indeed, by 1967 or so it was rare when any political figure attempted to run around the position taken by the Secretary of Health, Education and Welfare.

37. Memorandum on Reassignment of Civil Rights Functions, p. 1019.
38. This is based on the writer's interviews with Nicholas Katzenbach, Ramsey Clark, John Doar, Stephen Pollak, and Peter Libassi.

THE ATTORNEY GENERAL AS COORDINATOR

Presidential delegation of the Council's Title VI co-ordination responsibilities to the Attorney General was rather sudden and took the entire Justice Department by surprise. According to Ramsey Clark, they were never given the opportunity to consider if they wanted the co-ordination role—they "were never asked."[39] Moreover, the Council's Executive Secretary, Wiley Branton, was transferred to the Justice Department, where he served as a special assistant to the Attorney General on voting matters.[40]

Katzenbach believed that the President gave the coordination task to the Attorney General because Johnson felt that others in the Cabinet "did not know much about the problem . . . somebody had to see how to get the job done fast." Moreover, Katzenbach thought that the President did not want "to have an uneven job." He said it could not be given to the Secretary of HEW because his own workload was too big. The operations of the Council on Equal Opportunity, according to Katzenbach, were unsuccessful because Humphrey's staff had uncertain powers, and not knowing the details, still had to depend on other departments for information. He said that additional staff and power could have helped, but Humphrey "was trying to maintain his own political credentials." Nicholas Katzenbach Interview.

39. Ramsey Clark Interview.

40. Branton said that during the September 24 meeting in which the Vice President told him of the Council's abolition, Humphrey told him that the President wanted him on the White House staff to work with voter registration. Branton refused. A few hours later, the President personally asked Branton if he wanted to work with the Attorney General as his special assistant—not mentioning a White House position. Branton accepted the offer. Soon after, during his first meeting with Katzenbach, Branton was asked by the Attorney General if he would "head-up" the entire coordination function that Justice had. He refused this offer, preferring to handle voter registration which, he believed, he could manage with more vigor. Branton's role at Justice, however, was a limited one, especially when Katzenbach and Doar were in charge. He told the writer: "I was a lone wolf over in Justice," being attached to the Civil

Thus, by early 1966 the civil rights responsibilities of
the Justice Department were greatly increased, having
absorbed the Community Relations Service, and being
given the Council on Equal Opportunity's Title VI duties.
Neither Attorneys General Katzenbach nor Clark found
favor with the role of coordinator that was trust upon
him.[41] Katzenbach felt that he could not *tell* other Cabi-

---

Rights Division for administrative reasons, "but not really attached to
CRD." He reported directly to Katzenbach, and had freedom to travel
and speak down South, but, he said, "nobody really cared if I came or
went. I was never invited to a single staff meeting of the Civil Rights
Division, even when they knew I was going to oversee elections." However, he found that "the attitude was different under Ramsey Clark . . .
he invited me to staff meetings of the Attorney General. . . . I was now
much more involved with him . . . he would frequently confer with me.
My role took on an entirely new meaning. Before nobody cared if I
came or went." When Clark was Attorney General, Branton met every
Tuesday and Thursday with the assistant attorneys general in the Attorney General's dining room, and met once a month with the Leadership
Conference on Civil Rights. Wiley Branton Interview.

John Doar, head of CRD, said that Branton understood that the "fellow who runs the Civil Rights Division can't have someone come in and
tell me what county to go in." Interview.

Nicholas Katzenbach also saw that the entrance of Branton was apt
to create a problem because "John Doar ran the division, and here I
have Wiley Branton." Katzenbach said that the Vice President had built
Branton up and had given him a high grade, which made a certain degree
of diplomacy necessary. Thus, Katzenbach had to find a job for him
without changing the Department's policies. Branton's new position,
according to Katzenbach, was to explain Justice Department policies
concerning voting and telling Negroes how to do the job but not doing
the registration for them. Nicholas Katzenbach Interview.

Ramsey Clark said that Branton was "not fully utilized, perhaps never
utilized—he was out of the main stream." Interview.

41. An example of Katzenbach's limited view of his coordination role
is found in an incident involving HEW's revision of school desegregation
guidelines for fall 1966. HEW Secretary John Gardner had proposed the
establishment of a percentage quota system for the Southern school districts which would stipulate suggestions for annual increases in integration. Katzenbach, in a conversation with Gardner, strongly urged him

net heads what to do. He could not, for example, "police the Department of Agriculture," because the secretary of that department was equal in position to him. He could, however, because of the prestige of the Justice Department, "discuss things with them."[42] Clark, though more active as coordinator of Title VI, similarly believed that the Attorney General lacked the power to do the job properly. "To get the job done," he said, "you need all the muscle you can command—at the White House." He thought that the Vice President was ideally suited for this type of job—if given proper Presidential backing, because "the Attorney General does not have the same leverage." Clark felt that White House support and adequate staff were vital prerequisites for this type of operation. Enforcement of civil rights, he said, "had to be ramrodded from there regularly," an area that had "more leverage." The White House, and not the Attorney General, he believed, could tell the Bureau of the Budget to give them "200 more men [because] it is a high priority item of business."[43]

However, the Chief Executive had already decided to give this duty to the Attorney General when he declared in Executive Order 11247 that:

---

not to use the percentage system, but did not insist on its abandonment. Katzenbach told the writer: "I could have stopped them . . . after all, the President threw the whole thing into my hands. . . . I spoke to Gardner . . . he would have caved in if I strongly insisted . . . and the President would have backed me. Katzenbach, however, decided not to dictate policy to the head of another department, but rather "held them back [and] eased down what they wanted to do." Interview. John Doar, confirming this, said "Katzenbach diplomatically asked Gardner to reconsider the percentages." Interview.

42. Nicholas Katzenbach Interview.
43. Ramsey Clark Interview.

The Attorney General shall assist Federal departments and agencies to coordinate their programs and activities and adopt consistent and uniform policies, practices, and procedures with respect to the enforcement of Title VI of the Civil Rights Act of 1964. He may promulgate such rules and regulations as he shall deem necessary to carry out his functions under this Order.[44]

Katzenbach thereupon chose David Filvaroff, who formerly held the position of General Counsel to the Council on Equal Opportunity, to be special assistant to the Attorney General for Title VI.[45] Filvaroff soon organized a small unit (it never had more than a handful of attorneys) which was thereafter the Federal Government's official civil rights coordinating mechanism. According to an official Justice Department report, the unit was involved in the following activities. It

reviews, develops, formulates, and drafts regulations, policy statements, and other materials designed to set forth the obligations of recipients of Federal assistance, and the procedures for obtaining compliance. Significant Title VI amendments have been prepared and forwarded to the White House for the President's approval during 1967. In addition, the Office makes recommendations to the Attorney General, as to what policy statements, directives, and guidelines he should issue.

The Office collects quarterly and annual reports from each of the Title VI departments and agencies. Where those reports and other information show continued discrimination in programs assisted by a particular department or agency,

44. *Weekly Compilation of Presidential Documents,* September 24, 1965, 1:310.
45. Filvaroff was succeeded for a short term by Robert Owen. David Rose assumed charge of the unit in mid-1967.

the Office conducts an in depth analysis of its civil rights compliance activities, method of operation, staff, policy directives, and standard contractual materials.

Moreover,

> The Office also is normally consulted by each department or agency which seeks to institute enforcement proceedings both against a particular category of recipients, and individual recipients. . . . The Office also reviews proposed individual enforcement proceedings to determine whether sufficient facts have been developed to show discrimination warranting the termination of financial assistance;
>
> In addition . . . the Office . . . gives many informal opinions to the interested agencies on questions of the coverage of . . . [Title VI] and other civil rights obligations and the procedural requirements of the Act and the regulations. It also resolves differences in interpretation and inconsistencies between agencies, and develops methods and plans of coordination where different agencies have overlapping responsibilities. . . . In addition, in cooperation with the Civil Service Commission, it helps to formulate civil rights training programs for Title VI compliance officers, and for administrators and managers who have responsibilities for granting Federal assistance to programs or activities covered by Title VI.

In addition to defending administrative decisions,

> the Office's litigation responsibility includes the initiation of selected law suits to enforce specifically nondiscrimination assurance and requirements in cases where termination of assistance is unlikely to lead to compliance.[46]

However, despite this impressive list of activities, its

---

46. *Annual Report of the Attorney General, for the Fiscal Year ended June 30, 1967*, pp. 188–89.

role, in reality, has been quite limited.[47] No interdepartmental meetings were held until July, 1967, when Attorney General Clark called the first one.[48] Thereafter, Clark and his new Title VI assistant, David Rose, held a series of monthly meetings of special compliance assistants from the Departments of Agriculture, Defense, Labor, Health, Education and Welfare, and the Office for Economic Opportunity. This gathering, usually around 12 people, discussed such topics as discrimination in Federal contracts. They also exchanged information concerning departmental action that was taken since their previous meeting. If departmental initiative was shown to be lacking, Clark would, at times, telephone or visit a department secretary to try to bring about greater implementation efforts. This type of action by Clark was limited, however, because he felt that he "couldn't reach over in HUD and tell them what to do. I have power of persuasion; otherwise I have no power."[49] The meetings, according to Clark were useful as communication belts which gave the compliance people information about what their fellow enforcement officers were doing, and which civil rights cases were pending. Yet, even though Clark engaged in other similar meetings, he nevertheless described interdepartmental coordination as "loose."[50]

---

47. The same conclusion was reached in *George Washington Law Review*, "Title VI of the Civil Rights Act of 1964," p. 862.

48. Ramsey Clark Interview. Some 40 to 50 people assembled for the first meeting.

49. Ramsey Clark Interview.

50. *Ibid.* Clark believed that the meetings permitted compliance officers from the various departments to see what was being done in other quarters in Government. This, he believed, had the effect of either a spur or a brake, depending on the activities of the agency or department. For example, Clark felt that if a department such as HEW, usually an aggressive enforcer, saw that it was too far out in front, it would try to get in line with the others.

On another front, Justice Department contacts with HEW were minimal during the year following the July signing of the 1964 Civil Rights Act.[51] The Departments progressively grew closer, however, after the September, 1965, Chicago school affair. The Justice Department had been given Title VI coordination responsibilities, at this time, and Peter Libassi, soon to be appointed special assistant to HEW Secretary Gardner for civil rights, was determined to create a solid working relationship between the two organizations.[52]

The relationship that existed between the Justice Department and the Civil Rights Commission was quite uneven over the years. It was strained to the point of an open break with Attorney General Robert Kennedy, then moved to a rapprochement with Ramsey Clark, and is, at present, in a tenuous state with Attorney General John Mitchell.[53]

Moreover, Clark said that he had converted a monthly series of secretary conferences (on urban problems) into a discussion forum on Title VI. Clark felt that the heads of Labor, HEW, OEO, HUD, and Commerce "had some really vital discussions." The conferences, continuing through the summer of 1968, were a good information mechanism, but in Clark's opinion, nothing concrete came from them. He said that "all got excited," but "then they would go back and have 25 things to do." However, Clark arranged to have the members of this group talk to compliance officers in an attempt "to bolster their sagging morale." Clark saw the enforcement people as possibly being isolated in huge departments, and thus tending to feel discouraged in their daily work. The secretaries, when speaking to these groups, tried to develop a theory of enforcement operations, and thus attempted to "motivate them . . . build excitement." Ramsey Clark Interview.

51. St. John Barrett Interview.

52. Peter Libassi Interview. See chapter 4 for details.

53. The Civil Rights Commission's Mississippi hearings were periodically blocked by Robert Kennedy (see above, n. 25). An excellent study in this area is George Sulzner, III, "The United States Commission on Civil Rights."

Both Nicholas Katzenbach and John Doar thought that the Civil

While official civil rights coordination responsibilities were delegated to the Attorney General, another type of coordination took place in a governmental unit that is known to be very close to the President—the Bureau of the Budget.

BUREAU OF THE BUDGET[54]

Beginning in the latter part of 1965, examiners in the

Rights Commission was a thorn in their sides, but both men nevertheless agreed that the Commission had an important role to play. Interviews. Katzenbach found that the Commission was "not very careful with their facts . . . not as careful as the Justice Department." Moreover, he felt that CRC was unfair in their criticism of the Justice Department in that "Doar and others are putting in 18 hours a day and they say we're not doing half enough." In his opinion, John Kennedy and Lyndon Johnson would have gone along if the Justice Department asked for the Commission's abolition, "but Congress may not have." However, Katzenbach thought that the one definite asset derived from having a radical organization like CRC was that it "made the Justice Department seem more reasonable to Southerners in Congress . . . it made Justice look moderate." In general, he found the Commission to be "not pleasant, but helpful." Nicholas Katzenbach Interview.

Ramsey Clark recalled that when he became Attorney General there were "hard feelings" that existed between his Department and the Commission, because CRC had issued a study of voting implementation without consulting Justice. He found that "there were some real personality conflicts." Clark began a campaign to better relations between the two organizations. He said that when he was in office, "Justice had more contact with them . . . worked hard for their extension . . . fought to increase their budget . . . and tried to get help for them on the Hill." Clark believes that he had "established a communication we did not have before." Ramsey Clark Interview.

Concerning the Nixon Administration, CRC stated that "the new procedures and recent actions involving Federal efforts to bring about school desegregation appear to be a major retreat in the struggle to achieve meaningful school desegregation." *New York Times,* September 13, 1969.

54. Most of this section is based on a lengthy telephone interview with Karen Nelson from Washington, D.C., on September 22, 1969. Miss Nelson is a staff assistant in the Office of Statistical Standards, Bureau of the Budget.

General Government Division of the Budget Bureau began challenging various departments and agencies as to the adequacy of their civil rights enforcement staff. Division personnel urged department and agency representatives to ask for more manpower. This resulted, for example, in a 100-man increase in HEW civil rights personnel for fiscal year 1967, and, according to Ramsey Clark, greater departmental awareness of this area.[55]

Another part of the Bureau, the Office of Statistical Standards (OSS), was also involved in civil rights activities. It is responsible for "the improvement, development, and coordination of Federal statistical services . . . for minimizing reporting costs to the Government and the public," and for the review of all forms, questionnaires, and other like data which are designated to be used for more than ten people.[56]

The personnel in OSS (the only Budget office that is

---

55. Peter Libassi said that the Bureau, in December, 1965, called him over to their offices and gave HEW an unrequested 100-man increase in its enforcement staff. Interview. Libassi, Ramsey Clark, and Karen Nelson all believed that the examiners initiated this action on their own volition. Interviews. However, it also appears that Attorney General Katzenbach, acting under his Title VI coordination powers, discussed the matter with the Bureau. In a letter accompanying the Attorney General's guidelines for the enforcement of Title VI, Katzenbach, on December 27, 1965, reported to department and agency heads that he had

. . . discussed with the Bureau of the Budget the critical importance of assuring that each agency with Title VI or other substantial civil rights responsibilities has the personnel and funds necessary to assure that it can fulfill its obligations promptly and effectively; representatives of the Bureau may have already contacted, or soon will be contacting, members of your staff to make certain that these needs have been fully provided for in your current and future budgeting. (Civil Rights Commission, *Compliance Officers Manual for Title VI*, p. 28)

56. U.S. Government, *United States Government Organization Manual, 1968–69* (Washington, D.C.: Government Printing Office, 1968), p. 57.

specifically designated to handle civil rights) have, because of their personal inclinations, actively worked for civil rights advances. For example, upon receipt of departmental or agency proposed civil rights questionnaires, OSS would, voluntarily and informally, immediately send copies over to the Civil Rights Commission and the special assistant to the Attorney General for Title VI for their comments and suggestions. Thereafter, if either of these units requested revision of the questionnaire, a meeting was called to iron out the differences. These meetings usually had representatives from the following five areas: (1) OSS; (2) the department or agency that initiated the questionnaire; (3) the Federal Program's Division of the Civil Rights Commission; (4) the Justice Department's Office of Title VI coordinator; and (5) an examiner from the Budget Bureau's General Government Management Division.

Generally, the parties present at these frequently convened meetings agreed on a compromise version of the originally submitted data. An example of OSS's success was the expansion of the United States Office of Education's survey on racial integration in Southern schools to cover the entire nation. However, there was virtually no follow-up after a questionnaire was approved by the Bureau.[57]

Why did the departments and agencies involved accede to this pressure? Karen Nelson, staff assistant at OSS, believes that the whole matter was "a very delicate situa-

---

57. Karen Nelson Interview. The Office of Statistical Standards did not initiate questionnaires or other data, and, in general, there was no follow-up to see if the departments: (1) abided by the agreement made with OSS; (2) used the questionnaire or other data; or (3) did anything with the information if they had in fact used the questionnaire.

tion—nothing overt." Success was primarily based on the questionnaire-submitter's fear that a recalcitrant position might result in a cut budget. Thus, the power of OSS, and its compatriots from the Civil Rights Division and the Department of Justice, was derived from the support given it by the people who had jurisdiction over departmental and agency budgets—the budget examiners. According to Miss Nelson, younger examiners tended to be more liberal in matters relating to civil rights, and thus offered greater support to OSS.[58]

INFORMAL COORDINATION

During the Kennedy and Johnson Administrations there were many informal efforts by civil rights minded Government officials to coordinate their enforcement activities. Meetings, for example, took place every four to six weeks during 1967 and 1968, in which the following people participated: Peter Libassi, director of HEW's Office for Civil Rights; Roger Wilkins, Assistant Attorney General in charge of the Community Relations Service; Edward C. Sylvester, director of Labor's Office of Federal Contract Compliance; William L. Taylor, staff director of the Civil Rights Commission; M. Carl Holman, special assistant to the staff director of CRC; and Lisle Carter, Jr., Assistant Secretary, Individual and Family Services, HEW. These luncheon gatherings brought together a cross section of the Federal Executive, and were held, according to Roger Wilkins, because the participants shared a community of interests in which they "formed bonds of respect and

58. Karen Nelson Interview. Most agreements were later approved by higher echelon Bureau clearance officers.

trust."[59] Their informal meetings were originally started by Peter Libassi because he felt that there was a need for informal communication.[60] Topics that were covered included progress and direction of civil rights programs, and strategy for effective implementation. The meetings, according to several participants, were an effective means for keeping abreast of the latest developments in civil rights.[61] Being "on the same wave length," they supported each other's ideas and offered help, where possible, with legislative items in Congress.[62] They were careful not to let the White House gain knowledge of their meetings,[63] in which they were also able to "size up who was friendly and who was an enemy."[64]

The group engaged in a major undertaking called the "Manhattan Project," in which they arranged for a spring, 1967, meeting between civil rights leaders and various representatives of several major funds. This assemblage, gathered at the New York Drake Hotel on a Sunday, consisted of 30 to 40 people, including the following: Libassi, Wilkins, Taylor, Holman, Sylvester, and Carter from the Executive Branch; Martin Luther King, Roy Wilkins, Whitney Young, Baird Rustin, Kenneth Clark, and others, from private civil rights organizations; and emissaries from

59. Roger Wilkins Interview.
60. Peter Libassi Interview.
61. Peter Libassi Interview; Roger Wilkins Interview. Wilkins, who gave the writer a good deal of information in this section said that the group had dealings in "90 percent of the [civil rights] action."
62. Wilkins said that he made his views known to such people in the White House as Harold Barefoot Sanders, who was Legislative Counsel to the President; and Wilkins also used his contacts outside of Government. Interview.
63. *Ibid.*
64. Told to writer by a former high HEW official.

the Field Foundation, the Rockefeller Fund, the Taconic Fund, and the Southern Regional Council.

The meeting was called in order to convince the foundations that they should give financial support to create an enforcement staff which would "monitor in close detail what the administration was doing."[65] Wilkins, and the others in the Washington group, believed that "civil rights groups in the country did not have as acute an understanding as to goings on in Washington." He said that these groups "did not have the staff. They needed the money to secure a much sharper staff to monitor what was going on in committees."[66] Results of the conference, however, were minimal, there being no follow-through.[67]

---

65. Roger Wilkins Interview.

66. *Ibid.*

67. *Ibid.* However, two main projects did come into being which may have been prompted by this meeting. One of them, called Project Enforcement, was a one-year research project at the A. Philip Randolph Institute. It was funded by the Office for Equal Opportunity, and directed in 1969 by Barney Sellers, who was formerly with the Office for Civil Rights, HEW, during the Johnson Administration. According to the 1968 *Annual Report* of the Leadership Conference's Committee on Compliance and Enforcement:

> Much time of the committee and staff were spent in an effort to secure foundation support for the committee's activities. Although no foundation grant has been received, the committee was able to assist in negotiating a contract with OEO for a study of civil rights enforcement by the A. Philip Randolph Foundation. The committee is cooperating in this study, known as Project Enforcement. (mimeograph copy dated January 28, 1969)

The second project that was formed, according to Peter Libassi, was the Washington Research Project of the Southern Center for Studies in Public Policy which was headed by Marian Wright Edelman, Harry Huge, and a former director of HEW's Office for Civil Rights, Ruby Martin. Following a six-month study this group co-issued a report which stated that Title I (ESEA Act) funds had been "wasted, diverted or otherwise misused by state and local authorities." *New York Times,* November 27, 1969.

Meetings between other members of the Washington "family" had taken place, during these years, at the Potomac Institute in Washington, D.C. On various occasions, for example, luncheon gatherings of 15 to 20 people in the GS 12 to GS 16 categories met to discuss the latest happenings in civil rights.[68] The Potomac Institute had played, according to Peter Libassi, an important role over the years as a place for civil rights minded people to meet.[69] Harold Fleming, president of the Institute, has been described by Elaine Heffernan (an active member of the Washington family) as a kind of consulting psychiatrist for Federal civil rights officials. She said he was instrumental in the development of

> ways and means of getting done what needs to be done—whether in Federal enforcement, or in civil rights movement, efficiency, etc. I suspect Fleming is consulted by about equal amounts of clients from within and without Government on civil rights. Thus, Fleming and Potomac are part of the small Washington "family" which cuts across various lines and includes public officials, private organization workers, civil rights leaders, movement "angels," and so forth. The Washington family has cousins and kin in other cities.[70]

68. Peter Libassi Interview; Roger Wilkins Interview.
69. Peter Libassi Interview.
70. Elaine Heffernan Interview. She said that some members of the Washington family were: Harold Fleming, Arthur Levin, and Eleanor Ambrose of the Potomac Institute; Cernoria Johnson of the National Urban League; Clarence Mitchell and Francis Polhaus of the Washington office of NAACP; Marvin Caplan and Yvonee Price of the Leadership Conference; James Hamilton of the National Council of Churches; Larry Speiser of ACLU; Don Slaiman of AFL-CIO; and the people who had been on the civil rights staffs of such Federal units as CRC, CRS, CSC, OCR, EEOP, OEO, Agriculture, HEW, HUD, and other granting agencies. The Justice Department staff "were never really incorporated into the Washington family—save by extension." Interview.

Thus, a great deal of informal coordination took place during the Kennedy and Johnson years, bringing together civil rights activists.[71] Moreover, many members of the Washington family worked in the civil rights field, whether in governmental or private employment.[72]

SUMMARY

Attempts to coordinate Executive branch civil rights implementation activities have been weak and infrequent. John Kennedy's Subcabinet Committee on Civil Rights, the first quasi-official coordinating unit, served as a useful channel of communication, but as little else. Lyndon Johnson's Council on Equal Opportunity was the first full-fledged official unit of coordination which had specific powers and responsibilities as stated in an Executive order. It, however, was created reluctantly by a President

71. Elaine Heffernan said that "this kind of thing has been typical since the New Frontier, since earlier probably—but it became a norm during the Kennedy years, so that at present it is a tradition." Interview.

72. Examples of this are: Peter Libassi went from the N.Y. State Commission Against Discrimination to CRC, to the Council on Equal Opportunity, to HEW's Office for Civil Rights, and is presently, in the private sector, executive vice president of the Urban Coalition; William Taylor went from the Legislation division of ADA to the Civil Rights Commission; Harold Fleming was director of the Southern Regional Council, deputy director of the Community Relations Service, and then president of the Potomac Institute; Derrick Bell had been an attorney on the NAACP Legal Defense and Educational Fund, then assumed the position of deputy special assistant to the secretary of HEW for civil rights; Ruby Martin went from CRC eventually to become director of HEW's Office for Civil Rights, and is now director of the Washington Research Project, a civil rights organization; Herman Edelsberg, first head of the Equal Employment Opportunity Commission, had previously been with the B'nai B'rith Anti Defamation League. There are numerous other illustrations of this type of interchangeability, and of at least part-time activity by former Government officials (who had enforced civil rights) in civil rights causes.

who always had reservations as to its need. Its short existence was an indication that the Administration preferred decentralized civil rights implementation, with White House control vested in the trusted Justice Department. This was further reflected in the delegation of Title VI coordination responsibilities to Attorney General Nicholas Katzenbach, who did not view his new duties as calling for czar-like action. Katzenbach, rather, saw the Justice Department as a moderating force which kept civil rights enforcement advancing at a steady and even speed. Thus, the Attorney General, as coordinator, did not engage in the pushing kind of operation that was desired by civil rights groups, but rather assumed a more passive coordination role, one in which he used his power to keep the various departments working in tandem, and in which he tried to prevent political embarrassment of the President.

Another type of coordination activity occurred in the Bureau of the Budget, where examiners prodded agency and departmental representatives to include or increase civil rights enforcement personnel in their budget estimates. In addition, civil rights activists in the Budget Bureau's Office of Statistical Standards, working closely with the Civil Rights Commission and Justice's Title VI coordinator, pressured the sponsors of questionnaires, and other such data, to include civil rights material in their finished product.

Furthermore, informal coordination types of activities have taken place between many official and nonofficial civil rights minded people, who constituted a civil rights family in Washington.

PART III

COMPARATIVE ANALYSES

UNITS OF IMPLEMENTATION

THE ACTIVITIES OF SEVERAL UNITS OF IMPLEMENTATION HAVE been examined in an attempt to understand and evaluate the role played by the Executive Branch in the enforcement of Southern Negro civil rights. There were various types of enforcement mechanisms created to effectuate the civil rights laws, each one using its own operational methods. The Civil Rights Division (CRD) in the Justice Department employed the litigation procedure as it dealt with voting rights and legally segregated public schools. HEW's enforcement units, the Equal Educational Opportunities Program (EEOP) and the Office for Civil Rights (OCR), on the other hand, used administrative methods. They attempted to establish workable plans for public school desegregation through the process of negotiation. On another front, the Community Relations Service (CRS) acted as a mediation agency that was ready to lend its services, in all phases of civil rights, to help conciliate racial disputes. Another mechanism, the President's Council on Equal Opportunity, was created to coordinate the efforts of the previously mentioned units of implementation.

Thus, several enforcement units had attempted, by litigative, administrative, and mediative means, to bring about compliance with the civil rights laws. But, why were some units of implementation more effective than others? What effect did factors relating to a unit's inception, the locale it was placed in, its philosophy of goals and methods, and its relations with other interested entities, have on the manner in which it carried out its enforcement operations?

A comparative analysis of the enforcement units, through use of the previously mentioned diagnostic factors, can give insight into the efficacy of the implementation efforts of the Federal Executive Branch.

INCEPTION AND LOCATION

Enforcement units that were established under unfavorable conditions, such as lack of provision for adequate staff and resources, limited statutory power, or placement in an inhospitable locale, were never able to overcome their restrictive beginnings.

Similarly, the Equal Educational Opportunities Program and the President's Council on Equal Opportunity seemed to be destined for short lives because of defects in their make-up at the time of their inception. EEOP, a unit created after passage of the 1964 Civil Rights Act, was granted a small staff and uncertain powers. In addition, it was located in the Office of Education, a milieu that was philosophically inhospitable for a program that called for the energetic implementation of civil rights. EEOP had to contend with a passive department secretary in addition to recalcitrant program people. These early obstacles, too great a burden for EEOP to overcome, helped bring about its untimely downfall two years after its inception.

In like manner, the President's Council, created by Executive order to coordinate Federal civil rights implementation, was given few definite powers to carry out its responsibilities effectively. Its activities, limited by its having a small staff and inadequate facilities, were abruptly terminated after less than nine months of operation. It never had the full support of President Johnson, who had reluctantly established it on the counsel of Vice President Humphrey and Attorney General Katzenbach. This was another instance where poor conditions existing at the time of inception proved to be fatal.

On the other hand, enforcement mechanisms that were created under favorable conditions had far better chances to survive and possibly succeed. The Civil Rights Division was unobtrusively made part of the 1957 Civil Rights Act, coming into being with no substantial opposition mustered against it. Having previously been a section in the Justice Department, it was an experienced unit that remained in the same congenial and germane environment. These early favorable factors were important reasons for CRD's longevity and effectiveness.

Similarly, the Office for Civil Rights, a unit given EEOP's Title VI responsibilities, was better able to fulfill its delegated role because of favorable conditions that existed at the time of its inception. Unlike EEOP, the Office for Civil Rights operated in a friendly locale—the office of the secretary of Health, Education and Welfare, where it received encouragement and aid. Though never free from budgetary worries, OCR nevertheless enjoyed greater political insulation in financial matters than its predecessor because it was funded from the secretary's budget.

Thus, of the five enforcement units analyzed in this study, only two survived intact—the Civil Rights Division and the Office for Civil Rights. A major part of the reason for this was that CRD and OCR had favorable inception conditions. Moreover, these conditions that existed at the time of a unit's establishment had an important effect on how officials in the enforcement units viewed their roles, i.e., how they philosophically determined their goals and chose methods to achieve them.

PHILOSOPHY AND METHODS OF OPERATION

During the years that the Community Relations Service was in the Commerce Department, its officials viewed their mission as calling for the settlement of racial disputes. LeRoy Collins and Calvin Kytle, CRS's first two directors, believed that Congress and the President had given them a "fireman" type of role rather than a role that would oblige them to engage in preventive activities. Their methods of operation reflected their concepts of office. CRS's goals and methods did not change until it was transferred to the Justice Department, where its new director, Roger Wilkins, was permitted to participate in some preventive types of programs. However, the "fireman" concept, as originally envisaged by the President and Congress, still remained a prevailing force and continued to be an important part of the Service's activities.

Officials in the Equal Educational Opportunities Program, though also given loosely defined powers, saw their role as requiring an aggressive program of implementation. David Seeley, director of EEOP, was guided by the

Theodore Roosevelt concept of office, in which the incumbent is free to do anything that is not expressly prohibited. Collins and Kytle, of the Community Relations Service, however, preferred the William Howard Taft philosophy of not doing anything unless expressly permitted. Peter Libassi, director of the Office for Civil Rights, followed a pragmatic approach in which he did not arbitrarily assume unspecified powers, but rather worked to have powers that he wanted legally put within the province of his unit. Libassi's philosophy was shared, in many ways, by officials in the Civil Rights Division.

These approaches were applied in various ways by the enforcement units. Those in command at EEOP, for example, attempted to "bluff" the Southern school districts into compliance by threatening school officials with fund cut-offs. EEOP applied this hard-line philosophy when it issued standardized percentages that indicated what the Commissioner of Education considered a reasonable annual mixture of black and white students. Libassi, of the Office for Civil Rights, however, shunned this method for fear that his unit would be set back if it could not carry out its threats. Instead, he meticulously built legal support for OCR's actions, in the belief that this type of approach was a surer, albeit slower, way to desegregate public schools. For the most part, Nicholas Katzenbach, John Doar, and others in the Justice Department followed a course of action that was similar to Libassi's, for they also believed that a hasty, "shoot from the hip" method of enforcement was counterproductive. CRD's careful choice of and preparation for court cases were indications of their desire to methodically enforce the laws by building desirable precedent.

Hence, both the Civil Rights Division and the Office

for Civil Rights approached their implementation roles conservatively, thinking that civil rights compliance was best secured by careful application of the laws. Officials in these two units were pragmatic in their philosophy and politically sensitive in their choice of methods of operation. On the other hand, the operations of the Community Relations Service and EEOP were conducted with less awareness of possible political ramifications.

Administratively, the Civil Rights Division and the Office for Civil Rights were extremely well run, compared to the often disorganized operations at CRS and EEOP. Each man in CRD and OCR knew his duties and usually performed as part of a master plan. Personnel in EEOP and the Community Relations Service, however, often worked on a day-to-day basis, usually receiving no uniform written instructions. The disparity in the quality of organizations was, in part, a result of differences in the caliber of their leaders. Burke Marshall, John Doar, and Stephen Pollak, consecutive heads of the Civil Rights Division, were well versed in the intricacies of their work. Similarly, the directors of the Office for Civil Rights, Peter Libassi and Ruby Martin, were seasoned veterans in their sphere of activity. But EEOP's David Seeley and CRS's LeRoy Collins, Calvin Kytle, and Roger Wilkins were all comparatively new to their tasks. Collins had prior political experience, but Kytle and Wilkins were, for the most part, politically and administratively neophytes.

In addition, the Office for Civil Rights had a better chance to succeed because it had the hindsight privilege of learning from EEOP's mistakes. The Civil Rights Division also had a comparatively easier time because it had had a great deal of experience in its designated area, namely jurisprudence. But both EEOP and the Community Relations Service had to implement laws without the benefit of someone else's errors. They had to start fresh in an area heretofore untouched.

RELATIONS WITH THE PRESIDENT AND CONGRESS

The kind of relations that the units of implementation had with other interest entities gives further insight into the effectiveness of their operations. The Civil Rights Division and the Office for Civil Rights, the only units that had favorable conditions at inception, and which used sound organizational methods, also enjoyed good relations with the White House. Officials in CRD, through the Attorneys General, had close working relationships with Presidents Kennedy and Johnson, and were their main source of civil rights expertise and information. Leaders in the Office for Civil Rights, moreover, diligently and successfully labored to win the confidence and good will of the White House. In addition, both CRD and OCR, though often restricted in some ways by the men on the Hill, had bearable relationships with the Congressional committees that had jurisdiction over them. The Office for Civil Rights was better able to survive Congressional attacks because it had the legal support of the Justice Department. Libassi had established and nurtured a working relationship with the Department of Justice, being fully aware that OCR would fare badly without the backing of the Attorney General.

The Community Relations Service and EEOP, however, did not enjoy a close working relationship with either the White House or Congress. They were, in many ways, loners in the Federal Government, each struggling with insufficient resources to do a seemingly impossible job.

Neither heard from the White House unless an emergency situation necessitated the President's entrance into the unit's activities. President Johnson, for example, directed that school funds be given back to Chicago after EEOP had, without adequate legal proof, deferred the money. Moreover, although the Community Relations Service was established to mediate civil rights disruptions, it was not called upon by President Johnson to help resolve the racial crisis that had occurred in Watts. Instead, the President sent an ad hoc fact-finding commission to Los Angeles. In their dealings with Congress, EEOP and CRS had less success. They usually had their budgets cut by Congressional committees, never being able to convince Congress of their worth. EEOP, moreover, was constantly harassed by Southern Congressmen, who attempted to weaken its enforcement efforts. Thus, it is not surprising that EEOP was divested of most of its responsibilities, and that the Community Relations Service was swallowed up by the Justice Department, for neither unit had the support of the President, of Congress, or of any other powerful pressure entity.

The Civil Rights Division and the Office for Civil Rights were better able to survive than the other enforcement units because they were not stymied by unfavorable inception conditions, nor were they hampered by placement in an alien locale. Moreover, they shielded themselves from attack through the use of organizational methods which called for the careful preparation of each new step. Their unobtrusive and unemotional approach to enforcement of civil rights served at least to cool the indignation of their Southern opponents. In addition, the close ties that CRD and OCR had with the White House and their cordial relations with Congress helped to assure their staying power.

The Community Relations Service and the Equal Educational Opportunities Program, as earlier demonstrated, were in almost every way the opposite of CRD and OCR. CRS and EEOP suffered from unfavorable conditions at inception, were placed in inhospitable locales, were plagued by organizational inefficiency, and had poor relations with Congress and the White House.

EFFECTIVENESS

Which units were more effective? Generally speaking, no unit had accomplished its purpose, which was total enforcement of the civil rights laws. However, viewing the situation in a relative manner, the Civil Rights Division and the Office for Civil Rights were able to survive—a prerequisite for everything else. In addition, CRD was quite successful in the area of voting registration, helping to almost double Negro registration (in the 11 Southern states of the Old Confederacy) since passage of the 1965 Voting Rights Act. This success, however, may well be attributed to the strength of the law rather than the unit that enforced it.

The Office for Civil Rights was more effective than EEOP, in that OCR, since assuming its predecessor's Title VI school desegregation duties in 1967, tripled the percentage of black and white students that attended the same schools—approximately 35 percent for the 1969-70 school year.

It is very difficult to evaluate the effectiveness of the Community Relations Service, because it was obliged by statute to keep its activities secret. However, information derived from lengthy interviews with Roger Wilkins, one of its former directors, and from Congressional hearings and other documents leads to the conclusion that they had few successful experiences.

8

THE PRESIDENTIAL ROLE
IN CIVIL RIGHTS

WHAT CIVIL RIGHTS ROLES HAVE BEEN ASSUMED BY THE MEN who have sworn to faithfully execute the Office of President of the United States? How have their philosophical concepts of the role of the Presidency affected their civil rights actions?

Answers to these questions are essential for a full understanding of governmental implementation of civil rights, because the tone of an administration is usually set by its Chief Executive. Presidents Eisenhower, Kennedy, Johnson, and Nixon, all vested with *the* executive power, directed the operations of government as they saw fit. Their frames of reference, as determined by their views of the Presidency, the existing environment, and the question of civil rights, were guideposts for the type and degree of civil rights activity engaged in by officials in the Executive Branch.

It is difficult to properly compare the four Presidents, because each served under different conditions, in dis-

218

similar environments. There was not, for example, a viable civil rights law until Eisenhower's second term. Richard Nixon, however, has sworn to faithfully execute six civil rights laws, a host of Supreme Court holdings, several Executive orders, and numerous administrative actions in this area. Moreover, social, political, and economic conditions within and outside the United States differed during the terms of these four men. Within the United States, momentum for Federal civil rights action began at a slow pace during the Eisenhower years, but grew more rapid as time went on. The nation, similarly, was partially involved in Vietnam during the Eisenhower Administration, but progressively became more committed in the Kennedy and Johnson terms in office. Vietnam had an effect upon all phases of American life. Moreover, each President inherited a 535-member group called Congress, and a vast bureaucracy of permanent civil service workers.[1] Eisenhower had to deal with a Democratic Senate and House of Representatives (during his last six years), as does Nixon; while Kennedy had the mixed blessing of having a Congress dominated by conservative members of his own party. Johnson's successful legislative boxscore with the Democratic majorities that controlled Congress during his years in office indicates the type of relationship he enjoyed.[2] In addition, the Presidents who served dur-

1. *U.S. News & World Report* (December 30, 1968) calculated that Mr. Nixon was limited to the appointments of about 2,200 people out of approximately three million civilian employees. Of the 2,200 jobs, almost ⅓ are private secretaries and confidential aides, and ¼ are open to Presidential appointment—but 115 of this latter group are ambassadors, of whom 70 percent are career people. One hundred forty-nine posts, for example, out of 36,000 in the Justice Department, are open. In HEW there will be 85 vacancies from a total of 110,000 positions. Pp. 40–41.

2. Johnson had an average 57 percent of his submitted proposals to Congress approved. This compares to 40 percent for Kennedy and 49

ing these two decades, though representatives of the entire country, were, nevertheless, more indebted to certain ethnic groups and geographic areas. Eisenhower's second-term victory was so widespread that no single part of the population could claim credit for his election. Kennedy, not so fortunate, was a minority President who owed his election to Negroes as well as other groups. Johnson, though sharing the same basic constituency that Kennedy had, received an overwhelming majority of electoral and popular votes in the 1964 Presidential election, and was thus freer from interest-group pressure. Richard Nixon, however, narrowly winning office, has achieved a limited mandate. His poor performance in the black community and his success in the white South are certain to influence his actions as President.[3]

Thus, a President begins his term with preestablished conditions and obligations that constitute a type of rider on his oath of office. This can either help or hinder him, depending upon, among other factors, his conception of office.

CONCEPTIONS OF OFFICE

All evidence indicates that Dwight Eisenhower favored a weak Presidency, that is to say, an institution that

percent for Eisenhower (omitting 1953). Congressional Quarterly Service, *Guide to Current American Government*, p. 43.

3. Robert Finch, as Secretary-designate of HEW, said that the Nixon Administration could deal with racial problems with "a new kind of candor and a new kind of directness," because "it is perfectly clear that we hardly owe our election to the Negro community." He added that "in a way we get a kind of freedom out of this in terms of options because we can deal directly with this problem without any hint of political obligation." *New York Times*, December 25, 1968.

would have as few dealings as possible with the other branches of Government, and would not try to force its will on Congress.[4] He wanted to assume a position above the partisan politicking that took place, for he "dislike[d] all struttings of power, all histrionics of politics."[5] Eisenhower applied his philosophy to the area of civil rights, where he could not envisage himself using the power of the Presidency to forcefully bring about something that he thought could best be effectuated through persuasion and education.[6] He said that he would uphold the Consti-

4. Louis W. Koenig believes that "in public pronouncement and personal act, Eisenhower was respectful of Congressional prerogative and the doctrine of separation of powers." He quotes Eisenhower as stating to the Convention of the National Young Republican Organization in 1953 that "our very form of Government is in peril unless each branch willingly accepts and discharges its own clear responsibilities—and respects the rights and responsibilities of others." Dwight D. Eisenhower, *Mandate for Change* (Garden City, N.Y.: 1963), p. 193, as quoted in *The Chief Executive,* rev. ed. (New York: Harcourt, Brace & World, 1968), p. 11.

Robert J. Donovan, after intensive research and interview, wrote that Eisenhower "brought to the White House a genuine respect for Congress and a traditionalist's conception of the separation of powers. In talks with associates he has referred to himself more than once as a 'Constitutional President.'" *The Inside Story* (New York: Harper and Brothers, 1956), p. 83.

5. Emmet John Hughes, *The Ordeal of Power: A Political Memoir of the Eisenhower Years* (New York: Atheneum, 1963), p. 347.

6. Everett Frederic Morrow, a Negro who held the White House position of Administrative Officer for Special Projects from 1955 to 1961, wrote in his diary (*Black Man in the White House* [New York: Coward-McCann, 1963]) that in May, 1958, Eisenhower told a Negro publishers association the following (in Morrow's words):

while laws should not be ignored in bestowing citizenship rights upon Americans, it had to be acknowledged that prejudice because of race and color is deeply rooted in the hearts of men and can only be changed by education and by constant work on the part of enlightened citizens. . . . He asked Negroes to be "patient" and to use forbearance in their efforts to gain citizenship privileges." p. 218.

tution as interpreted by the Supreme Court in the *Brown* decision, but believed that it was not part of his duty to comment on the morality of the issue.[7]

John F. Kennedy, on the other hand, believed that the man in the White House should get fully involved in affairs of state and practice the art of politics. Theodore Sorensen, who was a close adviser to him, commented on this:

> His philosophy of government was keyed to power . . . the primacy of the White House within the Executive Branch and of the Executive Branch within the Federal Government, the leadership of the Federal Government within the United States and of the United States within the community of nations.[8]

Lyndon Johnson, like his two Democratic predecessors, Franklin Roosevelt and John Kennedy, put himself in the

7. Emmet Hughes, an Eisenhower aide in the 1956 Presidential campaign, wrote that the General, at that time, said to him:

> I am convinced . . . that the Supreme Court decision *set back* progress in the South *at least fifteen years.* . . . It's all very well to talk about school integration—if you remember you may be also talking about social *dis*integration. Feelings are deep on this, especially where children are involved. . . . We can't demand *perfection* in these moral questions. . . . All we can do is keep working toward a goal and keep it high. And the fellow who tries to tell me that you can do these things by *force* is just plain *nuts. The Ordeal of Power,* p. 201.

Sherman Adams, in his powerful role as Assistant to the President, had found that "Eisenhower himself took a moderate view and was convinced in his own mind that progress toward school integration had to be made with considerable deliberation." Adams recalled that when the trouble in Little Rock, Arkansas, broke out, Eisenhower said: "You cannot change the hearts of people by law." *First-Hand Report* (New York: Harper and Brothers, 1961), pp. 331–32.

8. *Kennedy,* p. 389.

thick of governmental activities. Unlike Eisenhower, he did not try to separate the Executive from the Legislative branch—on the contrary, Johnson maintained close ties with his former colleagues in Congress.[9] Moreover, he had no philosophical qualms about getting the Office of the Presidency, and the rest of the Executive Branch, involved in the quest for civil rights. When asked his position at a news conference, Johnson said:

> I think the Federal Government must be a leader in this field and I have three years that I've been President tried to by word and action do everything I could to bring about equality among the races in this country and to see that the Brown decision affecting the integration of our schools was carried forward expeditiously and in accordance with the law.[10]

Richard Nixon's conception of the Presidency has not thus far become fully evident. To date, he appears to have a philosophy that combines some of the ideas of the previously mentioned Presidents. On the one hand he has voiced the Eisenhower approach, in which the President is viewed as being above politics. Near the end of the 1968 Presidential campaign Nixon said:

> I want the Presidency to be a force for pulling our people back together once again, and for making our nation whole by making our people one. We have had enough of discord and division, and what we need now is a time of healing, of renewal and of realistic hope.[11]

---

9. See Koenig, *The Chief Executive*, chapter 6, "Legislative Leader," pp. 124ff.

10. *New York Times*, October 7, 1966.

11. Sidney Wise, ed., *Issues 69–70: Documents in Current American Government and Politics* (New York: Thomas Y. Crowell Co., 1969), p. 12.

On the other hand, he has been deeply involved in partisan politics by his apparent appeal to the South. This was illustrated by the Nixon Administration's proposal to broaden the Voting Rights Act of 1965, whereby it would not only apply to the South, and by the nominations of Clement Haynsworth and G. Harrold Carswell, both Southerners, for the United States Supreme Court.

However, the views of both Eisenhower and Nixon minimize the use of Presidential power as a means for bringing about greater civil rights for the Negro—but for different reasons. Eisenhower thought that he was Constitutionally restricted from engaging in such activities, while Nixon seems to have the political fear that such action would alienate the South—a potential Republican vote area. Contrarily, Kennedy, though personally and politically inclined to move on the civil rights front, found himself checkmated by a recalcitrant Congress, and hampered by his own inexperience. Lyndon Johnson, however, had the skill (that his years in Government and his personality enabled him to develop) and the philosophical temperament to bring into being an unprecedented array of civil rights laws.

The methods by which the Presidents executed the civil rights laws were often a reflection of their philosophical conceptions of office.

METHODS OF OPERATION

The Presidents, generally, made little organizational provision for the handling of civil rights. This area rarely received a high priority status.[12] Eisenhower utilized the

12. Richard Longaker was told in an interview with Mrs. Eleanor Roosevelt that her husband "apparently by conscious decision, subordi-

services of Maxwell Rabb, an all-around trouble shooter
on minority problems, who had quite a difficult job, being
in a generally conservative Republican Administration.[13]
During Kennedy's first year in office, Harris Wofford spe-
cialized in White House civil rights problems. Wofford,
who was sponsored for the position by Father Theodore
Hesburgh of the Civil Rights Commission, remained for
approximately one year. Thereupon, Lee White combined
Wofford's civil rights function with his own domestic

---

nated the direct civil rights program of Negro groups to the indirect
benefits of economic and social gain of the New Deal and later to the
world wide struggle for liberty in World War II." Mrs. Roosevelt also
told Longaker that the President, despite his personal sympathy for the
Negro "placed civil rights legislation down the list . . . because he did
not want to lose Southern support in Congress for the overwhelming
necessities of defense preparation." Interview on June 4, 1958, as cited
in *The Presidency and Individual Liberties* (Ithaca, N.Y.: Cornell University Press, 1961), pp. 9, 41–42.

    According to Theodore Sorenson, Kennedy refrained from pressing
for civil rights legislation for two years. *Kennedy*, pp. 475–76.

    Lee White, former White House assistant Special Counsel, told Donald
Sullivan in an interview on February 7, 1964, that "as the Kennedy Administration began, civil rights was not given a priority position." Cited
in "The Civil Rights Programs of the Kennedy Administration," p. 198.

    13. E. F. Morrow, in *Black Man in the White House*, wrote that Raab
"was perhaps the only one on the White House staff who showed deep
personal concern about the plight of the Negro and other minorities in
the country." Morrow's diary, in December 1955 carried the following
comment: "Rabb outlined the difficulty he was having in trying to get
prominent members of the White House staff who are close to the President to go along with him on the matter of civil rights. He said he had a
tremendous job in trying to convince the Cabinet that a forthright stand
should be taken." Pp. 223, 31, respectively.

    Gordon Tiffany, staff director of the Civil Rights Commission, in a
*Report of the Staff Director to the President and the United States Com-
mission on Civil Rights: 1958–1960*, said that the departure of Sherman
Adams and his administrative assistants from the White House made a
difference in the attention given to civil rights problems, the area then
becoming a "White House orphan." Cited in Sulzner, "The U.S. Commission on Civil Rights," p. 108.

White House duties.[14] This, in effect, meant that there would be no specialist handling this area, which was consistent with the generalist type of staff system used by Kennedy.[15] Burke Marshall, Assistant Attorney General in charge of the Civil Rights Division and an adviser to President Kennedy, touched upon the staff matter in the following letter:

President Eisenhower had a Special Assistant in the White House on civil rights matters, and so did President Kennedy

---

14. In "The Civil Rights Commission—New Life or Last Rites?", a mimeograph study prepared for submittal to the *Administrative Science Quarterly*, 1965, Kent Watkins wrote that Father Hesburgh in 1961 told Kennedy that communication between CRC and President Eisenhower was poor. Kennedy tried to remedy this situation by appointing Harris Wofford, who was legal assistant to Hesburgh, to the White House post of special civil rights assistant. Cited in Sulzner, "The U.S. Commission on Civil Rights," p. 108.

Wofford wrote Donald Sullivan, on March 25, 1964, the following letter:

Generally, I saw the President for brief talks either before or after taking various civil rights leaders in to see him, or in connection with immediately pending issues. This averaged about once a month. One could see the President if he wished simply to sit around his office at the end of the day, which I never did. . . . The negative factor for me was simply that the center of power and decision making in civil rights was in the Department of Justice. (as cited in "The Civil Rights Programs of the Kennedy Administration," pp. 206–7)

15. Sorensen wrote that "the President wanted a fluid staff. Our jurisdictions were distinguishable but not exclusive, and each man could and did assist every other." *Kennedy*, p. 262.

Arthur Schlesinger found that Kennedy "liked to regard his staff as generalists rather than specialists. . . . But a measure of specialization was inevitable. . . ." *A Thousand Days*, p. 687.

For more detailed analyses see: Richard E. Neustadt, "Approaches to Staffing the Presidency" (mimeographed speech delivered at the APSA Convention, New York City, September 6, 1963), and Koenig, *The Chief Executive*, chapter 7, "Administrative Chief."

for a time. Specification of function in the White House was
not, however, in keeping with the manner in which President Kennedy liked his staff to function, so that since some
time in 1962, civil matters in the White House have been
handled by the Special Counsel to the President, or a member of that staff.[16]

A formal mechanism that was created by Kennedy in
1961—the Subcabinet Committee on Civil Rights, served
primarily as a discussion forum in which participants exchanged information. These monthly gatherings of senior
staff members from 17 departments and agencies tapered
off after Wofford left office.[17]

Lyndon Johnson put civil rights responsibilities into
the hands of many people, his choice depending upon the
specific task to be performed. Lee White, Joseph Califano,
Hubert Humphrey, Nicholas Katzenbach, and others, were
called upon to provide information and opinions in this
sphere. Johnson, moreover, reluctantly created the President's Council on Equal Opportunity in 1965 as a mechanism to coordinate the civil rights activities of the
Executive Branch. Nicholas Katzenbach said that in the
latter months of 1964 the President was going to put all
coordination responsibilities in the hands of the Attorney
General, but that he, Katzenbach, changed Johnson's mind
by persuading him to set up the President's Council.
Katzenbach did not think that the Justice Department was
the proper place for this type of activity. However, he
said that the President "never really wanted to set up"
the Council, and was "always grumbling" about it.[18] Thus,

16. Letter to Donald Sullivan on April 24, 1964, as cited in "The
Civil Rights Programs of the Kennedy Administration," p. 207.
17. See chapter 6 for details.
18. Nicholas Katzenbach Interview.

this formal mechanism, which was headed by Vice President Humphrey—the only one of its kind that was ever established in the Executive Branch—was abolished after less than nine months of operation. It did not fit into President Johnson's conception of how the Chief Executive should handle civil rights implementation. Johnson, in his desire to keep control of civil rights in his hands, gave the Council's Title VI coordination duties to Attorney General Nicholas Katzenbach, (as he originally wanted to do), who was not only experienced in the area of civil rights, but was a man the President knew he could trust.[19]

Thus, the historical record indicates that Presidents Eisenhower, Kennedy, and Johnson made very little organizational provision for the handling of civil rights problems. The mechanisms that were established often came as an afterthought, or as the result of pressure on the White House.

Methods employed by the Presidents in the legislative and administrative areas also indicate that civil rights was never given total backing. Eisenhower, as stated earlier, tried not to become involved in the civil rights struggle. The 1954 *Brown* decision was as much a surprise to him as to many others,[20] and the 1957 Civil Rights Act was, to a large extent, the result of the determination and drive of Attorney General Herbert Brownell.[21] President Eisenhower, moreover, did not have a face-to-face private

---

19. Nicholas Katzenbach Interview.

20. Sherman Adams frankly states that "Eisenhower had nothing to do with the Supreme Court's decision. . . . The decision came to him, as it did to most people, as somewhat of a surprise." *First-Hand Report*, p. 331.

21. See Anderson, *Eisenhower, Brownell and the Congress*.

meeting with civil rights leaders until 1958—the middle of his second term in office.[22]

John Kennedy was aware of his limitations in the Congressional sphere, and thus early decided not to use the legislative avenue for civil rights. Instead, he employed his executive powers in efforts to create a congenial civil rights climate.[23] Some of his actions included: pressure to increase Federal employment of Negroes; placement of Negroes in various high Federal positions; the moral denouncement of segregation; frowning upon his official family belonging to racially segregated private clubs; and attempting to induce civil and other leaders to take a stand against racial discrimination.[24] His administrative

---

22. Morrow, *Black Man in the White House*, p. 228.

23. Schlesinger wrote that Kennedy favored the administrative approach because "it fitted his conception of an activist Presidency and because the 1957 and 1960 civil rights debates had left him pessimistic about further progress in Congress." *A Thousand Days*, p. 929.

Sorensen pointed out that "what he could not accomplish through legislation . . . he sought to accomplish through Executive Orders, proclamations, contingency funds, inherent powers, unused statutes, transfers of appropriations, reorganization plans, patronage, procurement, pardons, Presidential memos, public speeches and private measures." *Kennedy*, p. 390. See above, p. 35.

24. Kennedy stated that segregation was morally wrong in a now-famous May, 1963, speech. Schlesinger wrote that Kennedy "had prepared the ground for that speech ever since he became President. . . . He had quietly created an atmosphere where change, when it came, would seem no longer an upheaval but the inexorable unfolding of the promise of American life." *A Thousand Days*, pp. 965–66.

Sorensen stated that Kennedy, in preparation for national acceptance of the civil rights bill proposed in 1963, "immediately resumed the hard, practical job of creating the political, legislative and educational climate that would transform the bill into law and the speech into a new era of racial justice." This meant that Kennedy, Vice President Johnson, and Attorney General Kennedy "embarked on an unprecedented series of private meetings in the White House—seeking to enlist the cooperation and understanding of more than sixteen hundred national leaders: edu-

actions in civil rights appear in sharp contrast to the silence of Eisenhower, but were, in reality, quite limited. The narrow scope and calculated timing of his long-delayed Executive Order on housing, for example, were indications of his reluctance to fully commit himself.[25] Furthermore, his role in relation to what became the 1964 Civil Rights Act was prompted by explosive local incidents that had aroused the nation. At the time the bill was sent to Congress, Kennedy admitted to a group of civil rights leaders:

> I don't think you should all be totally harsh on Bull Connor . . . after all he has done more for civil rights than almost anybody else. . . . A good many programs I care about may go down the drain as a result of this—we may all go down the drain as a result of this—so we are putting a lot on the line.[26]

Moreover, according to several sources, Kennedy included the public accommodations and Title VI provisions in the 1963 bill only after civil rights leaders insisted that

cators, lawyers, Negro leaders, Southern leaders, women's organizations, business groups, governors, mayors, editors and others, Republicans as well as Democrats, segregationists as well as integrationists. . . . He pressed for action from the leaders of the American Labor movement . . . from the blue-ribbon Business Council." *Kennedy*, pp. 496, 501–2.

25. Executive Order 11063, Equal Opportunity in Housing, November 24, 1962. The Order, because it did not cover housing financed through savings and loan, and commercial bank loans, applied to approximately 18 percent of new housing, compared to 80 percent anticipated coverage for the 1968 Housing Act. *Revolution in Civil Rights*, 4th ed., pp. 52, 84. Moreover, Kennedy announced the Order unexpectedly at a news conference that was dominated by the Cuban missile crisis; and, furthermore, it came after the mid-term Congressional elections, and almost two months before the new Congress convened.

26. Schlesinger, *A Thousand Days*, p. 971. Bull Connor was the police chief of Birmingham, Alabama, whose repressive actions against Negro

he do so.[27] John Kennedy was in many ways, during the early part of his Administration, a neophyte feeling his way around. He had not only to learn how to use and control the Executive bureaucratic machine, but also to develop a working relationship with members of Congress. According to Theodore Sorensen, Kennedy

> particularly in his first year . . . felt somewhat uncomfortable and perhaps too deferential with these men who the previous year had outranked him . . . he knew that he had always been too junior, too liberal, too outspoken and too much in a hurry to be accepted in their inner ruling circles. . . . Many of his efforts to bridge this gap seemed futile.[28]

Lyndon Johnson, on the other hand, was able to take advantage of the preparatory work that Kennedy did in civil rights, and also capitalize on the national sympathy that followed his predecessor's assassination. Moreover, Johnson was a Southern, seasoned Congressman who had proved himself to be an expert at legislative legerdemain. In addition, his positive view of Presidential power and of civil rights helped set the stage for the forthcoming

demonstrators brought about a national outpouring of sympathy for the black cause. Schlesinger also wrote that "Birmingham and the Negroes themselves had given him the nation's ear." p. 966.

27. Clarence Mitchell Interview and Whitney Young Interview. Young said that the President and Robert Kennedy, at a meeting with civil rights leaders, tried to convince them not to include public accommodations and Title VI provisions in the 1963 civil rights bill.

Gary Orfield was told by White House aide Lee White that Title VI was not seen by the Administration as a "make or break item," but as something "kind of tucked away among some giants." Based on his interview with White, Orfield wrote that "had Kennedy lived, it was one of the segments of the bill that might possibly have been traded to the South for an end to the Senate filibuster." *The Reconstruction of Southern Education*, p. 39.

28. *Kennedy*, p. 345.

array of civil rights laws.[29] Roy Wilkins, Executive Director of the NAACP and a man who had worked closely with the President, found that there was

> no better informed man on the functions of the Government. He knew where all the trails went, where all the bodies were buried. He knew where power was, who had the power to do what. He was exceptionally well informed. No President knew all that he knew about the Federal establishment.[30]

Furthermore, in his efforts to garner Congressional votes for new civil rights laws and in his actions to implement the existing statutes, Johnson made full use of his Southern background. James Reston reported on June 19, 1964 (two weeks before the 1964 Civil Rights Act was signed), that all of Johnson's "understanding and knowledge of the South is now being brought to bear in a torrent of personal and telephone conversations with Southern leaders with the single purpose of urging compliance."[31]

---

29. The writer found, in interviews with former public officials and civil rights leaders, that there was a unanimity of opinion that Lyndon Johnson was sincere in his civil rights efforts. Nicholas Katzenbach, for example, said that Johnson "bent over backwards" to wipe out the Southern part of his background, and had once asked Katzenbach if the opponents of Negro equality realized that two-thirds of the world was colored. Johnson then said: "How long can this inequality last in the United States." Interview.

NAACP assistant director John Morsell said: "We could doubt his strategy but not his intent." Interview.

Whitney Young felt that he was the most trusted of the Presidents, and that Johnson was "fully committed even if it would put him at a political disadvantage." Interview.

30. Roy Wilkins Interview.

31. *New York Times*, June 19, 1964. Johnson, during a May, 1964, trip through the South, while speaking to a Georgia audience reportedly "identified himself wholeheartedly as a Southerner with family roots in

Moreover, he was also able to maintain high credentials with the civil rights community.[32]

---

the red earth of Georgia, where one of his forebears was sheriff of Henry County; and when his daughter, Lynda Bird, rose to speak, she said, 'y' all' as naturally as she smiled." *New York Times,* May 9, 1964.

Tom Wicker, a Southerner, wrote in his book *JFK and LBJ: The Influence of Personality Upon Politics* (New York: William Morrow and Co., 1968) that "Southerners knew he had shared their bitter alienation; among other things, it had helped lose him the Democratic nomination they and he thought he deserved in 1960. . . . Johnson might play politics in the North, but he did not come to the South with vindictiveness in his heart; there might be a little Scalawag in him but a Carpetbagger he could never be. He was one of the South's own; he had a sympathy for their outlook that many Southerners could believe was genuine. He understood them, and they him." P. 175.

Ramsey Clark, Texas born, said that enforcement of civil rights laws "is harder for a President from Massachusetts than a President from Texas." Interview.

32. See above, n. 29. Sorensen wrote that President Kennedy, Robert Kennedy, Burke Marshall, Assistant White House Counsel Lee White, and Democratic National Committee Deputy Chairman Louis Martin "were constantly in touch with Negro leaders." *Kennedy,* p. 476. This was not so with President Eisenhower, who had his first face-to-face meeting with civil rights leaders during June 1958. Morrow, *Black Man in the White House,* p. 228. Moreover, Roy Wilkins said that he had had little contact with Eisenhower. Interview.

President Nixon does not seem to be trusted by the civil rights community. Roy Wilkins said that he had "an uncertainty and uneasiness" about Nixon; and Whitney Young believes that now under Nixon's policies, "Southerners think all of these things can be diluted, rescinded, or revoked." Interviews. Marvin Caplin of the Leadership Conference on Civil Rights said that civil rights enforcement "gets little assistance" from the White House or the Justice Department. Caplin found that White House aides "Harry Dent and Ehrlichman have little feeling for civil rights enforcement and considerable power. The situation is very dangerous." Letter to writer, August 11, 1969.

Clarence Mitchell, legislative director of the NAACP, said, after the House of Representatives approved a weak Administration substitute for the expiring Voting Rights Act of 1965, that the vote was "engineered by the President of the United States who was supposed to be bringing the people together, but instead has consigned Negroes to a political doghouse whose roof leaks." Clarence Mitchell further added

Johnson's execution of the voting and school desegregation laws was, according to people who were directly involved, indicative of a genuine desire to see them fully complied with. Furthermore, he gave a great deal of autonomy to the civil rights enforcement units, having stepped in only during times of emergency, or when a matter was poorly handled.[33]

SUMMARY

Presidential implementation of Southern Negro civil rights has varied, being dependent upon the outlook and ability of the man in the White House and upon environmental conditions that existed during his incumbency.

President Eisenhower had sufficient popular support and confidence to fortify strong civil rights action that he may have chosen to take, but he was limited by his own strict interpretation of his Constitutional duties and by his personal beliefs. President Kennedy was not bound by such philosophical limitations, but, rather, was stifled by his inability to cope with a recalcitrant Congress. His successor, Lyndon Johnson, was able to make great strides in civil rights because: he philosophically viewed the Presidency as an institution which could take this type of affirmative action; he had been elected to office by a large margin and thus felt he had a popular mandate to act; he had the support of a Congress that was more

---

that under the proposed bill the responsibility for initiating court action will "now rest with a foot-dragging Attorney General who has shown that he lives in the 19th century." *New York Times*, December 12, 1969.

33. Departments of Justice and HEW officials said that they had felt little pressure from the White House and were usually permitted to handle civil rights matters in their own way. Interviews with Nicholas Katzenbach, John Doar, Francis Keppel, and David Seeley.

liberal minded than the one his predecessor had to work with; and Johnson was an experienced and skillful politician who had many contacts in Congress.

Richard Nixon, on the other hand, possesses no strong mandate, is faced by an unsympathetic Congress, and his philosophical appearance is that of a practical politician.

PART IV
CONCLUSION

9

CONCLUSION AND RECOMMENDATIONS

IMPLEMENTATION OF SOUTHERN NEGRO CIVIL RIGHTS BY THE Executive Branch of the Federal Government has been a limited operation. From the Eisenhower years to the Administration of Richard Nixon there have been only qualified, partial attempts to bring about compliance in this area. The enforcement of civil rights laws was never designated as a must action which took priority over all other programs. There have been, relatively speaking, greater efforts made by some Chief Executives than by others. The expressed moral commitment of President Kennedy and the executive civil rights action taken during his Administration appear in sharp contrast to enforcement efforts expended by the Eisenhower people. Moreover, progress made during Johnson's Presidency, especially in the legislative area, far surpassed the accomplishments of all who served in that office before him. Nevertheless, even though there was a progressive advance in civil rights, there were always restraining forces which prevented a total commitment on the part of any of the above Presidents.

In some instances these restraining forces were of a personal nature, having involved the individual President's conception of his role in office, or his attitude toward the problem of civil rights. Dwight Eisenhower's view of government, for example, in contrast to Kennedy's and Johnson's called for a wall of separation between its main organs so that one branch would not impose its will on another. His philosophical approach had a deterrent effect on the performance of his Administration in the enforcement of civil rights.

However, there were two major restraining forces which commonly affected and limited, in varying degrees, the civil rights activity of all the Presidents. Each President had to cope with: (1) the political power of Southern leaders as practiced in Congress (and in the national electoral process); and (2) the defiant attitudes of many white Southerners.

The South's political power—always prevalent, often organized, and consistently applied—was especially felt in the area of executive-legislative relations. From the time of the first *Brown* decision, in 1954, to the present, there have been Democratic majorities in both Houses of Congress. This has meant that Southerners, because of their electoral longevity and the seniority system, have held the bulk of major committee positions in that body. These entrenched Senators and Congressmen, considerable in number, have usually spoken with one voice in matters pertaining to Black civil rights. Their unrelenting drive to impede advances in this area has had a restraining effect on administrative implementation of civil rights.

President Kennedy recognized the committee power of Southern legislators, and, fearful that his other programs would be impaired, decided not to press for new civil rights laws. He preferred, instead, to use his executive powers and the Federal courts to bring about civil rights compliance. Lyndon Johnson had greater success in the legislative realm, having had more experience in such undertakings, and being fortunate to have had a more compatible Congress. However, he also did not use all the means at his disposal to fully and rapidly execute the civil rights laws.

The second major factor that had a constraining effect on the Chief Executives was the ever-present, perhaps exaggerated, display of grass-roots Southern intransigence. The Presidents, and their official families, were constantly besieged by local, state, and Federal Southern officials who demonstrated, in innumerable ways, their opposition to civil rights. Manifestos from Southern Congressmen, petitions from local townspeople, irate visiting delegations, and persistent political threats were but few of the pressures directed at those in the Executive Branch who had sworn to enforce the law. This seemingly unyielding display of emotions came from a large geographic area in the United States that consisted of tens of millions of Americans—a fact not unknown to those who had the responsibility for effectuating civil rights compliance.

Thus, a predicament was created for the man in the White House. Even if he had personally wanted to immediately bring about compliance with the existing laws, did he have the power to do so? In view of Southern opposition, would thorough civil rights implementation necessitate a second reconstruction of the South? However, were people in the South as adamantly opposed to equality for the Negro as Presidents Eisenhower and Kennedy (and Nixon) seemed to believe? Did these Chief Executives truly know the mind of the South or were they the objects of a stupendous bluff perpetrated by a vociferous minority of Southern whites?

Hence, the Presidents had to consider many tangible and intangible factors preceding their choice of implementation methods. Their enforcement arsenal ranged from the use of overt force to the educational method of weaning obstinate Southerners from their environmental way of life. President Eisenhower believed that the Government could not successfully force the South to change its style of life. He therefore advocated the slower course of social education. The innovative civil rights actions that occurred during his years in office were not initiated by Eisenhower, for he bore no responsibility for the *Brown* decision, had given tacit approval for the Civil Rights Acts of 1957 and 1960, and had reluctantly sent Federal troops into Little Rock, Arkansas.

President Kennedy also tried to create a climate in which those south of the Mason-Dixon line would accept the idea of equal Negro rights. Kennedy also did not want to push too hard or too fast. His reluctance to use Federal might was illustrated in his following actions: his limited Housing order; his initial reluctance to include public accommodations and Federal fund withholding (Title VI) provisions in the 1963 Civil Rights bill; his many statements in praise of Southern moderates for their acts of voluntary compliance; and his attempt to get citizens in all walks of life to solve the problem of civil rights locally. John Kennedy used overt executive power only when conditions dictated such action. He delayed, for example, his long-promised Housing order until pressure mounted for its issuance, and sent troops to the University of Mississippi when inaction on his part would have appeared as Presidential inability to execute a Federal court order. In addition, Kennedy freely admitted to civil rights leaders that the national revulsion which followed the violent suppression of black demonstrators in Selma, Alabama, was an important factor in his decision to send the 1963 Civil Rights bill to Congress.

Lyndon Johnson inherited what became the 1964 Civil Rights Act from his predecessor, and, keeping its provisions intact, pushed it through Congress. Soon after, he sponsored the 1965 Voting Rights Act, which was the only 20th-century civil rights law that was not in some way tied in with a pending Presidential election. Yet, Johnson refused to extend Kennedy's Housing order by similar executive fiat, insisting instead on Congressional action. His strategy, contrary to most predictions, resulted in the Housing Act of 1968. He, unlike Kennedy, chose the legislative route because it was an area in which he had great skill and powerful contacts, and thus the best chance to succeed. Moreover, he probably did not want to appear to be going over the heads of his former Congressional brethren by arbitrarily issuing Executive orders. He had publicly stated that he did not think he could make an act stand up and be effective if he could not get Congress to embrace it. There is also the possibility that he, being from the South and familiar with the behavior and thoughts of people from this section of the country, was not convinced of the intractibility of the Southern mind. Perhaps he was better able to judge, compared to Eisenhower and Kennedy, how far a President can go in the area of civil rights.

Indications are that the route desired by officials in the Nixon Administration similarly calls for the use of noncoercive methods to bring about Southern compliance. Nixon's Attorney General, John Mitchell, has inaugurated what he considers to be a slower but surer procedure to bring about public school desegregation—court litigation. Kennedy had also hoped to execute the *Brown* decision through the courts. In addition, Mitchell has stated the Administration desire to end regional legislation and has thus proposed an alteration of the 1965 Voting Rights Act.

Thus, Southern power and emotions have played a dominant role in the implementation activities of Presidents Eisenhower, Kennedy, Johnson, and Nixon. They were all restrained by Southern Congressional pressure, and by the display of emotional intransigence on the part of many Southerners. These dual pressures on the Presidents also had a restraining effect on others in the Executive Branch.

It is extremely difficult for a President to induce people in the bureaucracy to proceed along *proven* paths, but it is a herculean task for him to make them tread on new ground—which is what was called for in civil rights enforcement. Moreover, if the Chief Executive does not fully commit himself and his Administration to an all-out stringent enforcement of the civil rights laws, then neither will members of his Cabinet or his bureau chiefs or the people on the lowest rung of the Government service ladder. The bureaucratic machine, if pushed, can perhaps move as fast as its chief, but not faster. During the 1950s and 1960s the actions of the people in the bureaucracy reflected the behavior of the Presidential incumbent.

The Civil Rights Division, for example, engaged in few cases during the Eisenhower Administration, and although it progressively grew more active through the Kennedy and Johnson years, it never fully committed its resources to the enforcement of civil rights. There was great hesitancy by the Justice Department to cut off school funds, they having preferred other less direct means. Even at the height of its compliance activities, which took place when Ramsey Clark was Attorney General, the Department of Justice continued its policy of the sparing use of Federal voting examiners. Moreover, although Civil Rights Division officials periodically expressed the need for additional enforcement attorneys, they rarely requested more than a 20 percent annual increase in personnel.

Other official organs of implementation, the Community Relations Service, the Equal Educational Opportunities Program, and the Office for Civil Rights—all established as a result of the 1964 Civil Rights Act—similarly never operated at full speed. These mechanisms were not given adequate power and resources to fully meet their responsibilities. President Johnson rarely interfered with their operations, but neither did he exert pressure on Congress to get them money and men. The implementation units had to survive by their own ingenuity, using inadequate resources in what were often makeshift operations. For the most part, they were afforded no special treatment from the Bureau of the Budget, and as a general rule their budget requests were cut by Congressional appropriations committees. Thus, it is not surprising that, in a relatively short amount of time, the Community Relations Service was absorbed by the Justice Department, and the Equal Educational Opportunities Program's Title VI duties were taken over by the Office for Civil Rights.

The absence of strong Presidential leadership was further reflected in the lack of provision made by the Chief Executives to coordinate civil rights activities. Dwight Eisenhower, for example, had only one man handling minority problems, while John Kennedy used a civil rights specialist for only one year. Kennedy, moreover, established a type of coordination unit called the Subcabinet

Committee on Civil Rights. It turned out to be an innocuous forum that petered out not long after it was organized. This, in effect, left the settlement of civil rights problems that occurred during the Kennedy Administration to be handled by generalists on an emergency basis. Lyndon Johnson, similarly, used many people to oversee this area, until he reluctantly created, in early 1965, the President's Council on Equal Opportunity. This mechanism, headed by Vice President Humphrey, was the only full time, overall civil rights coordinating unit ever established in the Federal Government. Created on a trial-and-error basis with a small staff, it began to make itself felt by prodding departments and agencies to enforce the laws. However, the Council never really had an opportunity to prove itself, for it was abolished less than nine months after its inception, apparently having not fulfilled the expectations of President Johnson. Its Title VI coordinating duties were thereupon summarily thrust on an Attorney General (Nicholas Katzenbach) who had preferred not to handle this aspect of enforcement.

Thus, efforts to coordinate civil rights activities within the Executive Branch were extremely lax, with the White House, in most instances, having treated such problems on an ad hoc basis. Moreover, there was little preventive action to deter jurisdictional and other types of conflicts that erupted between agencies. Interdepartmental meetings generally took place after a pressing emergency brought matters to a head.

Most units of implementation were also thrown together in a haphazard manner, since the President did not take the necessary time and effort to see that they were organized on a sound administrative basis. The thought of the mechanics of implementation usually came after passage of a specific civil rights law was assured. This type of situation took place with the Title VI provision of the 1964 Act, and the Federal examiner provision of the 1965 Voting Rights Act. Moreover, units of implementation were often created in a random manner without adequate consideration as to their place in a grand design of enforcement. There was no grand design!

Another aspect of civil rights implementation concerns the negative attitude of many in the Federal Government toward this area. It seems as though almost everyone wanted to pass the buck. Eisenhower said that it was not the job of the Federal Government because people had to see the light themselves. Kennedy, though not so extreme in his Federal philosophy, was quite reluctant to impose the power of his office to bring about conditions which he believed could be eventually worked out through court litigation. Johnson used his legislative skills to get Congress to act, but then assumed somewhat of a laissez-faire attitude in which he allowed enforcement to proceed without his help or hindrance. Nixon has indicated his desire to let the Federal courts handle the dilemma.

This "hot potato" attitude was also expressed by the heads of various departments. HEW Secretary Wilbur Cohen, for example, suggested to the Bureau of the Budget in the latter part of 1968 that HEW's enforcement duties be given to the Justice Department. His counterpart in the Nixon Administration, Robert Finch, has expressed the same sentiments. Attorneys General Katzenbach and Clark would rather have not been burdened with the Title VI coordination task. Katzenbach held President Johnson off in the latter part of 1964, when the President stated his intention of giving him this function. This negative attitude permeated the entire bureaucracy where civil rights enforcement duties were regarded as an unwanted and politically harmful burden. Even the United States Federal Court of Appeals for the Fifth Circuit, in general a positive force for the effectuation of the civil rights laws, expressed the hope that HEW would take over the burden.

However, there were two organs in the Federal Government (besides the Fifth Circuit), that showed consistency in their civil rights efforts—the Supreme Court and the Civil Rights Commission. In their individual ways, they have been the most staunch supporters of civil rights.

In all fairness, it must be stated that this was a very difficult area to enforce. Officials had to deal with numerous obstacles that militated against an orderly execution of the civil rights laws. Mechanically, an operation of this size and nature was never attempted by the Federal Government. This meant that the program had to proceed in an experimental manner: new methods were tried; personnel were trained for freshly created positions; and budgetary requests had to be conjectured. The bureaucratic machine was technically ill equipped and psychologically ill prepared to engage in this type of program. People who were in charge of Federal programs and responsible for the disbursement of Federal funds were, in general, reluctant to force recalcitrant recipients to adhere to the prerequisite civil rights provisos.

Even in a utopian situation, where political and emotional barriers did not exist, there would still be the task of establishing an efficient organizational structure to enforce the civil rights laws. However, the bureaucracy was not politically or emotionally neutral, nor was such a structure created. This, in effect, left a large part of the implementation operation uncoordinated and decentralized.

Moreover, during this entire period, a running battle

took place between those who wanted to bring about change and those who had attempted to prevent the effectuation of the civil rights laws. The opposition forces, usually from the South, and having great strength in Congress, applied consistent daily pressure to render implementation efforts ineffective. In numerous instances, Southern chairmen were able to subvert enforcement operations through their control of Executive appropriations, and by their skillful use of Congressional oversight.

The liberal forces, on the other hand, were scattered and inconsistent. They united only for special purposes, such as to push through a major piece of legislation or to prevent a rout. However, when the civil rights army of liberal Congressmen, Federal officials, and representatives from various civic, religious, labor, and civil rights organizations worked together, their combined strength was formidable. This was attested to by their efforts to get the 1964 and 1968 Civil Rights bills passed, and by their success in blocking the Supreme Court appointments of Clement Haynsworth, Jr. and G. Harrold Carswell—two conservative Southern Nixon nominees. However, they lacked the power to effectively counter the day-by-day actions of their opponents. The number of liberal Congressmen who had important positions in the House and Senate did not constitute a force capable of preventing the injurious actions of Southern opponents. Similarly, there was no united national civil rights bloc which equaled in numbers, determination, and zeal the seemingly relentless army that existed in the Southern states.

Thus, the following three central themes run through the civil rights implementation picture: (1) the lack of full Presidential commitment because of Southern power and pressure; (2) a similar attitude on the part of many in the bureaucracy; and (3) insufficient efforts by civil rights proponents to effectively counter opposition. The result was the inadequate implementation of Southern Black civil rights.

What can be done to bring about greater implementation of civil rights?

Only when the idea of the inevitability of Negro rights becomes, like the New Deal social legislation, an irreversibly basic part of American life will it be possible to fully implement the civil rights laws. Laws that protect the rights of Negroes (and others) must be interwoven into the American social and political fabric. Implementation activities by the Federal Executive Branch must be institutionalized so that compliance work is made a natural, nonpolitical part of the bureaucratic way of life. Methods and mechanisms must be devised to create an organizational structure which can efficiently and diligently enforce the civil rights laws. Implementation must become, for the most part, a decentralized activity in which personnel throughout the Executive Branch fulfill their responsibilities. Thus, it is essential to make Federal personnel both aware of their legal responsibilities and fearful of punishment for failure to meet them. Hence, the specification of civil rights duties and penalties for poor performance must be incorporated into Federal job descriptions. However, an overseer will still be needed to check daily enforcement operations. This need could be met by the creation of a permanent bipartisan ombudsmen-like commission, which would be given statutory power to investigate all Executive Branch compliance efforts—below the White House. The members of the commission, in order to be effective, would be appointed for a 15-year period (without the right of reappointment), by the President with the consent of the Senate. Their positions must be full-time and high salaried. Moreover, they must be guaranteed adequate working funds for five-year periods, and must be given the right to choose their staff freely. Their powers must include the rights to observe Federal personnel at work, and immediate access to department and agency files. Finally, upon the Commission's determination of inadequate civil rights enforcement, the commissioners must have the right either to recommend that changes be made, or directly press charges against Government employees in the Federal courts. The ombudsmen-like commission, endowed with the powers of publicity and prosecution, can be an effective instrument.

However, such a mechanism does not obviate the need for strong Presidential leadership, because the man at the top sets the tone and temperament for the rest of the bureaucracy. Without his continuous aid, enforcement would be extremely difficult; and should he take a negative position, it would constitute an almost impossible task. Thus, until the concept of civil rights for Negroes is institutionalized, the actions of the man in the White House will have a great effect upon civil rights implementation efforts.

APPENDIXES

Department of Justice   *Date*

St. John Barrett*
  2nd Assistant Attorney General,
  Civil Rights Division   July 18, 1969

Ramsey Clark
  Attorney General   July 10, 1969
  August 21, 1969

John Doar
  Assistant Attorney General,
  Civil Rights Division   July 24, 1969
  August 6, 1969

Harrison J. Goldin
  Trial Staff,
  Civil Rights Division   July 3, 1969

---

* Interviewed in Washington, D.C. All other interviews were conducted in New York.

Nicholas de B. Katzenbach
  Attorney General

June 24, 1969
July 7, 1969
December 10, 1969
  (telephone)

Burke Marshall
  Assistant Attorney General,
  Civil Rights Division

May 13, 1969

Stephen Pollak*
  Assistant Attorney General,
  Civil Rights Division

July 16, 1969

Department of Health, Education & Welfare

Elaine Heffernan*
  Staff Assistant
  Office for Civil Rights

July 17, 1969

Francis Keppel
  U.S. Commissioner of Education

July 31, 1969

F. Peter Libassi*
  Director, Office for Civil Rights
  Assistant Staff Director, U.S.
    Civil Rights Commission
  Staff, President's Council on
    Equal Opportunity

September 9, 1969
  (telephone)

Ruby Martin*
  Director, Office for Civil Rights

July 17, 1969

David Seeley
  Director, Equal Educational
    Opportunities Program in the
  U.S. Office of Education

July 24, 1969

David Seeley & David Barus
  Barus: Legal consultant, Equal
  Educational Opportunities
  Program, U.S. Office of
  Education   July 24, 1969

Barney Sellers*
  Special assistant to Director,
    Office for Civil Rights   July 16, 1969

Bureau of the Budget

Karen Nelson*
  Office of Statistical Standards   September 22, 1969
                                                 (telephone)

Community Relations Service

Roger Wilkins
  Director   August 6, 1969
                                              August 13, 1969

President's Council on Equal Opportunity

Wiley Branton*
  Executive Director   July 17, 1969

Civil Rights Leaders

Norman C. Amaker
  1st Assistant Counsel, NAACP Legal
    Defense & Educational Fund   July 3, 1969

Arnold Aronson
  Secretary, Leadership Conference
    on Civil Rights   July 23, 1969

Jack Greenberg
  Director-Counsel, NAACP Legal
    Defense & Educational Fund   July 23, 1969

Floyd McKissick
  National Director, Congress of
    Racial Equality   July 30, 1969

Clarence Mitchell*
  Director, Washington office,
    NAACP   July 18, 1969

John Morsell
  Assistant Director, NAACP   July 10, 1969

Roy Wilkins
  Executive Director, NAACP   August 13, 1969

Whitney Young
  Executive Director,
    National Urban League   August 6, 1969

B. QUESTIONNAIRE

The following questionnaire was sent to approximately 150 Federal Government officials:

(1) What part did you have in the formulative stages of the 1964 and 1965 Civil Rights Acts?

(2) What effect did the formulative and lawmaking stages have on:

  (a) enforcement measures in the law
  (b) subsequent enforcement activity

(3) Which part or parts of the Executive Branch do you feel were most successful in fulfilling its enforcement duties? What do you base this judgment on?

(4) Which part or parts of the Executive Branch was least successful? Why? How can this be corrected?

(5) What effect did motivational encouragement by administration superiors have on successful enforcement?

(6) Have the various agencies, etc., of the Executive Branch worked in a coordinated way? Where is this most evident? Least evident?

(7) Were there administrative devices for checking and following up enforcement? What improvisation or alterations do you suggest?

(8) What restrictions were there on enforcement?

(9) What part did administration priorities have in the determination of scope and intensity of enforcement?

(10) Has there been a more appropriate time to push enforcement?

(11) In which of the Civil Rights areas was there more stringent enforcement?

(12) Did ambiguity of law, or detailed laws, hinder or help enforcement? In what type of case?

(13) What provisions were made for unforeseen factors? Were alternative methods considered and planned?

(14) Did the incumbent President attempt to enforce the civil rights policies of prior administrations?

(15) Did political differences (party, etc.) have an effect on the quality of enforcement? How?

(16) How did interest groups affect enforcement? Which areas of the Executive Branch were they most active in?

(17) What effect did Congress have on enforcement?

(18) What effect did the Federal courts have on enforcement?

(19) Additional comments.

C. SELECTED CHRONOLOGY

1954

    Brown v. *Board of Education of Topeka:* public school desegregation

1955

    Brown v. *Board of Education of Topeka:* enforce with "all deliberate speed."

1957

    Civil Rights Act:
        Civil Rights Commission

Civil Rights Division of Justice Department
Voting provisions
Federal troops sent to Little Rock, Arkansas
1958
Cooper v. *Aaron:* prompt and reasonable start with no schemes of racial discrimination in school desegregation
1960
Civil Rights Act
Voting provisions
Presidential election
1961
Freedom Rides
ICC prohibits discrimination in interstate buses and terminals
1962
Federal troops sent to University of Mississippi
Congressional elections
Executive Housing Order
1963
Civil Rights Commission report: cut off Mississippi funds
Demonstrations in Birmingham, Alabama
Katzenbach–Wallace confrontation at University of Alabama
Medgar Evers (NAACP) killed
Civil Rights bill sent to Congress
March on Washington "for jobs and freedom"
Kennedy assassinated
1964
Poll tax ratified
Civil Rights Act:
Public accommodations
Public facilities
Public education (Title IV)—desegregation
Federal fund withholding (Title VI)

Equal Employment Opportunity Commission
Community Relations Service
Voting
Riots: Harlem, Rochester, Jersey City, Paterson, Chicago,
     Philadelphia
Presidential election
Presidential approval of Government-wide civil rights en-
     forcement regulations

1965

Equal Educational Opportunities Program (USOE)
President's Council on Equal Opportunity
Civil rights march from Selma to Montgomery, Alabama
Elementary and Secondary Education Act
School desegregation Guidelines issued
Voting Rights Act
Watts riots
EEOP defers and then returns Chicago school funds
Johnson reorganized civil rights units:
     President's Council on Equal Opportunity abolished
     Committee on Equal Employment Opportunity
          abolished
     Attorney General given Title VI coordination role
     Community Relations Service's transfer to the Justice
          Department proposed
Roger Wilkins appointed acting director of Community Re-
     lations Service
Attorney General Katzenbach issues Guidelines for civil
     rights enforcement

1966

Singleton v. *Jackson Municipal Separate School District*
     School desegregation Guidelines upheld (5th Circuit)
Revised school desegregation Guidelines issued
South Carolina v. *Katzenbach*
     1965 Voting Rights Act upheld
Community Relations Service transferred to Justice De-
     partment

HEW Secretary John Gardner issues first school fund termination order under Title VI

Watts riots

White House Conference on Civil Rights

Meredith shot on civil rights walk

Summer riots: New York, Indiana, Illinois

Revised school desegregation Guidelines upheld by 5th
Circuit

1967

U.S. v. Jefferson County Board of Education
5th Circuit (*en banc*) upholds school desegregation
revised Guidelines

Office for Civil Rights (HEW) takes over EEOP's Title VI
school desegregation duties

Riots: Newark and Detroit

1968

4th school desegregation Guidelines released
National in scope

Martin Luther King killed

Johnson states he won't run

Housing Act

Poor People's Campaign in Washington, D.C.

Robert Kennedy assassinated

Presidential election

1969

HEW-Justice school desegregation white paper

Supreme Court Mississippi decision: "desegregate schools
now"

1970

Voting Rights Act

SELECTED BIBLIOGRAPHY

PUBLIC DOCUMENTS

U.S. Congress. House of Representatives. Committee on Appropriations. Subcommittee on the Departments of Labor, and Health, Education and Welfare, of the Committee on Appropriations. *Hearings, Appropriations for 1968.* Part 2, 3, 6. 90th Cong., 1st Sess., 1967.

U.S. Congress. House of Representatives. Committee on Appropriations. Subcommittee on the Departments of State, Justice, The Judiciary, and Related Agencies, of the Committee on Appropriations. *Hearings, Appropriations for 1963.* 87th Cong., 2nd Sess., 1962.

————. *Hearings, Appropriations for 1966.* 89th Cong., 1st Sess., 1965.

————. *Hearings, Appropriations for 1967.* 89th Cong., 2nd Sess., 1966.

————. *Hearings, Appropriations for 1968.* 90th Cong., 1st Sess., 1967.

————. *Hearings, Appropriations for 1969.* 90th Cong., 2nd Sess., 1968.

U.S. Congress. House of Representatives. Committee on Education and Labor. *Hearings* before a Subcommittee on Integration in Federal and Public Education of the Committee on Education and Labor. 87th Cong., 2nd Sess., 1962.

U.S. Congress. House of Representatives. Committee on Education and Labor. *Hearings* before a Special Subcommittee of the Committee on Education and Labor. 89th Cong., 2nd Sess., 1966.

U.S. Congress. House of Representatives. Committee on the Judiciary. *Hearings* before the Committee on the Judiciary, Executive Session. Part 4. 88th Cong., 1st Sess., 1963.

U.S. Congress. House of Representatives. Committee on the Judiciary. *Hearings* before Subcommittee No. 5 of the Committee on the Judiciary. Part 2. 88th Cong., 1st Sess., 1963.

U.S. Congress. House of Representatives. Committee on the Judiciary. *Civil Rights, Hearings* before Subcommittee No. 5 of the Committee on the Judiciary. 89th Cong., 1st Sess., 1965.

U.S. Congress. House of Representatives. Committee on the Judiciary. *Guidelines for School Desegregation, Hearings* before a Subcommittee on Civil Rights of the Committee on the Judiciary. 89th Cong., 2nd Sess., 1966.

U.S. Congress. House of Representatives. Rules Committee. *Policies and Guidelines for School Desegregation, Hearings* before the Rules Committee. 89th Cong. 2nd Sess., 1966.

U.S. Congress. Senate. Committee on Appropriations. *Hearings on Department of Justice Appropriations for 1961* before the Committee on Appropriations. 86th Cong., 2nd Sess., 1960.

――――. *Hearings, Appropriations for 1965.* 88th Cong., 2nd Sess., 1964.

――――. *Hearings, Appropriations for 1969.* 90th Cong., 2nd Sess., 1968.

U.S. Congress. Senate. Committee on Appropriations. *Hearings on Department of Health, Education and Welfare*

Appropriations for 1967 before the Committee on Appropriations. 89th Cong., 2nd Sess., 1966.

———. *Hearings, Appropriations for 1968.* 90th Cong., 1st Sess., 1967.

U.S. Congress. Senate. Committee on Commerce. *Hearings, Nomination of Roger Wilkins as Director of the Community Relations Service* before the Committee on Commerce. 89th Cong., 2nd Sess., 1966.

U.S. Congress. Senate. Committee on the Judiciary. *Hearings, Civil Rights* before the Committee on the Judiciary. 88th Cong., 1st Sess., 1963.

U.S. Congress. Senate. Committee on the Judiciary. *Hearings, Nomination of Ramsey Clark as Attorney General* before the Committee on the Judiciary. 90th Cong., 1st Sess., 1967.

U.S. Congress. Senate. Committee on the Judiciary. *Hearings, Nomination of Jerris Leonard as Assistant Attorney General, Civil Rights Division* before the Committee on the Judiciary. 91st Cong., 1st Sess., 1969.

U.S. *Government Organization Manual, 1968–69.* Washington, D.C.: Government Printing Office, 1968.

U.S. *Congressional Directory, 1966.* Washington, D.C.: Government Printing Office, 1966.

U.S. *Congressional Record 112.*

———. *Congressional Record 115.*

U.S. Department of Justice. *Annual Report of the Attorney General of the United States for the Fiscal Year ended June 30, 1961.* Washington, D.C.: Government Printing Office, 1961.

———. *Annual Report, 1962–1969.*

U.S. President. *Public Papers of the Presidents of the United States.* Washington, D.C.: Office of the Federal Register, National Archives and Records Service, 1961—. John F. Kennedy, 1961.

———. *Public Papers of the Presidents of the United States.* 1963—. Lyndon B. Johnson, 1963–1966.

BOOKS

Adams, Sherman. *First-Hand Report.* New York: Harper and Brothers, 1961.

Anderson, J. W. *Eisenhower, Brownell and the Congress: The Tangled Origins of the Civil Rights Bill of 1956–1957.* University, Alabama: University of Alabama Press for the Inter-University Case Program, 1964.

Bailey, Stephen K., and Mosher, Edith K. *ESEA: The Office of Education Administers a Law.* Syracuse, N. Y.: Syracuse University Press, 1968.

Bentley, Arthur. *The Process of Government.* Evanston, Illinois: Principia Press of Illinois, Inc., 1908.

Berman, Daniel. *A Bill Becomes a Law.* 2nd ed. New York: MacMillan Co., 1966.

Commager, Henry S. *Documents of American History.* 6th ed. New York: Appleton-Century-Crofts, Inc., 1962.

Congressional Quarterly Service. *Legislators and the Lobbyists.* Washington, D.C.: Congressional Quarterly Service, 1965.

———. *Revolution in Civil Rights.* Washington, D.C.: Congressional Quarterly Service, 1965.

———. *Revolution in Civil Rights.* 4th ed. Washington, D.C.: Congressional Quarterly Service, 1968.

———. *Guide to Current American Government.* Washington, D.C.: Congressional Quarterly Service, 1969.

Cushman, Robert E., and Robert F., eds. *Cases in Constitutional Law.* 2nd ed. New York: Appleton-Century-Crofts, 1965.

Donovan, Robert J. *Eisenhower: The Inside Story.* New York: Harper and Brothers, 1956.

Easton, David. *The Political System.* New York: Alfred A. Knopf, 1959.

Fenno, Richard F. Jr. *The Power of the Purse: Appropriations Politics in Congress.* Boston: Little, Brown and Co., 1966.

Hughes, Emmet John. *The Ordeal of Power: A Political Memoir of the Eisenhower Years.* New York: Atheneum, 1963.

Key, V. O., Jr. *Southern Politics in State and Nation.* Vintage Books. New York: Random House, 1949.

———. *Politics, Parties, and Pressure Groups.* 5th ed. New York: Thomas Y. Crowell Co., 1964.

Koenig, Louis W. *The Chief Executive.* rev. ed. New York: Harcourt, Brace and World, 1968.

Lindblom, Charles E. *The Policy-Making Process.* Englewood Cliffs, New Jersey: Prentice-Hall, Inc., 1968.

Longaker, Richard. *The Presidency and Individual Liberties.* Ithaca, New York: Cornell University Press, 1961.

Marshall, Burke. *Federalism and Civil Rights.* New York: Columbia University Press, 1964.

Morrow, Everett Frederic. *Black Man in the White House.* New York: Coward-McCann, 1963.

Neustadt, Richard E. *Presidential Power.* New York: John Wiley and Sons, Inc., 1960.

Orfield, Gary. *The Reconstruction of Southern Education.* New York: John Wiley and Sons, Inc., 1969.

Peltason, Jack W. *Fifty-Eight Lonely Men.* New York: Harcourt, Brace, and World, 1961.

Schlesinger, Arthur M., Jr. *A Thousand Days.* Boston: Houghton Mifflin Co., 1965.

Snyder, Richard C.; Bruck, H. W.; and Sapin, Burton. *The Decision Making Approach to the Study of International Politics.* Monograph No. 3 of the Foreign Policy Analysis Project Series. Princeton, New Jersey: Princeton Univ. Press, 1954.

Sorensen, Theodore. *Decision-Making in the White House.* New York: Columbia University Press, 1963.

———. *Kennedy.* New York: Harper and Row, 1965.

Truman, David. *The Governmental Process.* New York: Alfred A. Knopf, 1960.

Wicker, Tom. *JFK and LBJ: The Influence of Personality Upon Politics.* New York: William Morrow and Co., 1968.

Wilson, Woodrow. *Congressional Government: A Study in American Politics.* New York: Meridian Books, republished in 1956.

Wise, Sidney. ed. *Issues 1969–1970: Documents in Current American Government and Politics.* New York: Thomas Y. Crowell Co., 1969.

ARTICLES AND PERIODICALS

Drew, Elizabeth B. "Education's Billion-Dollar Baby." *The Atlantic Monthly* (July, 1966).

Fleming, Harold. "The Federal Executive and Civil Rights: 1961–1965." *Daedalus* (Fall, 1965).

Kommers, J. "The Right to Vote and Its Implementation." *Notre Dame Lawyer* (June, 1964).

Lindblom, Charles E. "The Science of Muddling Through." *Public Administration Review* 19 (1959).

Mitchell, Clarence. "The Warren Court and Congress: A Civil Rights Partnership." *Nebraska Law Review* 48 (1968).

Neustadt, Richard E. "Presidency and Legislation: The Growth of Central Clearance." *American Political Science Review* 48 (September, 1954).

————. "Approaches to Staffing the Presidency." Paper delivered at the American Political Science Association convention in New York City on September 6, 1963.

Sherill, Robert G. "Guidelines to Frustration." *The Nation* (January 16, 1967).

Steif, William. "The New Look in Civil Rights Enforcement." *Southern Education Report* (September, 1967).

"Title VI of the Civil Rights Act of 1964: Implementation and Impact." *George Washington Law Review* (September, 1968).

U.S. News & World Report. December 30, 1968; March 10, 1969; August 18, 1969.

NEWSPAPERS

New York Times. 1961–1970.

REPORTS AND PAMPHLETS

Compliance Officers Manual for Title VI, Act of 1964. Washington, D.C.: U.S. Government Printing Office for the U.S. Civil Rights Commission, 1966.

Executive Support of Civil Rights. Southern Regional Council, Atlanta, Georgia: Southern Regional Council, 1962.

Federally Supported Discrimination. New York: Leadership Conference on Civil Rights, 1961.

Hearings, Voting. Vol. 1. Washington, D.C.: U.S. Commission on Civil Rights, 1965.

Southern School Desegregation, 1966–67. Washington, D.C.: U.S. Government Printing Office for the U.S. Commission on Civil Rights, 1967.

Study on Equal Opportunity Programs and Activities of the Federal Government. Washington, D.C.: U. S. Commission on Civil Rights, 1969.

UNPUBLISHED MATERIALS

Annual Report, 1968, of the Leadership Conference's Committee on Compliance and Enforcement. January 28, 1969. (Mimeographed)

Filvaroff, David. "Memorandum to Vice President Humphrey," summarizing the accomplishments of the President's Council on Equal Opportunity, September 22, 1965. (in Wiley Branton's files)

Sullivan, Donald F. "The Civil Rights Programs of the Kennedy Administration." Ph.D. dissertation, University of Oklahoma, 1965.

Sulzner, George, III. "The United States Commission on Civil

Rights: A Study of Incrementalism in Policy-Making."
Ph.D. dissertation, University of Michigan, 1967.

OTHER SOURCES

Letter to the writer from Derrick Bell, former deputy Special
    Assistant to the Secretary of HEW for civil rights, Sep-
    tember 24, 1969.
Letter to the writer from Senator Edward W. Brooke, Repub-
    lican, Massachusetts, July 28, 1969.
Letter to the writer from Marvin Caplin, Director, Washing-
    ton, D.C. office, Leadership Conference on Civil Rights,
    August 11, 1969.
Letter to the writer from Douglas E. Chaffin, former director
    of Personnel, Housing and Home Finance Administra-
    tion, March 13, 1968.
Letter to the writer from Harold Howe, former U.S. Commis-
    sioner of Education, September 1, 1969.
Letter to the writer from Hubert H. Humphrey, May 7, 1969.
Letter to the writer from Senator Jacob Javits, Republican,
    New York, April 11, 1968.
Letter to the writer from Senator Jack Miller, Republican,
    Iowa, July 28, 1969.

INDEX

A. Philip Randolph Institute, 202n
Abbitt, Watkins, 124
Adams, Sherman, 222n, 225n, 228n
Agnew, Spiro, 49n, 148n, 177n
Agriculture, Department of, 192
Allen, James, Jr., 146, 153n
Amaker, Norman, 95n
Ambrose, Eleanor, 203n
Anderson, J. W., 67
Antipoverty programs, 39n
Aronson, Arnold, 55, 55n, 56, 76n,
  188n
Ashmore, Robert, 157
Attorney General as Coordinator,
  190–97

Bailey, Stephen, 23n
Barrett, St. John, 68n, 69, 102
Barus, David, 115n
Beatrice Alexander v. *Holmes
  County Board of Education*
  (1969), 41n
Bell, Derrick, 142, 204n
Bentley, Arthur, 20n, 21n
Birmingham, Alabama, 230n, 231n
Black attorneys, 94–95, 94n, 95n
Black, Hugo, 68n
Branton, Wiley, 76n, 182, 182n,

183, 183n, 184, 185, 185n, 186,
  186n, 190, 190n, 191
Brewer, Albert, 53n
Brimmer, Andrew, 174n
Brooke, Edward, 61
Brown v. *Board of Education*
  (1954, 1955), 22n, 40, 41, 41n,
  68, 84n, 85n, 107, 109, 150,
  222, 223, 228, 239, 240, 242,
  244
Brownell, Herbert, 65n, 66, 67n,
  228
Budgeting and Accounting Act
  (1921), 25n
Bureau of the Budget, 111n, 123,
  156, 192, 197–200, 205, 245,
  247
Burger, Warren, 97

Califano, Joseph, 97, 129, 132,
  176n, 227
Caplin, Marvin, 54, 59, 80n, 100,
  142, 203n, 233n
Carswell, G. Harrold, 58, 224, 249
Carter, Lisle, Jr., 200, 201
Cater, Douglas, 129, 132
Celebreeze, Anthony, 110, 111,
  112, 112n, 114n, 134

269

Celler, Emanuel, 50, 58, 125
Chaffin, Douglas, 47
Chicago fund dispute, 129, 130, 131, 132, 136, 137, 188, 188n, 196, 216
Civil Rights Act (1957), 32, 36, 65, 66, 82, 181, 211, 228, 242
Civil Rights Act (1960), 32, 36, 155, 242
Civil Rights Act (1964), 33–35, 37, 44, 50, 56, 58, 72, 82, 84, 108, 110, 111, 113, 115, 116, 134, 156, 178, 181, 196, 210, 232, 243, 245, 249
    Title IV, 107, 115, 123, 133, 137, 151
    Title VI, 19n, 27n, 84n, 88, 105, 110, 111, 111n, 113n, 114n, 115, 130, 133, 134, 135, 137, 139, 140, 146, 147, 152n, 153n, 154n, 179, 181, 182, 183n, 184n, 189, 189n, 190, 191, 192, 193, 194, 195, 196, 196n, 198n, 199, 205, 211, 217, 228, 230, 231n, 242, 245, 246, 247
    Title X, 159, 160
Civil Rights Act (1968), 18n, 36n, 37, 38, 50, 58, 60, 105, 243, 249
Civil Rights Cases (1883), 31n, 39, 39n
Civil Rights Commission (CRC), 19n, 32, 33n, 90, 91n, 92, 112n, 125, 156, 176, 184, 184n, 197n, 199, 205, 225n, 226n
Civil Rights Division (CRD), 20, 32, 65ff, 126, 137, 167, 173, 185n, 188, 189, 190n, 191n, 200, 209, 211, 212, 213, 214, 215, 216, 217, 244, 245

Civil Service Commission, 75, 90n, 196, 196n, 248
Civil War, 30
Clark, Kenneth, 201
Clark, Ramsey, 24n, 27n, 77, 77n, 78, 78n, 85n, 91, 92, 93, 94, 94n, 95, 95n, 98, 98n, 99, 100, 101, 102, 104, 105, 120n, 136, 138, 139, 165, 167, 167n, 169, 170, 171, 171n, 172, 173, 174n, 177, 187n, 190, 190n, 191, 191n, 192, 195, 195n, 196, 196n, 197n, 198, 198n, 233n, 245, 247
Cohen, Wilbur, 130, 133, 247
Collins, LeRoy, 157, 157n, 159, 159n, 160, 166, 166n, 169n, 180, 180n, 181, 186n, 212, 213, 214
Commerce, Department of, 156n, 157, 158, 160, 165n, 168, 169, 174, 212
Committee on Equal Employment Opportunity (1961), 35, 186n
Committee on Fair Employment Practices (1941), 31
Committee on Government Contract Compliance (1951), 32n
Committee on Government Employment Policy (1955), 33
Community Relations Service (CRS), 20, 105, 155ff, 180n, 186n, 191, 209, 212, 213, 214, 215, 216, 217, 245
Conners, Eugene ("Bull"), 230, 230n
Connors, John, 158
Constitution, Art. 1, Sec. 9, 30n
    Thirteenth Amendment, 30
    Fourteenth Amendment, 30
    Fifteenth Amendment, 30
    Twenty-Fourth Amendment (Poll tax), 33n, 38n, 51

Coordinating Committee for Fundamental American Freedoms, 58
Cox, Harold, 104
Cramer, William, 144, 145
Cushman, Robert, 40n

Daley, Richard, 130
Democratic Study Group, 23, 50, 58
Dent, Harry, 233n
Diagnostic factors, 25–27
Dirksen, Everett, 51, 51n
Doar, John, 18n, 69, 70n, 75, 76, 77, 78, 90, 90n, 92, 94, 97, 98n, 99, 122n, 126, 132, 137, 171n, 172n, 173, 177, 180, 185n, 187, 188, 190n, 191n, 192n, 196n, 197n, 213, 214
Donovan, Robert, 221n
Dred Scott v. *Sandford* (1857), 39, 39n

Eastland, James, 45, 50, 104
Easton, David, 21n
Ecclesiastes, 155
Economic Opportunity Act (1964), 38
Edelman, Marian Wright, 202n
Edelsberg, Herman, 204n
Ehrlichman, John, 233n
Eisenhower, Dwight D., 19, 32, 36n, 43n, 56, 56n, 69, 81, 82, 176n, 218, 219, 220, 220n, 221, 221n, 222n, 223, 224, 226, 228, 228n, 230, 233n, 234, 239, 241, 242, 244, 245, 247
Elementary and Secondary Education Act (1965), 39, 44, 44n
Title I, 39n, 129, 130, 130n, 146, 146n, 202n
Ellender, Allen, 101
Ellington, Bufford, 129

Elliott, J. Robert, 104
Employment Act (1946), 25n
Equal Educational Opportunities Program (EEOP), 20, 113ff, 209, 210, 211, 212, 213, 214, 216, 217, 245
Equal Employment Opportunity Council, 185, 185n

Fair Employment Board (1948), 33n
Federal Bureau of Investigation (FBI), 24n, 66
Federally Supported Discrimination, 55, 56
Field Foundation, 202
Fifth Circuit Court of Appeals, 116, 117, 117n, 118, 118n, 151, 153, 153n, 248
Filvaroff, David, 122n, 179, 182n, 183, 183n, 193, 193n
Finch, Robert, 81, 88, 139, 149, 150, 151, 152, 178n, 220n, 247
Flank assault, 39n
Fleming, Harold, 203, 203n, 204n
Flood, Daniel, 133
Fogarty, Daniel, 132, 133
Foster, G. W., 115, 115n
Frontal assault, 39n

Gardner, John, 120n, 121, 127, 131, 132, 133, 134, 138, 143, 146, 177n, 191n, 192n, 196
Golden, Harry, 103
Government Contract Committee (1953), 32
Greenberg, Jack, 95n, 99
Gronouski, John, 48
Guidelines for school desegregation, 115, 116, 116n, 119, 119n, 120, 120n, 127, 136, 150, 151

Hamilton, James, 54, 203n
Hart, Philip, 103
Haynsworth, Clement, Jr., 58, 224, 249
Health, Education and Welfare, Department of (HEW), 107ff. *See also* constituent units: USOE, EEOP, OCR
Heffernan, Elaine, 131, 131n, 132, 135, 137, 141, 142, 147, 203, 204n
Hennings, Thomas, 66n
Herbers, John, 146, 154n
Hesburgh, Theodore, 225, 226n
Hill, Lister, 52n, 101, 124
Holland, Spessard, 157n
Holman, Carl, 200, 201
Hoover, J. Edgar, 24n
Housing Act (1968), 18n, 36n, 37, 38, 58, 60, 105, 243
Housing and Urban Development, Department of, 49n, 171n, 195
Housing Executive Order (1962), 36, 36n, 38, 230n, 243
Howard University, 46
Howe, Harold, 120, 123, 124, 140, 140n, 144, 145
Huge, Harry, 202n
Hughes, Emmet John, 222n
Humphrey, Hubert, 76n, 127, 161n, 176n, 178, 179, 179n, 182, 182n, 183n, 185, 185n, 186, 186n, 187, 188n, 189, 190n, 191n, 211, 227, 228, 246

Interstate Commerce Commission (ICC), 35n
Isaiah, 155

Javits, Jacob, 50n, 59, 60n, 165n, 168n, 169, 172
Johnson, Cernoria, 203n
Johnson, Lyndon B., 19, 19n, 37,

38, 41, 42, 43n, 44, 44n, 45, 46, 52n, 57, 75, 89, 96, 97, 98, 101, 112, 127, 128, 129, 130, 136, 139, 142, 145n, 155, 157n, 158n, 163, 164, 164n, 170n, 171n, 176n, 178, 179n, 182, 185, 185n, 186, 186n, 187, 197n, 200, 202n, 204, 211, 215, 216, 218, 219, 219n, 222, 223, 224, 227, 228, 229n, 230n, 231, 232, 232n, 233, 233n, 234, 239, 241, 243, 244, 245, 246, 247
Justice Department, 36n, 37n, 60, 65ff, 120n, 122, 126, 127, 130, 135, 136, 137, 138, 139, 142, 151, 152, 164, 164n, 165, 166, 166n, 167, 168, 170, 171, 171n, 172, 172n, 173, 174, 184n, 186n, 188n, 189, 190, 190n, 191, 191n, 192, 193, 196, 197n, 203n, 205, 211, 213, 215, 216, 233n, 245, 247
    Civil Liberties Section (1939), 31, 66
    Civil Rights Division (CRD), 20, 32, 65ff, 126, 137, 167, 173, 185n, 188, 189, 190n, 191n, 200, 209, 211, 212, 213, 214, 215, 216, 217, 244, 245

Katzenbach, Nicholas, 24n, 45, 60, 60n, 74, 74n, 76n, 77, 77n, 78, 78n, 83, 84n, 88, 88n, 89, 90, 92, 93, 94, 97, 98n, 99, 101, 104, 105, 120n, 122n, 126, 136, 138, 157, 158, 164, 165, 165n, 167, 167n, 168n, 171n, 174, 176n, 184, 189, 190n, 191, 191n, 192, 192n, 193, 196n, 197n, 198n, 205, 211, 213, 227, 228, 232n, 246, 247

Kennedy, John F., 19, 33, 33n, 35, 36n, 37n, 38, 39n, 41, 42, 43, 43n, 45, 46, 48, 49n, 55, 56, 70, 70n, 83n, 87, 89, 96, 97, 98, 101, 103, 110, 111n, 155, 158, 176, 176n, 197n, 200, 204, 204n, 215, 218, 219, 219n, 220, 222, 223, 224, 225, 225n, 226, 226n, 228, 229, 229n, 230, 230n, 231, 231n, 233n, 234, 239, 240, 241, 242, 243, 244, 245, 246, 247

Kennedy, Robert, 35, 48n, 70, 70n, 71n, 72, 73, 74, 74n, 77, 77n, 78n, 82n, 86, 89n, 94, 104, 126, 158, 165n, 196, 196n, 229n, 231n, 233n

Keppel, Francis, 111, 111n, 112, 113, 116, 117n, 120, 125, 126, 128, 129, 130, 131

Key, V. O., 22n

King, Martin Luther, 76n, 166n, 168n, 201

Koenig, Louis, 221n

Kytle, Calvin, 156, 159, 159n, 160, 161, 162, 163, 167, 168n, 169, 169n, 211, 213, 214

Leadership Conference on Civil Rights, 54–55, 59, 100, 142, 202n

Leonard, Jerris, 80n, 87, 92n, 93, 100, 103, 105

Levin, Arthur, 203n

Libassi, F. Peter, 127, 131, 131n, 132, 134, 135, 136, 137, 138, 140, 141, 142, 147, 148, 177, 177n, 182, 182n, 183, 188n, 196, 198n, 200, 201, 202n, 203, 204n, 213, 214, 215

Lincoln, Abraham, 42

Lindsay, John, 58

Little Rock, Arkansas, 45, 104, 222n

Longaker, Richard, 224n, 225n

McC. Mathias, Charles, 58

McClellan, John, 123

McCormack, John, 51

MacGregor, Clark, 58

McKissick, Floyd, 75n, 76n, 168n

McLaurin v. Oklahoma State Regents (1938), 40n

McMurrin, Sterling, 109

"Manhattan Project", 201

Mansfield, Mike, 51, 51n

Mardian, Robert, 178n

Marshall, Burke, 35n, 70n, 71n, 72, 73, 73n, 74, 78, 82n, 86, 87, 89n, 92, 94n, 99, 101, 104, 182n, 214, 226

Marshall, Thurgood, 66

Martin, Louis, 233n

Martin, Ruby, 145n, 202n, 204n, 214

Mason, Norman, 47

Miller, Jack, 61

Missouri ex. rel. Gaines v. Canada (1938), 40n

Mitchell, Clarence, 44n, 46, 52n, 53n, 57n, 60, 61, 76n, 77n, 78n, 168n, 169n, 188n, 203n, 233n

Mitchell, John, 79, 80, 80n, 81, 88, 96n, 97, 100, 139, 150, 151, 152, 173, 174, 178n, 196, 243, 244

Montell, Sherwin, 27n

Morrow, Everett Frederic, 221n, 225n

Morsell, John, 57, 76n, 168n, 169n, 188n, 232n

"Most Solemn Petition", 52n

Murphy, Frank, 66, 67

Nash, Philleo, 176n

Natcher, William, 138

National Association for the Advancement of Colored People (NAACP), 49n, 89n

NAACP Legal Defense and Educational Fund, Inc., 99, 100, 146n

National Citizens Committee on Community Relations, 161

National Urban League, 179n

National Security Act (1947), 25n

Nelson, Karen, 197n, 198n, 199, 200

New Deal, 250

Niles, David, 176n

Nixon, Richard M., 19, 53n, 85n, 89, 95n, 96, 97, 139, 147, 148, 148n, 149, 152, 152n, 177n, 197n, 218, 219, 219n, 220, 220n, 223, 224, 233n, 234, 241, 243, 244, 247, 249

Northwest Ordinance (1787), 30n

O'Brien, Lawrence, 42

Office for Civil Rights (OCR), 20, 134ff, 209, 211, 212, 213, 214, 215, 216, 217, 245

Office for Equal Opportunity, 202n

Office of Statistical Standards (OSS), 198–200

Orfield, Gary, 110n, 231n

Owen, Robert, 193n

Page, Ray, 129

Panetta, Leon, 152n

Plessy v. *Ferguson* (1896), 40, 40n

Polhaus, J. Francis, 55, 55n, 203n

Poll tax, 33n, 38n, 51

Pollak, Stephen, 76, 77n, 78, 83n, 85, 85n, 89n, 92, 93, 96, 98n, 99, 165n, 171n, 173, 188n, 214

Potomac Institute, 203

President's Council on Equal Opportunity, 105, 161n, 178–89, 204, 209, 210, 211, 227, 246

President's Subcabinet Committee on Civil Rights, 176–78, 204, 227, 245, 246

Pressure Entities, 20ff

Price, Yvonne, 203n

Project Enforcement, 202n

Quigley, James, 111, 112n, 131

Rabb, Maxwell, 176n, 225, 225n

Rauh, Joseph, 168n

Regulations (HEW), 112, 113, 113n, 115, 116

Reston, James, 232

Ribicoff, Abraham, 36n, 108, 109

Rilling, Paul, 152n

Rockefeller Fund, 202

Rooney, John, 101, 123, 169

Roosevelt, Eleanor, 224n, 225n

Roosevelt, Franklin D., 31, 66, 176n, 222, 225n

Rose, David, 193n, 195

Rowe, James, 176n

Rustin, Baird, 201

Sanders, Harold Barefoot, 201n

Schattschneider, E. E., 45

Schlei, Norbert, 180, 180n, 181, 187

Schlesinger, Arthur, Jr., 39n, 43, 73n, 96, 104, 229n

Seeley, David, 111, 112n, 113, 114, 114n, 116, 120n, 122, 125, 126, 127, 129, 130, 131, 132, 143, 144, 145, 147n, 214

Sellers, Barney, 202n

Selma, Alabama, 243

Singleton v. *Jackson Municipal Separate School District* (1965), 117

Slaiman, Donald, 203n
Slaughterhouse Cases (1872), 31n
Sloane, Martin, 19n
Smathers, George, 45, 157n
Smith, Howard, 125
Sorensen, Theodore, 33n, 43, 55,
    82, 83n, 222, 225n, 229n, 231
Southern bloc, 23, 50, 50n, 52n,
    53, 53n, 59, 60, 123, 124, 125,
    140, 143, 149n, 197n, 232, 240–
    42
Southern Regional Council, 82n,
    202
Southern strategy, 148, 148n, 149,
    149n
Sparkman, John, 101
Speiser, Lawrence, 203n
Spottswood, Stephen, 153n
Statistics,
        employment, 85
        public schools, 17n, 18n,
            84n, 148, 154n
        voting, 18n, 36n, 78n, 79n,
            82, 83–84
Stewart, John, 182n
Sullivan, Donald, 176n, 225n, 226n
Supreme Court, 22, 31n, 39–41,
    39n, 68, 93, 105, 118n, 151,
    152, 153n, 219, 222, 222n, 224,
    228n, 248
Sweatt v. *Painter* (1950), 40
Sylvester, Edward, 200, 201

Taconic Fund, 82n, 202
Taney, Roger, 39n
Taylor, William, 156, 176, 184,
    200, 201, 204n
Theoretical approach, 20-28
Thurmond, Strom, 53n, 102, 157,
    157n
Tiffany, Gordon, 225n
Truman, Harry S., 31, 66n, 176n
Tyler, Harold, 69, 70n, 82

United States Attorneys, 93–94
United States Office of Education
    (USOE), 109, 110, 111, 111n,
    112, 112n, 114, 114n, 119, 123,
    124, 125, 126, 128, 129, 132,
    134, 138, 144, 199
University of Mississippi, 45, 104,
    242
U.S. v. *Jefferson County Board of
    Education* (1966), 117, 119

Vietnam war, 219
Voting registration, 74–78
Voting Rights Act (1965), 37–38,
    44, 46, 50, 58, 60, 74, 76, 79,
    83, 97, 217, 224, 233n, 243,
    244, 247

Wallace, George, 53, 53n, 124
Warren, Earl, 117n
Washington Family, 203, 203n,
    204, 205
Washington Research Project,
    146n, 202n
Watkins, Kent, 226n
Watts riot (Los Angeles), 186,
    216
Weaver, Warren, Jr., 197
Whiston, Frank, 130
White House Conference on Civil
    Rights, 185
White, Lee, 110n, 132, 176n,
    177n, 225, 225n, 227, 231n,
    233n
White, Wilson, 69
Wicker, Tom, 233n
Wilkins, Roger, 156, 157, 158,
    158n, 160, 160n, 161, 161n,
    164, 166, 167, 167n, 168, 169,
    169n, 170, 171, 172, 172n, 173,
    174n, 200, 201, 201n, 202, 214,
    217

Wilkins, Roy, 18n, 49n, 55, 56, 56n, 57, 89n, 168n, 169n, 188n, 201, 232, 233n

Willis, Benjamin, 130, 130n

Wilson, Woodrow, 24, 24n, 50, 153n

Wisdom, John, 117–18

Wofford, Harris, 176n, 177, 177n, 225, 226n, 227

Yarborough, Ralph, 45

Young, Whitney, 47, 57, 76n, 168n, 201, 231n, 232n, 233n

Zelenko, Herbert, 36n